Research Methods for Leisure and Tourism

a practical guide

A.J. Veal
University of Technology, Sydney

Series Editor: **Brian Duffield**

in association with
Institute of Leisure and Amenity Management

PITMAN PUBLISHING
128 Long Acre, London WC2E 9AN

A Division of Pearson Professional Limited

First published in Great Britain 1992

© Longman Group UK Ltd 1992
Reprinted 1995

British Library Cataloguing in Publication Data
A CIP catalogue record for this book can be obtained from the British Library.

ISBN 0 273 62009 6

Printed and bound in Great Britain by Ipswich Book Co.

The Publishers' policy is to use paper manufactured from sustainable forests.

Contents

Preface   v

Foreword   vii

1   Introduction: the what, why and who of
    leisure and tourism research   1
2   Approaches to leisure and tourism research   11
3   Starting out – research plans and proposals   27
4   The range of research methods   48
5   Existing sources: the literature   56
6   Existing sources: secondary data   69
7   Observation   81
8   Qualitative methods   93
9   Questionnaire surveys   104
10 Questionnaire design   120
11 Sampling   148
12 Survey analysis: preparation   160
13 Survey analysis: operation   170
14 Preparing a research report   201

References   213

Index   223

Preface

Recent years have seen the expansion of leisure services throughout Britain, whether they are provided by institutions in the public, commercial or voluntary sectors. Such leisure facilities and services are now recognised as of critical significance in the changing social and economic structure of contemporary Britain. The effectiveness of such provision, however, lies in the hands of leisure officers and managers and it is clear that there is a need to ensure the highest level of professional support for leisure services.

The Institute of Leisure and Amenity Management (ILAM) has been in the forefront of promoting a scheme of professional education and training leading to the qualifications of the ILAM Certificate and Diploma in Leisure Management. These professional qualifications are designed to ensure that leisure managers have a sound base of education and understanding in the operational and technical aspects of day-to-day management of leisure facilities and opportunities. Similarly there is a concern to ensure a thorough knowledge and understanding of the disciplines and skills appropriate to the manager in the leisure business.

The aim of this series is not only to provide texts which will cover constituent elements in the ILAM syllabuses but also to provide for all leisure professionals the opportunities to update and improve their practice and managerial skills. In that sense they will be relevant not only to ILAM courses but also to other educational programmes leading to Higher National Diploma and Degree qualifications as well as reference sources to the working professional.

Each volume deals with a different aspect of professional activity in the leisure field. As such the texts can be used on an individual basis to enhance skills and understanding in specific aspects of the day-to-day responsibilities of leisure managers. More significantly, however, taken together, the volumes in this series will constitute an integrated support system for professional development which will enhance the efficiency of individual managers and the effectiveness of the services they provide.

This text aims to provide the leisure manager/student with a practical insight into research methods that are relevant to the study of, and/or the management of, leisure and tourism. The book will allow those who wish to utilise research methods to do so with a confidence underpinned by the experience of the growing body of research studies.into leisure and -tourism that has accumulated in recent years. No less importantly, it will facilitate an understanding for both students and managers on how best to exploit, in an informed way, the research findings of others that they come across in their studies and/or day-to-day work.

The book's starting point is to provide a firm foundation of understanding of research and its relevance to leisure and tourism. Previous studies are reviewed and different approaches to research examined and a synoptic perspective provided of the 'research process', including the relationship between research management and project design. The book continues with a step-by-step examination of different methods; how to get the most out of existing sources; the role of observation techniques; and, the potential contribution of quantitative and qualitative techniques. A practical guide is then provided to some of the key elements of utilising questionnaire surveys; the variety of techniques that are available, questionnaire design and the principles of sampling.

The book concludes with the critical issue of how best to get the most from research investigations, firstly, by examining how to analyse research data and, secondly, how to prepare and present a research report.

Whatever the perspective — either as a potential research investigator or a practitioner wishing to benefit from the fruits of research — this book will illuminate the symbiotic relationship between research and the effective management of leisure and tourism.

Brian S. Duffield   Series Editor

Foreword

This book is based on experience in teaching research methods to undergraduate and graduate students in three institutions on two continents. The aims of the book are to provide a 'how to do it' text and to offer an understanding of how research findings are generated in order to assist the student or practising manager to become a knowledgeable *consumer* of the research of others.

The book does not include material on statistics beyond a conceptual introduction to the basics of sampling theory and a discussion of confidence intervals and their relationships with sample size. In addition some indication of statistical tests available in SPSSPC is given in Chapter 13. The reason for limiting the treatment of statistics in this way is mainly because the subject of statistics requires more attention than can be given in this book, and also because many suitable texts are readily available.

A J Veal
Sydney
December 1991

1 Introduction: the what, why and who of leisure and tourism research

This chapter examines what research is, who does it and why, and the role of research in the leisure and tourism planning and management process. To understand and utilise existing research it is necessary to be familiar with the world of research – how it is structured and how it is produced.

What?

What is research? The sociologist, Norbert Elias defines it in terms of its aims as follows:

> The aim, as far as I can see, is the same in all sciences. Put simply and cursorily, the aim is to make known something previously unknown to human beings. It is to advance human knowledge, to make it more certain or better fitting ...The aim is... *discovery*.
>
> (Elias 1986, p. 20)

Discovery – making known something previously unknown – could cover a number of activities, for instance the work of journalists or detectives. Elias, however, also indicates that research is a tool of 'science' and that its purpose is to 'advance human knowledge' – features which distinguish research from other investigatory activities. This book is concerned with research which can be viewed in three contexts.

1. Scientific research – research which is conducted within the rules and conventions of science. This means that it is based on logic and reason and the systematic examination of evidence; ideally it should be possible for research to be replicated by the same or different researchers and for similar conclusions to emerge (although this is not always possible or practicable); and it should contribute to a cumulative body of knowledge about a field or topic.

2. Social science research – research as carried out using the methods and traditions of *social* science, particularly as they relate to the field of leisure and tourism. Social science differs from natural science, such as physics and

chemistry, in that it deals with people and people are less predictable than non-human phenomena. People can be aware of the research being conducted about them and are not therefore purely passive subjects; and they can react to the results of research and change their behaviour accordingly.

3. Applied research – research geared to the solution of problems which arise in a policy, planning or management situation, and in particular those situations which arise in the areas of leisure and tourism.

Research can be defined as, firstly, the process of *finding out* and secondly the process of *explaining*. In this book, we are also concerned with a third function of research, namely *evaluating*. Three types of research can be identified corresponding to these three functions:

Descriptive research	finding out.
Explanatory research	explaining.
Evaluative research	evaluation.

In some cases particular research projects concentrate on only one of these, but often two or more of the approaches are included in the same project.

Descriptive research is very common in the leisure and tourism area. This is partly because this is a relatively new field and there is a need to 'map the territory'. Much of the descriptive research in the field might therefore be described as 'exploratory': it merely 'discovers' patterns of behaviour and the explanation is left until later or to other researchers.

A second reason for the preponderance of descriptive research is that the phenomena studied are subject to change. For example levels of participation in different leisure activities change over time; the patterns of participation among different social groups change; the importance of different tourism markets changes. A great deal of research effort in the field is therefore devoted to monitoring basic patterns of behaviour. The providers of leisure and tourism services must be aware of and respond to changing market conditions whether or not they can be explained or understood, although understanding and explanation would also, of course, be welcome.

Thirdly descriptive research is common because, in applied research, there is often – but not always – a gap between research projects and the policy, planning or management activity which gives rise to the research. So, for example, a company may commission a 'market profile' study or a local council may commission a 'recreation needs' study from a research team – but the use of the results of this research for marketing or planning purposes is a separate exercise with which the research team is not involved: the research team has simply been required to produce a descriptive study.

Explanatory research moves beyond description to the thorny issue of causality. It is one thing to discover that A has increased and B has decreased; but to establish that the rise in A has been caused by the fall in B is a much more demanding task. To establish causality, or the likelihood of causality, requires the researcher to be very rigorous in the collection, analysis and interpretation of data. The issue of causality is discussed further in Chapter 2 and in Chapter 13, which deals with data analysis.

Evaluative research arises from that part of the policy and management decision-making process (as discussed below) which involves making judgements on the success or effectiveness of policies or programmes – for example whether a particular leisure facility or programme is meeting required performance standards or whether a particular tourism promotion campaign has been cost-effective. *Evaluative* research is highly developed in some areas of public policy, for example education, but less well developed in the field of leisure and tourism (Shadish *et al.* 1991). Again the issues facing the evaluative researcher are discussed in later chapters, particularly Chapters 3 and 13.

Planning and management: the role of research

In general

While some readers of this book may engage in research in an academic environment – that is research conducted for its 'own sake' or in the interests of 'the pursuit of knowledge' – most will find themselves conducting or commissioning research for 'practical' reasons. It is therefore particularly appropriate to consider the role of research in the policy, planning and management process.

All organisations engage in planning what to do in the future and managing resources to achieve their goals. This process is considered in more depth in specialist planning and management books (e.g. Torkildsen 1983; Howard and Crompton 1980). Here the process is considered only briefly, in order to examine the part played by research.

The 'rational-comprehensive' process of planning/management is often depicted diagrammatically as in Figure 1.1. Research has a role to play in most of the six steps shown:

1. the setting of goals and objectives;
2. identification and evaluation of alternative courses of action;
3. choosing the preferred alternative;
4. implementing the preferred course of action;
5. controlling and monitoring the implementation process;
6. feedback and adjustment.

Planning can be seen as the process of deciding what leisure or tourism services should be provided in the future – mainly steps 1 to 3 in the diagram. Although planning is usually associated in the public mind with government bodies, it is also an activity undertaken by the private sector: organisations such as cinema chains, holiday resort developers or sport promoters are all involved in planning, but their planning activities are less public than those of government bodies (Henry and Spink 1990). And while private organisations are usually

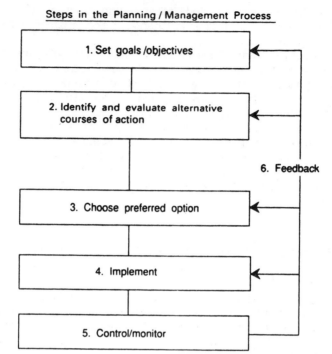

Figure 1.1　The role of research in the planning/management process

only concerned with their own activities, government bodies often have a wider responsibility to provide a planning framework for the activities of many public and private sector organisations.

Management can be seen as being mainly concerned with the implementation of plans – mainly steps 4 to 6 in the diagram. However, in some presentations management is seen as the all-encompassing process with planning, including the consideration of goals and objectives as one or more steps in the management process.

Research has a large part to play in the development of approaches to planning and many guides to planning advocate research as a key element in the planning process (e.g. Kelsey and Gray 1986a, Marriott 1987). Research certainly has a role to play in helping decision makers to:

- formulate goals, that is to decide broadly what they wish to achieve, by providing information on current problems (Step 1);
- identify and evaluate alternative courses of action best suited to achieving their goals and objectives, by providing information on such aspects as the views of the public and the likely consequences of alternative courses of action (Steps 2 and 3);
- monitor and evaluate the implementation process and its effects, to provide feedback which confirms the success of the operation or indicates the need for modifications (Steps 5 and 6).

Research for leisure and tourism planning/management is presented in many forms and contexts. A number of these are discussed briefly below, but they are not all mutually exclusive.

Position statements

Research can assist in helping decision makers become knowledgeable about an area or issue and to take stock of their own current policies and provision. For example if a local authority wishes to develop new policies for open space in an area, research should ideally be carried out to determine what open space exists, its quality and nature, existing policies, rules and regulations, and levels and types of use. Such a study is called a position statement.

Market profiles

If an organisation wishes to start a project in a particular tourism or sports market it will usually require a 'profile' of that market sector. How big is it? What are its growth prospects? Who are the customers? What sub-sectors does it have? How profitable is it? Who are the current suppliers? Such a profile will usually require considerable research. A market profile can be seen as one element in the broader activity of market research.

Market research

Research on the actual or potential market for a service can take place in advance of the service being established but also as part of the on-going monitoring of the performance of an operation. Market research seeks to establish the scale and nature of the market (the number of people who use or are likely to use the product or service and their characteristics) and consumer requirements and attitudes (the particular requirements or tastes of users or potential users of the product or service).

Market segmentation/lifestyle research

One area of market research is worth noting because of its particular relevance to leisure and tourism: this is the area of 'lifestyle' research. Traditionally marketers attempted to classify people into sub-markets or segments on the basis of characteristics, or 'variables', such as age, sex, occupation and income. While this approach can work to some extent, it can also leave a great deal of market variability unexplained. Market researchers have therefore recently attempted to classify people on the basis not just of such background social and economic characteristics but also their *attitudes*, *values* and *behaviour*. Behaviour includes such things as purchasing and voting, but also leisure activities and holiday behaviour.

Using appropriate statistical techniques it is possible to group people on the basis of all these factors, in short to identify them by their *lifestyle*. In market research this is also referred to as 'psychographics'. The most well-known of such studies, the 'VALS' typology (Values, Attitudes and Life Styles, Mitchell 1985), classified Americans into nine lifestyle groups: Survivor, Sustainer, Belonger, Emulator, Achiever, I-Am-Me, Experiential, Socially Conscious, and Integrated. This system has been widely used in market research, including tourism research (e.g. Shih 1986). Other lifestyle 'systems' include the 'ACORN', census based system developed in Britain (Shaw 1984) and the Australian Age lifestyle typology (*The Age* 1982).

Feasibility studies

Feasibility studies investigate not only consumer or user demands, as in a market profile, but also such aspects as the financial viability and environmental impact of proposed development or investment projects. The decision whether or not to build a new leisure facility or launch a new tourism product is usually based on a feasibility study (Kelsey and Gray 1986b).

Leisure/recreation needs studies

A common type of research in leisure planning is the phenomenon of recreation or leisure 'needs' studies. These are comprehensive studies, usually carried out for local councils, examining levels of provision and use of facilities and services, levels of participation in leisure activities and views and aspirations of the population concerning leisure provision. In some cases the 'needs' study includes a leisure or recreation 'plan', which makes recommendations on future provision; in other cases the plan is a separate document.

Tourism strategies/tourism marketing plans

In tourism the equivalent exercise usually forms part of a 'tourism strategy' or 'tourism marketing plan'. Rather than a 'needs' study, relating to the requirements of the local population, such studies usually involve a 'demand' study, relating to the regions from which tourists are generated or the wider destination region within which the host area is situated. In addition such studies usually consider the capacity of the local area to accommodate tourists, existing and potential attractions and environmental impacts.

Forecasting

A key input to many plans is a forecast of the future, for example the projected demand for a particular leisure activity or the demand for a particular type of tourist accommodation over a ten year period.

Research can be involved in predicting the likely effects of future population growth and change, the effects of changing tastes, changing levels of income or developments in technology. The forecasting of leisure and tourism futures, has become a substantial field in its own right (Veal 1987, Archer 1987).

Who and why?

This book is mainly concerned with *how* research should be done, but it also aims to provide an understanding of the research process which will help the reader to become a knowledgeable, critical consumer of research carried out by others. In reading research reports and articles, it is useful to bear in mind *why* the research has been done and to a large extent this is influenced by *who* did the research and *who* paid for it to be done. Leisure and tourism research is undertaken by a wide variety of individuals and institutions, including academics and students, government and commercial research units, consultants and managers of leisure or tourism facilities and services. The respective roles of these 'actors' are discussed in turn below.

Academics are members of the paid academic staff of academic institutions. They include professors, lecturers, tutors and research staff – in American parlance: the 'faculty'. In most academic institutions professors and lecturers are expected to engage in research, as well as teaching, as part of their contract. Promotion and job security depend partly (some would say mainly) on the achievement of a satisfactory track record in published research. Publication can be in various forms, including: refereed journals (where articles are assessed by academic peers before being accepted for publication – the most prestigious form in academic terms), unrefereed journals (such as professional magazines), books, reports/monographs (published by academic institutions or other agencies), and conference papers.

The main refereed journals in the leisure and tourism area are: *Journal of Leisure Research* (USA), *Annals of Tourism Research* (USA), *Leisure Sciences* (USA), *Tourism Management* (UK), *Leisure Studies* (UK), *Journal of Travel Research* (USA), *Society and Leisure* (Canada).

Some research conducted by academics requires little or no specific financial resources, for example the many studies using students as subjects. But much research requires financial support, for instance, to pay full or part-time research assistants, to pay interviewers or a market research firm to conduct interviews, to cover travel costs, costs of equipment and so on. The main sources are university/college funds; government research councils; trusts/foundations; government departments or agencies; commercial companies; and non-profit organisations.

Universities tend to use their own funds to support research which is initiated by academic staff and where the main motive is the 'advancement of knowledge'. Most universities and colleges have research funds for which members of their staff can apply. Governments usually establish organisations fo fund scientific research, e.g. the UK Economic and Social Research Council or -the Australian Research Council. A number of private trusts or foundations also fund research, for example the Ford Foundation and the Leverhulme Trust.

Funds may come from the world of practice, for instance from a government department or agency, from a commercial company or from a non-profit organisation such as a governing body of a sport. In this case the research will tend to be more practically orientated. Government agencies and commercial and non-profit organisations fund research to solve particular problems or to inform them about particular issues relevant to their interests.

Generally academics become involved in funded research of a practically orientated nature when their own interests coincide with those of the agency concerned. For instance an academic may be interested in ways of measuring what motivates people to engage in certain outdoor recreation activities and this could coincide with an outdoor recreation agency's need for research to assist in developing a marketing strategy. Some academics specialise in applied areas, such as marketing or planning, so they are very often in a better position to attract funding from the 'practical world'. Academics may use funds to employ one or more research assistants who may also be registered for a higher degree, usually a PhD. This leads to the second academic source of research, namely students.

PhD and Masters degree students can be a major source of research. Journals periodically publish lists of theses and dissertations completed in the area (Van Doren and Stubbles 1976, Van Doren and Solan 1979, Jafari and Aaser 1988). Theses from most USA and UK universities are available on microfiche.

PhD theses are the most significant form of student research, but research done by Masters degree and graduate diploma students and even undergraduates can be a useful contribution to knowledge. Leisure and tourism are not generally well endowed with research funds, so even, for example, a small survey conducted by a group of undergraduates on a particular leisure activity or in a particular locality, or a thorough review of an area of literature, may be of considerable use or interest to others.

Government and commercial organisations often have their own in-house research organisations – for example, the UK Office of Population Censuses and Surveys, the Australian Bureau of Tourism Research and the US Forest Service Experiment Stations. Commercial organisations in leisure and tourism tend to rely on consultants for their social, economic and market research, although equipment manufacturers, for instance in sport, may conduct their own research for product development.

Research conducted by commercial bodies is usually confidential but that conducted by government agencies is generally available to the public. Research reports from these organisations can therefore be important sources of knowledge, especially of a more practically orientated nature. For example, in nearly every developed country some government agency takes responsibility for conducting nation-wide surveys of leisure participation rates and tourism patterns. This is research which no other organisation would have the resources to undertake.

Consultants exist to offer their research and advisory services to the leisure and tourism industries. Some consultancy organisations are large, multi-national companies involved in accountancy, management and property development consultancy generally, who establish specialised units covering the leisure and/or tourism field. Examples are Coopers and Lybrand and Price-Waterhouse. But there are many other, smaller, specialised organisations in the consultancy field. Some academics operate consultancy companies as a 'side-line', either because of academic interest in a particular area or to supplement incomes or both.

Managers in leisure and tourism who recognise the full extent of the management process should see research as very much part of their responsibilities. Since most of the readers of this book will be actual or trainee managers, this is a most important point to recognise. Successful management depends on good information. Much information – for example sales figures – comes to the manager as a matter of routine and does not require 'research'. However, the creative utilisation of such data – for example to establish market trends – may amount to research. Other types of information can only be obtained by means of specific research projects. In some areas of leisure and tourism management even the most basic information must be obtained by research. For example, while managers of theatres or resorts routinely receive information on the level of use from sales figures, this is not the case for the manager of an urban park or a beach; to gain information on the number of users of the latter it is necessary to engage in a specific data gathering exercise. Such data gathering may not be very sophisticated and some would say that it does not qualify as 'research', but in the sense that it involves 'finding out', and sometimes 'explaining', it is research for the purposes of this book.

Most managers need to carry out – or commission – research if they also want to find out additional information about their users or customers, for example, where they come from (the 'catchment area' of the facility) or their socio-economic characteristics. Research is also a way of finding out customers' evaluations of the facility or service.

It might be argued that managers do not themselves need research skills since they can always commission consultants to carry out the research. However, managers will be better able to commission good research and evaluate the results if they are familiar with the research process themselves, and not all managers work in an ideal world where funds exist to commission research; often the only way managers can get research done is to do it themselves.

The relevance of published research to planning and management

Who does research is important because it affects the nature of the research conducted and hence has a large impact on what constitutes the 'body of knowledge' which students of leisure and tourism must study and which leisure and tourism managers must draw on.

Academic research and publication is, to a large extent, a 'closed system'; academics referee other academics' book proposals for commercial publishers; they are the editors of the refereed journals and serve on their editorial advisory boards: they therefore determine what research is acceptable for publication. Practitioners therefore very often find published 'academic' research irrelevant to their needs – this is hardly surprising since most of it is not designed specifically for the practitioner but for the academic world.

The student training to become a professional practitioner in the leisure or tourism field should not therefore be surprised to find that much, but not all, of the scholarly writing available on leisure and tourism is not suitable for direct practical application to policy, planning and management. This does not mean that it is irrelevant, but simply that it does not necessarily focus directly on immediate practical problems.

Research can be 'academic' or 'practical'; it can be theoretical or applied. Some research arises from academic interest and some arises from immediate problems being faced by the providers of leisure or tourism services. Academic research tends to be governed by the concerns of academics often working in the various disciplines, such as sociology, economics or psychology. The 'practical' or 'applied' area tends to be governed by the needs of particular parts of the management process, such as policy, planning, marketing or financial management. Each of these disciplines and applied areas has developed its own distinctive body of leisure and tourism research. Some of these are reviewed in the next chapter.

Further reading

Discussions of leisure research generally: leisure: Jackson and Burton (1989); tourism: Ritchie and Goeldner (1987).

Leisure and tourism forecasting: Archer (1987), Veal (1987), Kelly (1987), Martin and Mason (Annual), Henley Centre for Forecasting (Quarterly).

Conduct of feasibility studies: Kelsey and Gray (1986b).

Psychographics/lifestyle: Wells (1974), Veal (1991), Plog 1987.

2 Approaches to leisure and tourism research

In this chapter the approaches of a number of academic disciplines to leisure and tourism research are examined, including sociology, economics, geography, psychology and social psychology, history and philosophy. In addition some cross-disciplinary dimensions of research are discussed, including such aspects as induction versus deduction, descriptive versus explanatory research, experimental versus non-experimental methods, positivist versus interpretive approaches, quantitative versus qualitative methods, primary versus secondary data and self-reported versus observed data. The aim is to show that research always has a context and must always be thought of in relative rather than absolute terms.

The origins of leisure and tourism research

The bulk of leisure and tourism research has arisen, not from the demands of practising managers, but from the interests of academics who generally owe allegiance to a particular *discipline*. While this statement is broadly true of both leisure and tourism research it is more true of the former than the latter. Here we examine briefly the leisure/tourism research approaches of a number of the most significant of these disciplines: sociology, geography, economics, psychology and social psychology, and history. It is of course impossible to gain a full appreciation of the research contribution and methods of any discipline without understanding the discipline as a whole: an academic discipline is after all defined by its body of research. The discussions below are therefore inevitably somewhat superficial, but references to more detailed reviews are given in the guide to further reading at the end of this chapter.

Sociology

Why do men tend to play sport more than women? Why do middle class, more highly educated people make more use of arts facilities and outdoor recreation areas than other groups? To what extent do people freely choose their leisure activities and holidays and to what extent is their choice limited by economic and social constraints or commercial manipulation? Who is involved and who is excluded when major decisions are made on a leisure or tourism investment in local areas? Why do some groups in society engage in leisure activities which are viewed as 'deviant' or 'anti-social' by others? These are the sorts of questions which sociological research attempts to answer.

Leisure

Sociologists have probably been the most significant contributors to the area of leisure studies, but less significantly to the specific area of tourism. Much of the early research, and some current research, which appears to be 'sociological' has, however, not been carried out by sociologists trained in the discipline. This is true, for example, of many of the major leisure participation and tourism surveys which provide much of the basic factual information about patterns of participation. Much *apparently* 'sociological' research is therefore very pragmatic and lacks the theoretical framework which many properly trained sociologists would like to see.

Sociology is concerned with explaining or understanding social behaviour – particularly the behaviour of groups or classes of people. In the area of leisure, early sociologists or 'social researchers' produced survey evidence which showed that leisure behaviour had a number of uniform features but that it also varied considerably between different groups in the community, depending on such social characteristics as family status, age, sex, educational level and race – known in research jargon as *variables*. Early researchers pursued the idea that if only they could identify sufficient of these *variables* – to construct a 'model' of behaviour – they would be able to predict behaviour of different social groups. The research approach was known as 'quantitative' because it was highly statistical and concerned primarily with *numbers* of participants – and as 'modelling' – because it was based on the construction of mathematical 'models' of human behaviour (Christensen 1988). All the early social research on leisure was not of this quantitative /modelling type, for example Parker's (1971) influential work on the relationships between work and leisure was empirically based, but not particularly quantitative.

The modelling/prediction approach was eventually rejected by many sociologists partly because it did not work in its own terms (Kelly 1980), but also because it lacked a framework of sociological theory: it was too pragmatic; and it asked the wrong questions. Methodologically it was challenged by those sociologists who were not 'quantitatively' orientated but instead believed in the power of theoretical reasoning and in qualitative evidence from small groups of 'real people' rather than statistical evidence from large numbers of 'abstract' people. They were also less interested in 'predicting' behavior than in 'explaining' it. They wanted to know not just what people did with their leisure time but *why*, what leisure *meant* to them, and so on. In Britain the Rapoports (1975) epitomised this move while in the USA it was championed by Kelly (1983). The Rapoports indicated the new trend with their book, *Leisure and the Family Life Cycle*, which was based on in-depth interviews with only about thirty people altogether; detailed 'case-studies' of the motivations and feelings of individuals were reported. In fact the research moves into the area of social psychology.

In the 1980s the leisure research traditions which had developed up to that point were attacked from a critical, neo-Marxist standpoint – typified by Clarke and Critcher's The *Devil Makes Work* (1985). On the one hand this work relies on broader, often historically based, analysis of society and on the other hand it relies heavily on the findings of the 'ethnographic' style of research involving in-depth interaction with usually small groups of individuals – such as youth gangs, ethnic groups, young mothers. The intellectual sweep of the neo-Marxists is broader than that of their predecessors, even though it is based on what is, in some senses, a narrower empirical base.

The 1980s also saw an attack on the existing sociological leisure research by feminist sociologists, who noted that much of the empirical work to date had been based on samples of men and, in focusing on aspects such as occupation and work/leisure relationships, had ignored the day-to-day experience of women and their traditional responsibilities for child-care and unpaid domestic work, and, in focusing on 'choice' in leisure, had ignored the power relationships in society which limited or negated the range of choice for some groups, including women (Deem 1986, Talbot and Wimbush 1987, Green *et al.* 1990).

More recently the sociology of leisure has been characterised by the 'existential' approach of Kelly (1983) and examination of the work of 'post-modern' theorists such as Barthes, Foucault and Baudrillard (Rojek 1985, 1990) which leads to research addressing the significance of such phenomena as the media, fashion, design and style.

The result of this history is a wide range of 'social' or 'sociological' research conducted within what Rojek (1985) refers to as 'multi-paradigmatic rivalry', that is alternative, competing traditions, with different ways of looking at the world. In addition an enormous range of research approaches are now deployed by sociologists studying leisure: quantitative methods are still used (see any edition of *Journal of Leisure Research*), major surveys continue to be conducted (mainly for government/policy purposes), and a variety of qualitative and experimental methods are also used. In short, anything goes.

Tourism

It is notable that, while leisure includes the activity of 'going on holiday' – tourism – the general leisure literature rarely refers to this activity specifically. A further oddity in the leisure/tourism research tradition is that a great deal of North American research on leisure, or outdoor recreation, is in fact based on studies of people who are camping, or at least staying away from home to visit major attractions such as National Parks. So a great deal of what is recognised as 'recreation research' in North America could in fact equally be seen as 'tourism research', but this is rarely acknowledged. So research on the 'sociology of tourism' is conventionally seen as separate from research on the 'sociology of leisure'.

Dann and Cohen (1991) point out that there is 'no single sociology of tourism', instead 'there have been several attempts to understand sociologically different aspects of tourism, departing from a number of theoretical perspectives' (p. 157). They indicate that leisure is only one of the contexts in which tourism is studied; it is also viewed in the context of the sociology of migration and in the context of research on travel.

Cohen (1984) divides sociological research on tourism into four 'issue areas': the tourist, including work on the sociopsychology of tourist motivation and MacCannell's (1976) seminal work on tourism as a 'quest for authenticity'; relations between tourists and locals; the structure and functioning of the tourist system, particularly the various actors in the 'industry'; and the social and environmental consequences of tourism. Reflecting the situation in leisure research, he concludes:

> While a variety of often intriguing conceptual and theoretical approaches for studying the complex and manifold touristic phenomena have emerged, none has yet withstood rigorous empirical testing; while field-studies have proliferated, many lack an explicit, theoretical orientation and hence contribute little to theory building (p. 388).

Geography

What is the relationship between where people live, their access to leisure facilities and their patterns of leisure participation? How do people's perceptions of and appreciation of different landscapes affect their leisure travel behaviour? How are the leisure and tourism trips of the population of a region accommodated and distributed in such a region? How do people make use of outdoor recreation areas, how do they view crowding and congestion? What is the capacity of various environments to absorb visitors? These are the sorts of questions which geographical leisure and tourism research addresses.

Geographers have been very prominent in leisure research (Coppock 1982) and have not generally restricted their interests to the formal confines of their discipline. For example, the Tourism and Recreation Research Unit of Edinburgh University was a creation of the Geography Department of the University and was at the forefront of the development of the modelling techniques discussed under sociology above (Coppock and Duffield 1975). 'Social modelling' was extended to 'spatial modelling' with the aim of predicting not just levels of participation in activities in general, but levels of trips to particular recreation sites. This research was based on data gathered by interview surveys of the population in general or the users of particular recreation sites.

Of course geographers can be expected to be concerned primarily with spatial and environmental issues and also with large-scale natural and man-made phenomena such as the coastline, wilderness and human settlement patterns. Geography has indeed contributed a great deal of insight into these aspects of leisure research. Thus for instance a considerable amount of research has been completed on the catchment areas of different kinds of leisure facilities, that is, surveys which ask people how far they travel to use facilities and which therefore establish the area which the facilities serve (Cowling *et al.* 1983). Much of this research included tourism.

Tourism is of course quintessentially a geographical phenomenon and geography has made major contributions to research in that field (Mitchell 1987, Smith 1983, Pearce 1987, Mitchell and Murphy 1991), including studies of travel patterns and their modelling using the 'gravity model', tourism/recreation carrying capacity studies and regional development studies.

Geographers have been at the forefront of various types of observational research (Burch 1964, TRRU 1983). In particular they have demonstrated the use of aerial photography in examining the spatial distribution of recreational resources and utilisation and they have examined the way visitors make use of dispersed sites such as parks (Van der Zande 1985, Glyptis 1981a, b). More recently geographers have linked the concept of lifestyle with census information to create 'lifestyle maps' based on the common social characteristics of neighbourhoods; such characteristics being closely associated with leisure behaviour (Bickmore *et al.* 1980, Shaw 1984). A mixture of geography and psychological research has been responsible for a large amount of research on 'landscape perception', that is what it is that people find attractive about different kinds of landscape (Patmore 1983, p. 212).

Economics

How do increases in incomes affect leisure expenditure and behaviour? How can an annual subsidy of £10 million to an opera house or a sports centre be justified? What is the impact in terms of business turnover and jobs, of an event such as the Olympic Games? How significant is tourism, the arts, or sport, in the economy? How will a change in the exchange rate affect international tourist arrivals? These are the sort of questions which economic research on leisure and tourism attempts to answer.

Economics is the discipline concerned with the 'allocation of scarce resources' – that is with *what* is produced by a society and with the distribution of what is produced – who gets what. Since leisure and tourism products and services now account for between 20 and 30 per cent of consumer spending in modern western societies, the *economics* of leisure and tourism is of increasing importance. Most of the *economics of leisure* is, however, concerned with the public sector, where the free market forces with which economics is so concerned, are constrained or inoperative (Veal 1989). In the case of tourism, economists have drawn largely on macro-economics, that part of economics which is concerned with economies as a whole – levels of economic output, multipliers, unemployment, international trade and so on.

The major focus of research in the economics of leisure has been on the public sector, particularly rural outdoor recreation and the arts. One of the major concerns of this area of research has been the economic valuation of the recreational, natural and aesthetic values of public recreation lands and wildernesses or arts facilities, even though, because entrance to such areas is often free or less-than-cost, the users' willingness to pay is not immediately available as a measure of people's evaluation, as it is, say, with a commercial facility such as Disneyland. This therefore has spawned a great deal of research on 'cost-benefit analysis' – ways of measuring both the full costs and the full benefits to society of these publicly provided facilities.

As governments moved to the right in the 1980s and began to examine critically many areas of public enterprise with a view to expenditure cuts or privatisation, there was a burst of 'economic impact' studies, in which economists were engaged to establish the economic significance of the arts (Myerscough 1988) or sport (Henley Centre for Forecasting 1986, DASETT 1988a, 1988b).

Another distinct area of the economic study of leisure has been the work on the economics of professional sport. Professional sport is a 'peculiar' – and fascinating – industry sector to economists because of the nature of competition, which is unlike that in other industries (Cairns *et al.* 1986).

Of a more practical bent is the work of forecasters such as Martin and Mason (Annual) and the Henley Centre for Forecasting (Quarterly), who produce regular forecasts of consumer expenditure on leisure products and services as a service to the leisure industries. Demand forecasting has been a major focus of tourism research (Eadington and Redman 1991) and in most countries, at least one organisation exists to produce forecasts of domestic and overseas tourist trips and such forecasts are often based on primarily economic models (Archer 1987).

In terms of research techniques, economists have tended to use similar methods to other social scientists, including household and site interviews, but they tend to have access to more government-collected data, for example on consumer expenditure, and tend to make use of quantitative methods, such as regression.

Psychology/social psychology

What satisfactions do people obtain from their leisure? How do people's perceptions of tourist destinations affect their decision to travel? What motivates people to engage in one form of leisure activity rather than another? How do people's relationships with family and friends affect their leisure behaviour? These are the sort of questions which psychological and social psychological research addresses.

In discussing sociological research, we have already referred to the work of the Rapoports and Kelly as social-psychological in nature, based as it is on attempts to understand the underlying motivations of the individual as well as their social interactions.

Ingham (1986) has reviewed the contributions of psychology to leisure research and classifies the body of work into four main categories: motivation and needs ('why individuals do what they do'), satisfactions (the idea that 'particular types of leisure behaviour and experience lead to differential levels of satisfaction'), leisure as a state of mind (including Csikszentmihalyi's concept of 'flow'), and individual differences (including sex, age, personality and cultural differences). The field is divided into two general approaches, the 'experiential' approach of Neulinger and Csikszentmihayli and the broader approach dealing with reported motivations, satisfactions and attributions typified by the work of Iso-Ahola. Ingham points out that:

> By far the majority of psychological research has relied on the use of self-report questionnaire-derived data. ... Alternative methodological approaches are relatively rare: these could include detailed case studies, direct physiological recording, open-ended self-reporting, field experimentation, and careful observation and analysis of behaviour in different settings
>
> (Ingham 1986, p. 258).

In the second part of his review Ingham (1987) commends for the future the socio-psychological work of Kelly (1983) which involves viewing leisure as a medium in which individuals develop their identities, styles and social roles.

In the area of tourism Pearce and Stringer (1991) divide psychological research into four types; physiological and ergonomic (e.g. jet-lag and travellers' health problems); cognition (e.g. the use of maps and tourists' 'mindfulness' of areas visited); individual differences approaches (e.g. relationships between personality types and types of touristic experience sought, and links with motivation, psychographics and need); social psychology (including intra-individual, inter-individual and group processes); and environmental studies (e.g. perception of crowding). Pearce and Stringer argue that the psychology of tourism is not well developed but that: 'In the absence of a broad psychological thrust in tourism, geographers, sociologists, and leisure and recreation researchers are doing much work which at heart is psychological' (p. 150).

History

What are the historical roots of the practices, attitudes and institutions involved in contemporary leisure and tourism? To what extent has leisure time increased since pre-industrial times? How is change constrained by the effects of past actions and events?

Historians, in addressing such questions, have been influential in the development of leisure research. For instance, Huizinga's classic work on play, *Homo Ludens* (1950) is largely historical. Young and Willmott's study of *The Symmetrical Family* (1973) has a firm base in historical analysis. More recently, historians and theorists have produced histories of leisure, particularly in the nineteenth century (Cunningham 1980, Bailey 1978) which show how leisure has been integral to the development of western capitalist society. In fact one of the claims of the 1980s critics of earlier leisure studies was that they were ahistorical, or at least that their view of history was naive.

Most textbooks on tourism (e.g. Burkart and Medlik 1981) provide an historical overview of the development of travel and tourism. Tourism is tracked back to classical Greek and Roman times, to the emergence of the 'Grand Tour' in Europe in the seventeenth and eighteenth centuries and the development of spas and resorts. In Britain historical research has addressed some of the theoretical issues on social structure and change which have been addressed by sociologists, but in America studies have tended to be more descriptive case-studies (Towner and Wall 1991).

While reviews of the contributions of history to leisure and tourism research tend not to discuss techniques, in fact one of the major contributions of historical analysis is to illustrate the use of secondary data sources, such as diaries, official records and reports, and newspaper reports.

Political science

Despite the importance of public policy matters in leisure and tourism, the political dimension of the subject was neglected for many years. More recently, important contributions have been made to rectify this by Bramham and Henry (1985), Wilson (1988) and Coalter (1990) in relation to leisure generally, and by Richter (1987) in relation to tourism. While leisure studies research has focused on the relationships between political ideology and leisure policy, in tourism the focus is less ideological and more to do with the role of tourism in political behaviour (Matthews and Richter 1991).

Philosophy

Histories of leisure in standard textbooks often begin with 'classical' views and definitions of leisure as propounded particularly by Aristotle. Murphy's (1974) textbook *Concepts of Leisure*, is typical of this genre and has long been a standard. One of the most famous essays on leisure was by the philosopher Bertrand Russell, entitled *In Praise of Idleness* (1935). The most comprehensive review of the relationship between philosophy and leisure is by Dare, Welton and Coe (1987), which ranges from Aristotle to Sartre via Kant, Marx and many others.

Approaches and dimensions

A number of alternative approaches to and dimensions of leisure and tourism research cut across the disciplines; some of them are discussed here in the form of dichotomies. ˗

Induction versus deduction

It has been noted that research involves *finding out* and *explaining.* Finding out might be called the 'what?' of research – what is happening? what is the situation? Explaining might be called the 'how?' and the 'why?' of research – how do things happen? Why do they happen the way they do? What are the causes of different phenomena?

Finding out involves description and it involves gathering information. Explaining involves attempting to understand that information: it goes beyond the descriptive. Research methods should facilitate both these processes: describing and explaining.

Description and explanation can be seen as part of a circular model of research as illustrated in Figure 2.1. The research process can begin at point A, description, or at point C, explanation/theory formulation. And a research project may involve a single circuit; or a number of circuits, possibly in both directions. If the research process begins with description, at point A, and moves from there to explanation, the

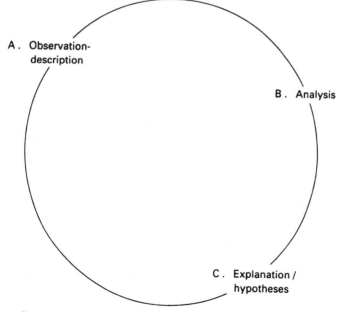

Source: Based on Williamson *et al* 1982, p. 7.

Figure 2.1: Circular model of the research process

process is described as *inductive*. The explanation is *induced* from the data – the data come first and the explanation later.

Case study 2.1: tennis versus golf – inductive approach

Suppose a descriptive piece of research shows that more people play tennis than play golf. This is just a piece of information; we cannot explain *why* this is so without additional information and analysis. If we added the information that it costs more to play golf than to play tennis then we could offer the explanation that tennis is more popular because it is cheaper.

However, this may not be the complete answer. It could be that more people perceive tennis as more fun to play than golf and that, even if it cost more than golf, it would still be more popular. Or it could be that there are more tennis courts available than golf courses and that if there were more golf courses available then golf would be more popular. More information (another circuit of the model) would help in confirming or refuting some of these explanations.

In its most fully developed form the explanation amounts to a theory – which is a considered set of related principles which explain how a social phenomenon operates or comes about. In this case we would need a theory of sports participation relating demand, supply of facilities, costs, perceived attractiveness of the activity and facilities, intrinsic satisfactions and so on.

This approach to research, where explanation arises from attempting to explain what is observed, where there is a toing and froing between data and explanation, is known as the *inductive* approach. Explanations are *induced* from the data.

If the research process starts at point C then it involves deduction, that is prior logical reasoning. This entails developing hypotheses as to how or why something might happen, then collecting the requisite data to test the hypotheses. In the case-study above, the possible explanations as to why one sport might be more popular than another would be set out in advance in the form of hypotheses. Hypotheses are statements which may be supported or refuted by evidence. The hypotheses might arise from informal observation and experience of the researcher or from the existing literature.

Case study 2.2: tennis versus golf – deductive approach

Hypothesis 1:   if sport A is more expensive to play than sport B, then sport B will be more popular.

Hypothesis 2:   if more facilities are available for sport B than for sport A then sport B will be more popular.

To test these hypotheses we have to design a research project to collect information on:

(a) the relative popularity of two sports,
(b) the costs of participating in the two sports,
(c) the availability of facilities for the two sports.

In this case the research is guided from the beginning by the initial hypotheses.

If the hypotheses form a coherent whole and possibly relate to other ideas about human behaviour then they may form *theories*.

In practice data are rarely collected without some explanatory model in mind (otherwise how would we know what data to collect?) so there is always an element of deduction. And it is not possible to develop hypotheses and theories without at least some initial information on the subject in hand, however informally obtained, so there is always an element of induction. So most research is partly inductive and partly deductive.

Whether hypotheses or theories containing the explanation are put forward at the start of the project or arise as a result of data analysis, they represent the key creative part of the research process. Data collection and analysis can be fairly mechanical but interpretation of data and the development of explanations requires – both before and after the collection of the data – at the least creativity and at best, inspiration!

Descriptive versus explanatory research

In Chapter one the difference between descriptive and explanatory research was discussed and it is appropriate to raise the issue again here.

Descriptive research aims to describe what is – what has been observed or reported. To explain the patterns in observed or reported data it is necessary to consider the question of *causality*: the question of whether A is *caused* by B.

Labovitz and Hagedorn (1971) state that there are '... at least four widely accepted scientific criteria for establishing causality. These criteria are association, time priority, nonspurious relation and rationale' (p. 4).

Association is a 'necessary condition for a causal relation' – that is, A and B must be associated in some way – for example, if A increases B decreases.

> There are two characteristics of an association that generally strengthen the conclusion that one variable is at least a partial cause of another. The first is *magnitude*, which refers to the size or strength of the association. ... The second ... is *consistency*. If the relation persists from one study to the next under a variety of conditions, confidence in the causal nature of the relation is increased.
>
> (Labovitz and Hagedorn, 1971:5)

Time priority means that for A to be the cause of B then A must take place before B.

A *nonspurious relation* is defined as '... association between two variables that cannot be explained by a third variable' (p. 9). This means that it must be established that there is no third factor, C, which is affecting both A *and* B.

Rationale means that statistical or other evidence is not enough; the conclusion that A causes B is not justified unless there is some theoretical or logical explanation to suggest *how* it happens.

These matters are taken up again in Chapters 3 and 13.

Empirical versus non-empirical research

Empirical research is research which uses data or specifically collected information to reach conclusions. But there is another type of research which is equally, if not more, important, which makes no explicit or formal reference to data as such. This is research which results from thinking and reading and contemplation. It is the research which develops ideas, hypotheses and theories.

A review of the contents of one or two editions of the main leisure or tourism journals will reveal the existence of both sorts of research – and the contributions which each can make. While the empirical studies provide the 'building blocks' of a great deal of research and knowledge the non-empirical contributions are needed to review and refine ideas and to place the empirical work in context. A book like this inevitably devotes more space to empirical methods, because they involve more explicit, technical processes which can be described and 'taught'. It cannot however be too strongly stressed that a good review of the literature or a thoughtful piece of writing arising from deep and insightful, inspirational thinking about a subject can be worth a thousand, unthinking, surveys!

Positivist versus interpretive approach

The positivist/interpretive dichotomy is related to the empirical/non-empirical dichotomy but is nevertheless distinct. It is primarily a reference to sociological schools of thought. *Positivism* is a framework of research similar to that adopted by the natural scientist in which the researcher sees people as phenomena to be studied from the outside, with behaviour to be explained on the basis of facts and observations gathered by the researcher and theories and models developed by the researcher. Many sociologists are highly suspicious of such attempts to translate natural science approaches into the social sciences (Rojek 1989, p. 70); they believe that it is dangerous to draw conclusions about the causes and motivations of behaviour on the basis of 'scientific' type evidence.

The *interpretive* model places more reliance on the people being studied to provide their own explanation of their situation or behaviour. The interpretive researcher therefore tries to 'get inside' the minds of subjects and see the world from their point of view. This of course suggests a less formalised approach to data collection and generally an inductive approach.

Experimental versus non-experimental

The popular image of the scientist is someone in a white coat in a laboratory, conducting experiments. The experimental method of research involves the scientist attempting to control the environment of the subject of the research and measuring the effects of controlled change. Knowledge progresses on the basis that, in a controlled experimental situation, change in A was brought about by change in B. The researcher aims to produce conditions such that the research will fulfill the requirements for causality discussed above.

In the world of human beings, with which the social scientist deals, there is much less scope for experiment than in the world of inanimate objects or animals with which natural scientists deal. Some situations do exist where experimentation with human beings in the field of leisure or tourism can take place. For instance it is possible to experiment with variations in children's play equipment; it is possible to conduct experiments with willing subjects; and it is possible to experiment in management situations, for instance by varying prices or advertising strategies in relation to leisure or tourism services. But many areas of interest to the leisure or tourism researcher are not susceptible to controlled experiment.

For instance the researcher interested in the effect of level of income on behaviour cannot take a group of people and vary their incomes in order to study the effects of income on leisure participation or tourism behaviour – it would be difficult to find people on executive salaries willing voluntarily to spend a year living on a student grant in the interests of research! Alternatively, unlike the scientist experimenting with rats, it is not possible to find two groups of humans identical in every respect except for their level of income. Even more fundamentally, it is of course not possible to vary people's social class or race. In order to study these phenomena it is necessary to use non-experimental methods, that is it is necessary to study differences between people *as they exist*. So in order to study the effects of income on leisure participation patterns or touristic behaviour it is necessary to study the behaviour of different groups of people with different levels of income; but people differ in all sorts of ways, some of which may be related to their level of income and some not. So in comparing the leisure behaviour of two groups of people, it is difficult to be sure which differences arise as a result of income differences and which as a result of other differences. The results of the research are therefore likely to be less clear-cut than in the case of the controlled experiment.

Some areas within the broad field of leisure and tourism do lend themselves to experimental research: these are the areas which are closest to the natural sciences, namely psychology and the human movement aspect of sports research. Thus in the case of psychological research, it is possible to set up experiments in which people are subject to 'stimuli' – for example photographs or video – and to study their reactions. In the case of human movement, subjects can be asked to engage in particular forms of physical exercise and their physical reactions can be measured. Although some of the techniques and approaches described in this book are applicable to experimental as much as non-experimental research, in general the experimental method is not dealt with.

Primary versus secondary data

In planning a research project it is sensible to consider whether it is necessary to go to the expense of collecting new information (primary data, where the researcher is the primary user) or whether existing data (secondary data, where the researcher is the secondary user) will do the job. Sometimes existing information is in the form of research already completed on the topic or a related topic. A fundamental part of any research project is therefore to scour the existing published – and unpublished – sources of information for related research. Existing research might not obviate the originally proposed research, but it may provide interesting ideas and points of comparison with the proposed research.

Even if new information is to be collected it will usually also be necessary to make use of other existing information – such as official government statistics or financial records from a leisure or tourism facility or service. Such information is generally referred to as *secondary data*, as opposed to the *primary* data, which is the new data to be collected in the proposed research. Secondary data and their analysis are dealt with in Chapter 6.

Self-reported versus observed data

The best, and often the only, sources of information about individuals' leisure or tourism behaviour or aspirations are the individuals' own reports about themselves. Much leisure and tourism research therefore involves asking people about their behaviour, attitudes and aspirations.

There are some disadvantages to this approach, mainly that the researcher is never sure just how honest or accurate people are in responding to questions. In some instances people may deliberately or unwittingly distort of 'bend' the truth – for instance in understating the amount of alcohol they drink or overstating the amount of exercise they take. In other instances they may have problems of recall – for instance in remembering just how much money they spent on a recreational or holiday trip some months ago. Generally self-reporting research methods involve interviews or survey methods.

The alternative to relying on people to tell the researcher what they do, is for the researcher to use an alternative source of evidence. For instance, to find out how children use a playground or how adults make use of a park or resort area it would probably be better to watch them than to try to ask them about it. Patterns of movement and crowding can be observed. Sometimes people leave behind evidence of their behaviour, for instance the most popular exhibits at a museum will be the ones where the carpet is most worn, and the most used beaches are likely to be those where the most litter is dumped. Generally these techniques are referred to as *observational* or *unobtrusive* techniques and are dealt with in Chapter 7.

Qualitative versus quantitative research

Much leisure and tourism research involves the collection, analysis and presentation of statistical information. Sometimes the information is inately quantitative – for instance the numbers of people engaging in a list of leisure activities in a year or the number of people visiting a particular holiday area. Sometimes the information is qualitative in nature but is presented in statistical form – for instance 'scores' calculated from asking people to indicate levels of satisfaction with different services.

One approach to research – the quantitative approach – involves statistical analysis, such that the results of the research from sample studies are generalisable to the whole population with a certain degree of confidence; it relies on numerical evidence to test its hypotheses. To be sure of the reliability of the results it is often necessary to study relatively large numbers of people and to use computers to analyse the results.

Another approach to research is not concerned with this sort of statistical analysis. It involves gathering a great deal of information about a small number of people rather than a limited amount of information about a large number of people. The information collected is generally not presentable in numerical form. It is based on the belief that a full and rounded understanding of the leisure or tourist behaviour and situation of a few individuals, however unrepresentative they may be, is of more value than a limited understanding of a large, 'representative' group.

Non-quantitative research is generally referred to as qualitative; more specifically, research studying groups of people using non-quantitative anthropological approaches, is referred to as ethnographic research or ethnographic fieldwork. The methods used – such as observation, informal interviewing and participant observation – were initially developed by anthropologists, but have been adapted by sociologists for use in their work. These methods are considered in Chapter 8.

While the debate between protagonists of qualitative and quantitative research can become somewhat partisan, many believe that the two approaches complement each other and even that quantitative research should be based on initial qualitative work. It is even possible that the two approaches are moving together, as a recently published book entitled *Using Computers in Qualitative Research* (Fielding and Lee 1991) suggests.

Further reading

The journal *Leisure Studies*, has published a number of articles which review the contributions of various disciplines to leisure research; these are by: Coppock (1982) on geography, Parry (1983) on sociology, Vickerman (1983) on economics, and Ingham (1986, 1987) on psychology. And in 1989 it published an analysis and review of the contribution of historians to leisure studies in Britain by Bailey (1989).

The journal *Annals of Tourism Research* devoted a special issue to

Tourism Social Sciences in 1991 (Graburn and Jafari, 1991), covering such disciplines as sociology (Dann and Cohen, 1991), geography (Mitchell and Murphy, 1991), history (Towner and Wall, 1991), psychology (Pearce and Stringer, 1991), political science (Matthews and Richter 1991) and economics (Eadington and Redman, 1991).

Recent books edited by Barnett (1988) and Jackson and Burton (1989) provide disciplinary reviews of leisure research in more detail than those presented above.

For discussion of qualitative versus quantitative research see Kelly (1980), Henderson (1990), Borman et al (1986), Krenz and Sax (1986).

For a discussion of the experimental method in leisure research see Havitz and Sell (1991).

3 Starting out – plans and proposals

In this chapter the process of formulating research proposals is examined. Because a proposal must indicate how a research project is to be conducted in its entirety, this involves examination of the whole research process from beginning to end, so a certain amount of cross-referencing is required to later chapters where elements of the process are dealt with in detail. The relationship between management and research problems and research design are considered. Time and financial budgetting and the role of the tendering process are also outlined.

Introduction: steps in the research process

Essentially the research process should proceed as follows:

1. preparation and planning;
2. investigation;
3. analysis;
4. writing up/presentation of results.

This can be broken down into more detailed steps, as indicated in Figure 3.1. However, as discussed in Chapter 2, there is an enormous variety of approaches to research, so all research projects do not follow the same procedures. For example, not all research involves the collection of new data. Some research is entirely theoretical, so writing – exploring ideas, constructing theories, developing models – does not come at the end, but is the basic activity of the research. Not all research involves 'measurement' in a conventional sense. Consulting the literature may happen at a variety of points in the research process – indeed it may be the main activity of the research. Not all research is conducted for a 'client'. Research is not nearly as 'tidy' and well-organised a process as lists of stages and procedures would imply. In fact the most important aspects of research are often the ones which do not 'conform' to the plan and do not appear in lists and schedules –

the inspired thought; the chance conversation that leads you to a book or article which says it all; the remarks by an individual in an interview which make sense of all the other interviews. It is not possible to put these in lists of procedures, but they are what makes the difference between good research and just ordinary or competent research.

The list of steps outlined in Figure 3.1 is therefore just a guide and must be adapted according to the particular situation and should not be slavishly adhered to if an alternative would produce better research! In particular the order in which tasks are undertaken may vary a great deal and there will usually be a great deal of iteration between decisions made in different steps – for example, a decision made in Step 13 on sample size, may have to be revised in the light of considerations in Step 18, the preparation of the budget. Indeed some

---

Preparation/planning stages
1. Identify research topic/issue.
2. Clarify research questions – with client if applicable.
3. Identify key concepts, working hypotheses, models, theories, evaluative framework.
4. Review existing research/literature/secondary data sources.
5. Refine ideas on concepts/relationships/hypotheses/theory/models in light of Step 4.
6. Statement of objectives/terms of reference.
7. Determine ways of measuring concepts.
8. Formulate research strategy.
9. Specify population.
10. Specify type of data collection method(s).
11. Decide sampling method.
12. Specify sample size.
13. List data items to be collected.
14. Design data collection 'instrument(s)'.
15. Plan fieldwork management arrangements.
16. Specify proposed data analysis procedures.
17. Prepare a budget (which may need to be approved).
18. Prepare a timetable/work schedule.

Investigation stages
19. Recruit and train interviewers and supervisors.
20. Conduct pilot survey(s) and, if necessary, revise steps 10 to 15.
21. Conduct main data collection exercise.
22. Collect any secondary data.

Analysis stages
23. Code data and enter into computer.
24. Prepare computer programs.
25. Specify analysis, related to initial research questions/hypotheses.
26. Run computer (or other) analysis.

Write-up/preparation stages
27. Prepare draft report/article(s)/presentation.
28. Submit draft for comment (to colleagues/supervisor/client).
29. Prepare final report/article/presentation.

Figure 3.1   Steps in the research process

steps – such as Step 13 and Step 18 – may be so interdependent that they are considered at the same time rather than sequentially.

The middle part of the list of tasks set out in Figure 3.1 (Steps 9 – 26) is largely mechanical, although carrying out the tasks competently is not necessarily easy. Large parts of this and other research methods texts are devoted to offering a 'cookbook' approach to these mechanical tasks. To do them well requires attention to detail, patience, and practice. However, in many ways the most important aspects are at the beginning and the end of the list. If the research is not properly specified in conceptual terms all the most painstaking data collection and analysis in the world will not save it. Equally, the most brilliant piece of research will be wasted if it is not adequately communicated to others.

Each of the stages listed above is now discussed in turn.

Preparation/planning stages

The first five stages are set down as discrete, sequential steps in the process, but in practice they can be anything but discrete and sequential. There may be much 'toing and froing' between the literature, the initial ideas and final ideas. The important aspect is the emergence in Stage six of a clear statement of objectives or terms of reference.

1. Identify research topic/issue

The research topic or issue will arise from the researcher's own interests or from a policy or management issue. It may be very specific or very general; it may be in the form of a question, a problem or an area of interest.

Students or academics, deciding on a topic to pursue 'for its own sake' or for a thesis, get ideas from the literature or from their own personal interests. They might decide, for example, that they would like to do research on 'leisure centres' or on 'tourism and the elderly'.

Policy or management-related topics arise from the world of practice where leisure or tourism service delivery organisations identify problems which they wish to solve or areas of information deficiency. Topics or issues arising from this source might relate to evaluation, for example, 'to assess the effectiveness of marketing practices' in a particular organisation; or they could be explanatory, for example: 'identify reasons for and possible means of reversing the decline in the number of visitors to x'.

2. Clarify research questions

In Chapters 1 and 2 the role of research was discussed in relation to policy, planning and management and in relation to academic disciplines. It should be emphasised here that research is not an isolated process; ideally it should be linked to either the policy/planning/management process or to a disciplinary or inter-disciplinary theoretical framework, or both. Research questions do not arise in isolation, they arise in an applied or theoretical context. It is therefore difficult, and probably impossible, for someone who knows nothing about the applied management or theoretical disciplines to frame good research questions.

The initial statement of the topic or issue is not always clear or in a form which is suitable for research. It will be helpful to discuss this stage in two contexts: firstly where the research topic arises from the researcher's own interest – researcher based – and secondly where it arises from a client – client based.

Researcher based

In some cases the researcher begins with a research question which is already clear and specific – for example: 'Why do most public leisure centres not make a profit?' or 'What is the role of 'the holiday' among retired people?' In that case they would proceed to Stage three.

In other cases the researcher is at the stage of having identified only a broad area of interest, such as 'Leisure centres' or 'Tourism and the elderly'. The problem is to identify questions/issues which are interesting and which merit research. To identify such questions/issues the researcher might refer to practitioners or existing researchers in the area or to the literature. In this case therefore they would go to Stage 4 at this point and return to Stage 3 when more specific questions/issues have been identified.

For example, following examination of the literature, it may be decided that the issue/question to be followed up in relation to the example of leisure centres is the proposition that most public leisure centres are constrained because they have to serve the wider community and political masters and are not able to 'target' their potentially most profitable 'market segments'. In relation to the example of tourism and the elderly it could be decided that an interesting issue to explore is how the motivation of the retired in taking holidays differs from the motivation of people with paid jobs. Note that the first of these statements implies explanatory research, whereas the second implies research which is more descriptive in nature. Evaluative research tends to be more the province of client-based research as discussed in the next section.

The research questions could be as follows. 'What is the influence of community accountability and political control on leisure centre management and profitability?' and 'What is the pattern of holiday-taking among the retired, compared with those in paid work?'.

Client based

Client organisations which are experienced in commissioning research can produce briefs which are clear and 'ready to roll' – as in the example given at the end of the discussion of Stage 1, above. In other situations it is necessary to clarify the client's meanings and intentions. For example a client might ask for a study of the 'leisure needs' of a community – in which case it would be necessary to clarify what the client means by 'leisure'. For example do they wish to include home-based leisure, holidays, entertainment, restaurants and nightclubs? If a client asks for the effectiveness of a programme to be assessed it may be necessary to obtain from them a statement of objectives of the sort presented in the case study under Stage 3 below, or a list of performance criteria.

Paradoxically, problems can arise when client organisations are over-specific about their requirements. For example an organisation may ask for a 'user survey' or 'visitor survey' to be conducted. It is not easy to decide what should be included in such a survey without information on the management or policy questions which the data are meant to answer – is the organisation concerned about declining attendances, is it wanting to change its 'marketing mix', is it concerned about the particular mix of clientel being attracted, is it concerned about future trends in demand? It would be preferable for the client to indicate the problem and leave the researcher to determine the most suitable research approach to take.

Sometimes there is a hidden agenda which the researcher would do well to become familiar with *before* embarking on the research. For example, research can sometimes be used as a means to defuse or delay difficult management decisions in an organisation. An example would be where a leisure or tourism service is suffering declining attendances because of poor maintenance of facilities and poor staff attitudes to customers; this is very clear to anyone who walks in the door, but the management decides to commission a 'market study', in the hope that the answer to their problem can be found 'out there' in the market – when in fact the problem is very much 'in there', and their money might be better spent on improving maintenance and staff training than on research!

A situation where the client's requirements may seem vague is when the research is not related to immediate policy needs but to possible future needs or simply to satisfy curiosity. For example, a manager of a leisure or tourism facility may commission a user survey (perhaps because there is spare money in the current year's budget) without having any specific policy or management problems in mind. In that case the research will need to specify hypothetical or potential policy/management tasks and match the data specifications to them.

3. Identify concepts, hypotheses, models, theories, evaluative framework

Concepts
Concepts are general representations of the phenomena to be studied – the 'building blocks' of the study. For example, 'leisure' is a concept; 'tourism' is a concept; 'social class' is a concept; 'power' is a concept; 'sport' is a concept; 'efficiency' is a concept, and so on.

The statement of the research question(s) will inevitably involve concepts. The researcher must identify all the concepts involved in the research problem and adopt working definitions of the concepts. To a large extent concepts arise not from the research process *per se* but from the researcher's or others' knowledge of the substantive subject of the research and relevant disciplines. literature

In the examples discussed above a number of concepts can be identified:

	Concepts
Leisure centres	Public leisure centre
	Management
	Community accountability
	Political control
	Profitability
Tourism and the elderly	Retired person
	Holiday
	Motivation
	Paid job

Descriptive research

In descriptive research, while concepts must be clear, they may not have any explicit relationships. The research task is to identify concepts clearly and measure them accurately.

Explanatory research: hypotheses/theories/models

In the case of explanatory research, as discussed in Chapter 2, the aim is to establish causality and one of the necessary conditions for establishing causality is that there be a consistent relationship between the concepts or variables concerned. A proposition concerning a relationship between one or more concepts is a *hypothesis*. The classic scientific procedure is to propose a hypothesis and test its validity against the data (the deductive approach). If the data are consistent with the hypothesis then the hypothesis is accepted; if not it is rejected.

Hypotheses for the examples discussed above are shown in Figure 3.2.

When the relationships between concepts are quantifiable a hypothesis or set of hypotheses may be referred to as a 'model'. For example, the proposition that individuals' expenditure on tourism is related to their level of disposable income can be conceived of as a model because both income and expenditure are quantifiable and it would be possible to produce a mathematical model of the type:

$$T = a + bI$$

where T is expenditure on tourism, I is disposable income and a and b are 'parameters' which would be determined from empirical research.

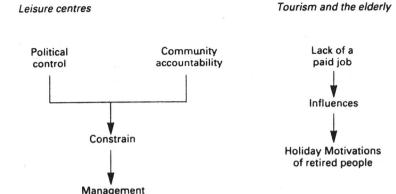

Leisure centres   **Tourism and the elderly**

Figure 3.2 Example hypotheses

A further condition for the establishment of causality is the existence of some sort of rationale or theory – that is, it cannot be concluded that A is the cause of B simply because there is a relationship between A and B. There must be some explanation of the mechanism by which A affects B. How elaborate this explanation is and the extent to which it is related to social theory generally – including the various disciplinary traditions outlined in Chapter 2 – will vary. In the deductive approach the hypotheses will have been generated in some sort of explanatory context. The origins of the research may be theoretical. The review of the literature may also provide a theoretical context. While limited, 'common sense', hypotheses may be of value, the research can be strengthened if it is related to wider theoretical explanations of human behaviour.

For example, the question of the control of public leisure centres discussed above could be related to 'public choice' theory, which relates public decision-making to the idea of different groups or 'actors' in the system pursuing their own interests (Wade 1983); and the elderly and holidays research might be related to 'disengagement theory', which sees ageing and retirement as a process of disengagement from previously significant and meaningful activities and relationships (Cumming and Henry 1961). In the case of the quantified model relating tourism expenditure to income, the model might be related to general economic theory on consumer income and expenditure.

The question of how data relate to the testing of hypotheses and theories and the various deductive and inductive processes involved are discussed more fully in Chapter 13 on data analysis. At this stage of the planning of research it is necessary to set out a conceptual and/or theoretical basis for the research design.

Evaluative framework

In evaluative research the concepts involved do not necessarily relate to each other but to established performance criteria – for example, in the private sector a common performance criterion is the requirement to produce a minimum rate of return on capital. The research design must therefore be guided by some sort of evaluative framework – a set of rules which will determine whether or not the programme, service or project being evaluated meets the agreed performance standards. The case study sets out an example of how this might work.

Case study 3.1: concepts in evaluative research: Part 1

Hatry and Dunn (1971) give an example of how concepts can be isolated from a set of objectives for a public recreation service. Their suggested objectives for a public recreation service are:

> Recreation services should provide for all citizens, to the extent practicable, a variety of adequate, year-round leisure opportunities which are accessible, safe, physically attractive, and provide enjoyable experiences. They should, to the maximum extent, contribute to the mental and physical health of the community, to its economic and social well-being and permit outlets that will help decrease incidents of antisocial behaviour such as crime and delinquency, (p. 13).

A research task which might be set by an organisation with such objectives would be to evaluate the effectiveness of its recreation programmes. From this statement a number of concepts, which constitute criteria for effectiveness, can be isolated:

(a) adequacy;
(b) enjoyableness;
(c) accessibility;
(d) (un)crowdedness;
(e) variety;
(f) safety;
(g) physical attractiveness;
(h) crime avoidance;
(i) health;
(j) economic well-being.

The question of devising measures to assess the organisation's effectiveness in terms of these concepts is discussed under Step 6.

4. Review existing research/literature

The process of reviewing existing research/literature is sufficiently important for a complete chapter to be devoted to it in this book, Chapter 5. Reviewing previous research or the literature can play a number of roles.

1. It may be the entire basis of the research – there is no intention of collecting new data in the current project.
2. It can be the source of ideas on what topics need researching.
3. It is an exercise to ensure that the proposed research has not already been done by someone else.
4. It may be a source of ideas about the proposed topic of research, either in terms of theories or methodology.

5. It may be a source of comparison, that is where findings from previous related studies are compared with those from the proposed project.

6. The information may be an integral or supportive part of the research, complementing the newly collected data - for example the use of population census data or leisure or tourism facility or service records in conjunction with survey data.

In many cases this has to be seen as an 'interim' literature review only. Time does not always permit a thorough literature review to be completed in the early stages of the project. Having investigated the literature as thoroughly as possible, it is usually necessary to proceed with the proposed research in the hope that all relevant material has been identified. Exploration of the literature will generally continue for the duration of the project. Researchers always run the risk of coming across some previous, or contemporaneous, publication which will completely negate or upstage their work just as they are about to complete it – but that is part of the excitement of research!

Where possible, attempts should be made to explore not just published research – the literature – but also unpublished and on-going research. The process is very much 'hit and miss'. Knowing what research is on-going or knowing of completed but unpublished research usually depends on informal networks, although some organisations produce registers of on-going research. Once a topic of interest has been identified it is often clear, from the literature, where the major centres for such research are located and to discover, from direct approaches or from annual reports or newsletters, what research is on-going. This process can be particularly important if the topic is a 'fashionable' one. However, if this is the case, the 'networks' are usually very alive through conferences or seminars. In fact research in the leisure and tourism field can rarely be replicated exactly – unlike the situation in the natural sciences. In the natural sciences research carried out in, say, California can reproduce exactly the findings of research carried out in, say, London. In leisure and tourism research however, this is not the case – a set of research procedures carried out in California could be expected to produce very different results from identical procedures carried out in London – or even New York – simply because leisure and tourism research is involved with people in varying social settings.

5. Refine ideas

This stage involves 'circling back' to Stages 1, 2 or 3 and, if necessary, reviewing the conclusions of those stages in the light of findings from the literature review. For example, in the case of the leisure centres study, the literature could reveal that narrow measures of 'profitability' using just monetary income and expenditure are not sufficient when analysing public facilities, but that the economist's 'public goods' aspects (costs and benefits which are generated but are not paid for by the recipients) should be taken into account – so 'public good' should be added to the list of concepts involved.

6. Statement of objectives

In the case of client-based research clear objectives may be available from the start, but in the case of researcher-based topics it is usually necessary to pause, somewhere around this stage of the process, and ensure that the objectives of the research are absolutely clear and have been written down.

To continue the two examples, the objectives of the 'leisure centres' project might be along the lines:

To investigate the extent to which community accountability and political control affects the marketing and hence the profitability of public leisure centres.

And in the case of the elderly and holidays:

To investigate the effect of the absence of a paid job on holiday motivations of the elderly.

7. Measuring concepts

Introduction

If empirical research is to be conducted then it is necessary to be precise about what is to be observed or measured. Some 'measures' are quantitative, others are simply definitional – for example the age limits of men and women. Some general considerations in measuring the phenomena of leisure and tourism are set out below.

1. The participation rate – the proportion or percentage of the population which engages in a particular activity in a given time period, e.g. the proportion of the population that plays tennis or the proportion of the population that takes an overseas holiday in a year.
2. Number of participants – measure (1) multiplied by the population, e.g. x million people attend the cinema at least once in the course of a year or y million people take overseas holidays in a year.
3. Volume of activity/trips – measure (2) multiplied by the frequency of participation or visits per head, e.g. there were n million attendances at cinemas in Britain in 1990, or m million overseas holiday trips made by Britons in 1990.
4. Time – measure (3) multiplied by the time spent per participant, e.g. the number of person-hours spent at the cinema per annum or the number of nights spent on overseas holidays in a year.
5. Expenditure – measure (3) multiplied by expenditure per visit per head, e.g. the amount spent per annum on cinema tickets or the amount spent per annum on overseas holidays.

Validity and reliability

Two aspects should be taken into consideration when devising means of measuring concepts: validity and reliability. Validity is the extent to which the measure truly reflects the phenomenon being considered. Leisure and tourism research are fraught with difficulties in this area, mainly because empirical research is largely concerned with people's behaviour and with their attitudes, and for information on these the researcher is, in the main, reliant on people's own reports in the form of responses to questionnaire-based and other forms of interview. These instruments are subject to a number of imperfections, which means that the validity of leisure and tourism data can rarely be as certain as in the natural sciences. Various steps can however be taken to attempt to test validity, as discussed in Chapter 10.

Reliability is the extent to which research findings would be the same if the research were to be repeated at a later date or with a different sample of subjects. Again it can be seen that the model is the natural sciences where, if experimental conditions are properly controlled, repetition of an experiment should produce identical results. This is rarely the case in the social sciences, because they deal with human beings in ever changing social situations. This means that the social scientist, including the leisure and tourism researcher, must be very cautious when making general statements on the basis of empirical research. Strictly speaking, any research findings relate only to the subjects involved, at the time and place the research was carried out. Hence the importance of sampling procedures which are an attempt to ensure that research findings are to some degree generalisable.

Case study 3.2: concepts in evaluative research, Part 2

Under Stage 3 above, Hatry and Dunn's illustration of the relationship between recreation objectives and evaluation concepts was outlined. Hatry and Dunn (1971) continue by devising measures of the concepts identified. They produce a set of 'illustrative measures of recreation effectiveness', as follows (letters cross-reference the concepts listed in Part 1):

Measures
1. attendances (re concepts a, b);
2. participants/non-participant numbers (a, b);
3. persons living within x mins and y miles of facilities (a, c);
4. crowdedness indices (waiting times, numbers turned away, ratios of use to capacity, user perceptions) (a, d);
5. number of different activities catered for (e);
6. accidents (f);
7. index of attractiveness of facilities (g);
8. citizen satisfaction (b);
9. crime rates (h);
10. illness (i);
11. business income, jobs, property values affected (j).

Some of these items of data could be collected routinely – for example the number of attendances at swimming pools – but others would require special data collection exercises – for example attendances at parks or citizen or user attitudes. Actually deciding whether or not the service was 'effective' or had 'improved its effectiveness' would involve comparing the measures with set targets, with similar measures from other organisations or with measures from previous years.

Concept	Measure/definition
Leisure centres	
Leisure centre	A facility open to the public, publicly owned, and including indoor sports and other leisure facilities.
Community	Population of a local authority area.
Accountability	Production of annual reports and accounts; instances of public influence on management via politicians and press.
Politician	Elected councillor.
Control	Issuing of instructions, laying down of rules/policies/practices.
Constraint	Rules, procedures, practices, which prevent certain actions (e.g. certain marketing or programming strategies).
Profitability	Difference between income and expenditure, including financial and 'public good' aspects.
Tourism and the elderly	
Retired person	Person in receipt of pension and/or superannuation, not in paid employment.
Holiday	Trip away from home of at least four nights, for leisure purposes.
Motivation	Reasons given for activity.
Paid job	Paid employment of at least 30 hours a week

Figure 3.3   Example concepts

Examples
Each of the concepts identified in Step 3 should be considered in turn and definitions and proposed methods of measurement determined. In relation to the two examples, the exercise might be as shown in Figure 3.3. Measurement in evaluative research is illustrated in Case study 3.2.

8. Formulate research strategy
Data requirements should flow fairly logically from the list of concepts and their measures. At this stage the researcher should be asking: what information is required in order to answer the research questions or to test the working hypotheses established?

At the same time it is necessary to consider the whole approach to how information will be gathered and analysed. In Chapter 4 the range of possible research methods and approaches is considered, and Chapters 5 to 9 give more detailed consideration to specific methods. To a large extent these discussions consider alternative sources of information or methods of data collection. In order to come to a decision on the most appropriate approach the researcher should consider carefully the type of information required and how that information will ultimately be used. It is very easy to begin thinking about particular data collection techniques without considering whether the information gained will provide answers to the research questions posed.

A further review of the literature can be valuable at this stage. What techniques have previous researchers used? Have their chosen methods been shown to be limiting or even misguided? What lessons can be learned from past errors?

The range of data collection methods dealt with in this book are:

- existing information, including existing published and unpublished research and secondary data (see Chapters 5 and 6);
- observation (see Chapter 7);
- qualitative methods: including ethnographic methods, participant observation, informal and in-depth interviews, group interviews or focus groups (see Chapter 8);
- questionnaire based surveys; including household face-to-face surveys, street surveys, telephone surveys, user/site surveys, postal surveys (see Chapter 9–13).

These individual techniques are not discussed further here since they are discussed in detail in later chapters. The task here then is to link the ideas and questions arising from previous steps with possible research methods or data collection techniques.

In the case of the leisure centres study the central task is to establish the relationship between level of political control and profitability, the main hypothesis being that a high level of control/accountability produces low profitability and vice versa. So the research must be designed to produce a range of situations of varying levels of control and profitability, so that the relationship between these two concepts can be determined. One approach would be initially to classify leisure centres into, say, high, medium and low profitability groups and then examine levels of control in each group. Obtaining initial information on the level of profitability (or net cost) of centres would probably involve a postal or telephone survey of local authorities or centres to obtain financial information on centres. The study would then proceed with detailed studies of selected centres. This initial selection process would not, however, include 'public good' aspects and it might have to be accepted that this would be explored in the second stage. An alternative would be to assume that a random sample of all centres would produce an adequate variety of profitable and unprofitable centres.

With regard to the detailed study of individual centres, it would be necessary to establish: financial profitability (or net costs); a measure of 'public good', which might modify the profitability status; and the amount of control by politicians and the effects of public accountability requirements on management and profitability. Financial profitability should be easily obtainable from documents produced by the centre management or councils. 'Public good' may be decided by some proxy measure related to level of use and the size of the community served, or it could be determined by user and non-user surveys of each centre. Investigation of the political control and public accountability aspects would involve study of documents – such as committee reports and minutes – and interviews with managers, politicians and possibly user or community representatives. The proposed scale of the study would determine whether these interviews were of an informal, in-depth nature or whether they would be based on questionnaires and analysed by computer.

It can be seen therefore that the leisure centre study involves the consideration of a wide range of data sources and data collection techniques.

The elderly and holidays example is logistically a simpler project. The main task is to establish what motivates retired people to take holidays and to see whether this differs from the motivations given by people in work. The motivation of the retired can be studied by means of a fairly straightforward questionnaire based survey. But a decision would need to be taken on whether this should be conducted by mail, by telephone or by face-to-face interview, and also whether the design of the questionnaire would be assisted by some preliminary qualitative research, such as one or more focus groups. The difficult aspect would be to decide how to compare the motivations of retired people with those in work. Information on the latter might be available from existing research, in which case it would be necessary to use similar research techniques so that the findings from the retired people would be compared with the existing data. It might be possible to ask retired people themselves to compare their motivations before and after retirement (even to conduct a longitudinal study, involving the same people before and after retirement), or it could be decided to interview a sample of working people in this study. The question of matching of samples, for example by occupation, would need to be considered as would the question of the position of non-employed spouses.

9. Specify population
It is necessary to indicate the whole population to which the research relates even if, as is usually the case, only a relatively small sample of that population is to be directly studied. As outlined in Chapter 10, sound selection of the study sample depends on adequate definition of the overall population. For example, the population in the 'leisure centres' example might be specified as all leisure centres (as defined in Step 5) wholly owned and directly managed by local authorities in England and Wales, as indicated by the Sports Council. In the case of the elderly and holidays example, the population might be specified as all people aged 60 and above in receipt of old age pensions and/or superannuation in England and Wales.

10. Specify type of data collection method(s) to be used
In most cases the specification of data collection methods will be a restatement of decisions made in outlining the overall research strategy in Step 8. However, this will not always be the case. For example, in the research strategy it may have been decided to collect certain information by means of a survey and certain other information by means of qualitative methods, but the type of survey and the type of qualitative method may not have been specified. To make decisions on

such matters the researcher must be familiar with the material presented in Chapter 4, which reviews alternative research methods, and Chapters 5–9, which discuss particular methods in more detail.

11. Decide sampling method
Again the question of sampling method may be implicit in decisions made in earlier steps, but precise detail may still need to be determined. For example, it may have been decided to select a sample of leisure centres for study, but how they should be selected – for example by region or size. Sampling is discussed in Chapter 11.

12. Decide sample size
The criteria for deciding sample size are discussed in Chapter 11. Here it is sufficient to indicate that the decision will depend on the type of analysis to be undertaken (Step 17) and the resources available (Step 18).

13. List data items to be collected
As a result of the consideration of concepts, hypotheses, theories or models in Steps 3 and 5 and the consideration of how to measure concepts in Step 7, it should be possible to produce a consolidated list of data requirements related to each data collection method to be used.

14. Design data collection 'instrument(s)'
The data collection 'instrument' is usually a questionnaire, but may be a checklist or some other type of form for the recording of information from observations or secondary documents. In some qualitative research there is no 'instrument' as such, information being recorded in the form of field notes. The design of questionnaires is considered in detail in Chapter 10; it is sufficient here to stress that the contents of a questionnaire should be based firmly on all the thinking and planning which has gone into the previous 13 steps.

15. Plan fieldwork arrangements
The demands of this step will depend on the scale and complexity of the proposed fieldwork – that is data collection etc. It may involve:

- seeking permissions – to visit sites, obtain records, etc.;
- obtaining lists for sampling – e.g. voters lists;
- arranging printing – of questionnaires etc.;
- preparing written instructions for interviewers;
- appointing interviewers and supervisors;
- training interviewers and supervisors;
- obtaining quotations for any fieldwork to be conducted by other organisations;
- appointing and training data coders.

16. Specify proposed data analysis procedures
Thinking ahead to just how data are to be analysed is a useful exercise in itself and should emerge to some extent in Stage 8. However, if

analysis is to be done in-house it is necessary to ensure that, if required, appropriate computer equipment, software and expertise are available and that the sorts of data to be collected lend themselves to the sorts of analysis envisaged, and that the analysis will indeed produce answers to the project's research questions. It is not good practice to collect data and then say, 'How am I going to analyse this?'

Where an outside agency is being used to collect and/or analyse data it is even more important to have a clear view of the required analysis in advance, because this will affect the budget. Computer time is money and the more tables and other forms of analysis required the more costly it will be.

17. Prepare a budget

As with much of what has been discussed so far, the question of budget will have been under consideration throughout most of the preparatory stages; little planning can be done without some consideration being given to the resources available, and usually these are fixed from the beginning. Where the only staff resource involved is the lone researcher the budget will be concerned primarily with 'consumables', such as the costs of printing questionnaires, postage, travel costs and so on. In some cases a reward is given to interviewees – such as payment for attendance at a focus group discussion or a prize to encourage returns to a postal questionnaire.

When considering costs of field staff – that is interviewers, counters, observers – careful consideration must be given to the rate at which people can reasonably work. For example, a typical interview may take only five minutes, so it might therefore be calculated that a single interviewer can conduct 12 interviews in an hour and 96 in a working day. But in reality interviewers need to take breaks, and some interviews may take longer than the standard five minutes, so that it might be found that, say 50 interviews is a more realistic daily target. Pilot exercises can be used to test such management aspects of fieldwork (see Chapter 9).

Where the time of the research staff must be budgeted for – which is the case with consultancy and some public agencies – it will generally be found that the costs per day are very much higher than the basic salary costs of the researcher. This is because office and other overheads must be taken into account, including superannuation, managerial overheads, office rent, secretarial and other support services, telephone and, often, a car, and it must be born in mind that researchers/consultants must be paid for 52 weeks a year even though, in practice, they work 'productively' for less than that. They have holidays; they spend some time preparing proposals/tenders (some successful and some not) and they may spend some time in staff development (in training, going to conferences etc.). Thus a typical researcher may need to earn their year's salary and overheads in, say, 40 weeks. It is these considerations which often make consultants' daily or weekly fees look deceptively high.

Where a budget is being prepared in order to seek funding or in response to an invitation to tender it is advisable to present a budget in terms of tasks rather than in terms of types of cost. For example a project involving some focus groups and a questionnaire survey might have the following headings, each with a total cost:

- Preparatory work (literature review/discussions with client etc.).
- Focus groups.
- Pilot survey.
- Main survey – design conduct and analysis.
- Preparation of report.

18. Prepare a timetable

A timetable should take account of the various steps in the research process as outlined in this chapter. Especially where a team is involved, some tasks may be carried out concurrently and this needs to be conveyed in the timetable – Figure 3.4 is one way of showing this. Figure 3.5 is one way of conveying not just the timetable but the overall structure/approach of a complex project.

The main fault in timetables is to fail to give enough time to analysis and report writing. This is not just common but almost universal, even among experienced researchers. It is impossible to give specific advice on this aspect of research because projects vary so much, but suffice it to say that the researcher should always allocate more time than is initially thought necessary for analysis and writing up! Having said that, the rush and panic that often sets in as the project deadline looms is often self-inflicted because researchers leave the writing of their report too late. As discussed in Chapter 15, some aspects of the final report can be written very early on in the process.

Week	1	2	3	4	5	6	7	8
Stage 1								
Review brief	-----							
Review existing research	-----	-----	---					
Define concepts etc.	---	---						
Steering committee meeting		•						
Stage 2								
Collect inventory data		---	-----	---				
Focus groups			--					
Design questionnaires		--	---					
Resident survey			---	----				
Survey analysis				--	----			
Stage 3								
Report write-up					--	-----	--	
Steering committee meeting							•	
Finalise report							---	----
Present report								•

Figure 3.4 Example of research project timetable

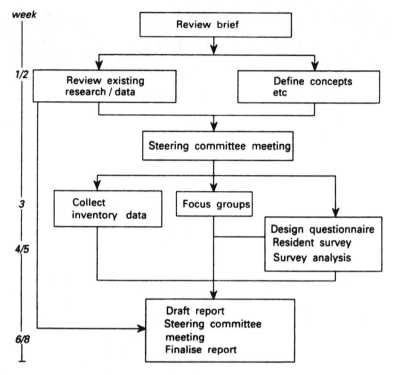

Figure 3.5 Diagrammatic presentation of research programme

Stages 19–29 investigation, analysis and write-up

It is not proposed to discuss these stages in detail here because they are discussed specifically in the chapters which follow.

Research proposals

Research proposals must be prepared by the academic seeking funds, by the PhD student seeking approval for research for a thesis, by planners and managers seeking 'in-house' resources, and by consultants responding to research briefs put out by clients. The latter is discussed first.

Briefs and tenders

A brief is an outline of the research which an organisation wishes to be undertaken. Usually briefs are prepared by an organisation with a view to a number of consultants competing to obtain the contract to do the research. In some cases potential consultants are first asked, possibly through an advertisement, to indicate their 'expression of interest' in the project; this will involve a brief statement of the consultants' capabilities, their experience in the field and staff available. In some cases public bodies maintain a register of accredited consultants with particular interests and capabilities, who may be invited to tender for particular projects. In the light of such statements of interest or information in the register, a 'shortlist' of consultants is sent the detailed brief and invited to submit a tender.

Briefs vary in the amount of detail they give. Sometimes they are very detailed, leaving little scope for consultants to express any individuality in their proposals. In other cases they are very limited and leave a great deal of scope to consultants to indicate proposed methods and approaches.

Successful consultants are not usually selected on the basis of price alone (the budget is often a fixed sum anyway) but on the quality of the submitted proposal.

What should a good proposal contain? The first and golden principle is that it should *address the brief*. It is likely that the brief will have been discussed at great length in the commissioning organisation; every aspect of the brief is likely to be of importance to some individual or section in the organisation, so every aspect of the brief should be considered. So, for example, if the brief lists,say,four objectives, the proposal must indicate how each of the four objectives will be met.

A research proposal must indicate clearly:

- what is to be done;
- how it is to be done;
- when it will be done;
- what it will cost;
- who will do it.

A broad outline of contents of a proposal would include a description of many of the steps outlined in this chapter. Clearly it is necessary to be fully familiar with the research process in its entirety in order to write a successful proposal. A typical proposal might therefore include the following elements:

1. Restatement of the key aspects of the brief.
2. Interpretation of key concepts in the brief. Overall 'approach' to the problem(s). Division of project into elements/stages/tasks.
3. Data requirements.
4. Data collection methods:
    - types of data collection;
    - sampling methods, measures to ensure data quality;
    - sample sizes;
    - data to be generated by each method.
5. Timetable (note some tasks will be concurrent):
    - meetings with clients;
    - other meetings with interested parties;
    - preparatory work;
    - fieldwork, data collection;

- analysis;
- draft report;
- feedback on draft;
- final report.
6. Budget – costing of each element/stage/task:
   - project staff costs (n days at £x per day, gross, including normal office overheads/support);
   - fieldwork/data collection costs;
   - additional items – e.g. travel, printing;
   - report preparation costs, if significant.
7. Report chapter outline.
8. Resources available:
   - project and supervisory staff – curricula vitae, especially experience relevant to the proposed project;
   - support staff/backup resources/organisation capability.

Academic research proposals

Academic research proposals, for student theses/projects or for academics seeking funding, will contain many of the elements included in the sort of consultancy proposals discussed above. The main difference is however, that academic proposals are not based on briefs prepared by another organisation – the academic proposal must begin with a justification for the research.

The justification for a piece of academic research will generally be couched in terms of the literature, in social terms, in policy or management terms or in popular terms.

Justifications in terms of the literature can take a variety of forms. It may be that X's theory has been tested in the USA but not in England; that Y's widely accepted theory is based on research on men and ignores women; that Z's widely quoted theory has never been tested empirically. It may be that a certain theory or methodology has never been applied to leisure or tourism, that a certain concept has not been fully investigated historically, or that certain assumptions in the literature have not been questioned.

Social justifications can be equally wide-ranging, justifying research, for example, on the leisure needs or behaviour of certain deprived or neglected groups in society or on the environmental or social impact of tourism.

Policy and management justifications may well overlap with the sorts of research commissioned by leisure or tourism agencies. For example, tourism forecasting is done not only by government and private tourism bodies but also by academics; user surveys of leisure facilities or cost-benefit analyses of programmes can be conducted by interested academics as well as organisations. The difference is that the results of the academic research will be made public – which agency research may not be – and will generally be presented so as to have more general implications than the particular application to the facility or programme studied. Academic studies are also often more concerned with methodology than with the substantive findings of the research.

Finally popular justification means that research may be sparked by the desire to explore popular beliefs or conceptions, especially where it is suspected that these may be inaccurate – for example this might be seen as the motivation for much research on media portrayals of such phenomena as sporting crowd violence.

Thus the academic research proposal must include an explanation of why the research should be done, that is, how it contributes to knowledge or understanding of theoretical or practical problems. An academic proposal would therefore contain the following elements:

1. Background and justification for the research, including appropriate references to the literature. Statement of research problems/questions and/or hypotheses.
2. Outline of key concepts. Overall research strategy. Division of project into elements/stages/tasks.
3. Data requirements.
4. Data collection methods:
   - types of data collection;
   - sampling methods – measures to ensure quality;
   - sample sizes;
   - data to be generated by each method.
5. Timetable (note some tasks will be concurrent):
   - preparatory work;
   - fieldwork – data collection;
   - analysis;
   - draft report/thesis;
   - feedback on draft;
   - final report/thesis.
6. Budget – where applicable – costing of each element/stage/task:
   - project staff costs (n days at £x per day, gross, including normal office overheads/support);
   - fieldwork/data collection costs;
   - additional items, e.g. travel, printing.
7. Report chapter outline.
8. Resources (necessary when seeking funds and when seeking accreditation for PhD).
   - Researcher(s) – curricula vitae, especially experience relevant to the proposed project.
   - Availability of computers/equipment etc.

Further reading

The best reading material for this chapter would be examples of successful research grant applications and proposals written in response to tenders.

For a discussion of approaches to tourism research see Pizam 1987.

Most general and specific research methods texts deal with the stages in the research process, for example, Kidder (1981), Kraus and Allen (1987), Williamson *et al.* (1982), Burgess (1982), Hudson (1988), Kelsey and Gray (1986a), Frank Small and Associates (1988).

4 The range of research methods

In this chapter the range of alternative research methods and criteria for the use of particular methods are examined. It covers the question of the roles of scholarship and research, 'just thinking', the use of existing literature, secondary data, observation, qualitative methods, and questionnaire based surveys and considers the qualitative–quantitative debate.

Horses for courses

Choosing appropriate research methods or techniques is clearly vital. In this book the principle is espoused that every technique has its place; the important thing is for the researcher to be aware of the limitations of any particular method and not to make claims which cannot be justified. There has been much debate in recent years, especially in the sociological literature, about appropriate methods for leisure research. In particular commentators have sought to denigrate quantitative research and extoll the virtues of qualitative research (Rojek 1989, Henderson 1990, Kelly 1980). The commentaries have often been very partisan in tone, as if there were a contest going on between the two approaches and as if there were some sort of conspiracy at work to maintain quantitative methods as the dominant research mode in leisure studies. While this domination may be apparent in leisure studies in the United States, it is less apparent in the literature emanating from other countries. In tourism research quantitative and qualitative research approaches seem to co-exist without the sort of apparent rivalry seen in leisure studies.

There is a tendency, in the methodological literature, for commentators to defend the methods in which they themselves are skilled. It is rare to find a researcher who is experienced in the full range of techniques as, for example, discussed in this book. It is hoped that the new generation of researchers in leisure and tourism will be competent in a full range of skills and will therefore adopt a balanced and non-partisan approach to their use. As Henderson points out in discussing qualitative versus quantitative methods:

> It is possible ... to mix the characteristics of the approaches in order to conduct a research study .... Ideally, a researcher who understands the array of methods available through both quantitative and qualitative approaches will be able to address the ways to best study the issues related to leisure (1990, p. 179).

It is therefore possible for research to be conducted entirely quantitatively, entirely qualitatively, or using a mixture of both approaches. It is quite common for large-scale quantitative research to be planned on the basis of prior, exploratory, qualitative studies.

In this book a 'horses for courses' approach is adopted; techniques are not considered to be intrinsically 'good' or 'bad', but are considered to be 'appropriate' or 'inappropriate' for certain situations. Further it is maintained that it is not a question of good or bad techniques but of good or bad *use* of techniques.

Scholarship and research

Although the dividing line between the two can be difficult to draw, it is useful to consider the difference between scholarship and research. Scholarship involves being well informed about a subject and also thinking critically and creatively about the subject and the accumulated knowledge on it. Scholarship therefore involves 'knowing the literature', but also being able to synthesize it, analyse it and critically appraise it. Scholarship is traditionally practised in the role of teacher, but when the results of scholarship are published they effectively become a contribution to research. Research involves the generation of new knowledge. Traditionally this has been thought of as involving the gathering and presentation of new data – empirical research – but clearly this is not a necessary condition for something to be considered 'research'. New insights, critical or innovative ways of looking at old issues, or the identification of new issues or questions – the fruits of scholarship – are also contributions to knowledge. Indeed, the development of a new framework or 'paradigm' for looking at a field can obviously be more significant than a minor piece of empirical work using an old, outmoded paradigm.

Recognising therefore that research does not have to be empirical, the first method discussed below is called 'Just thinking'.

Just thinking

There is no substitute for thinking! Creative, informed thinking about a topic may be the only process involved in the development and presentation of a piece of research, although it will usually also involve consideration of the literature, as discussed below.

But even when data collection is involved, the difference between an acceptable piece of research and an exceptional piece of research is usually the quality of the creative thought that has gone into it. The researcher needs to be creative in identifying and posing the initial questions or issues, creative in conceptualising the research and developing a research strategy, creative in analysing data and creative in interpreting and presenting findings. Books such as this can provide a guide to mechanical processes, but creative thought must come from within the individual researcher – in the same way that the basics of drawing can be taught but 'art' comes from within the individual artist.

The literature

There is virtually no research that can be done which would not benefit from some reference to the existing literature and indeed, for most research, such reference is essential. It is possible for a research project to consist only of a review of the literature. In comparatively new areas of study such as leisure and tourism, especially when they are multi-disciplinary as leisure and tourism are, there is a great need for the consolidation of existing knowledge which can come from good literature reviews.

The review of the literature often plays a key role in the formulation of research projects; it indicates the state of knowledge on a topic and is a source of or stimulator of ideas, both substantive and methodological.

A review of the literature can be important even when it uncovers no literature on the topic of interest. To establish that no research has been conducted on a particular topic considered to be of some importance can be a research finding of some significance in its own right.

The literature review process is discussed in detail in Chapter 5.

Existing information – secondary data

Clearly, if information is already available which will answer the research questions posed, then it would be wasteful of resources to collect new information for the purpose. As discussed in Chapter 6, vast quantities of information are collected and stored by organisations as routine functions of management, including sales figures, income and expenditure, staffing, accident reports, crime reports, and health data. Such data are referred to as 'secondary' data, because their primary use is administrative and research is only a secondary use. Even when such data are not ideal for the research in hand, they can often provide some answers, and more quickly and at less cost than new data.

It should be noted that existing information need not be quantitative. Historians for example, use diaries, official documents or newspaper reports as sources. In policy research such documents as the annual reports or minutes of meetings of organisations might be utilised.

In other cases data have been collected for research
administrative purposes but have not been analysed ;
analysed, or only analysed in a particular way for partic
Secondary analysis of research data is a potentially frui
neglected activity.

The use of secondary data sources is considered in Chapter 6.

Observation

The technique of observation is discussed in Chapter 7. Observation
has the advantage of being unobtrusive – that is it is possible to gather
information about people's behaviour without their knowledge. While
this may raise ethical questions in some instances, it clearly has
advantages over those techniques where the subjects are aware of the
researcher's presence and may therefore modify their behaviour or
where reliance must be placed on subjects' own recall and description
of their behaviour.

Observation is also capable of presenting a perspective on a
situation which is not apparent to the individuals involved. For example,
the users of an overcrowded part of a recreation or tourist area may
not be aware of the uncrowded areas available to them – the pattern
of use of the site can only be assessed by observation.

Observation is therefore an appropriate technique to use when
knowledge of the presence of the researcher is likely to lead to unacceptable modification of subjects' behaviour, and when mass patterns
of behaviour not apparent to individual subjects are of interest.

Qualitative methods

Qualitative methods are discussed in detail in Chapter 8. Four particular techniques or methods are examined:

1. ethnographic techniques, which are really a collection of the techniques
listed below and which have traditionally been used by anthropologists to
study groups of people or communities – the techniques have been utilised
in leisure and tourism research to investigate such communities as youth
groups or gangs, sporting sub-cultures and suburban neighbourhoods, and
tourism host communities;
2. participant observation, in which the researcher becomes a participant in
the phenomenon being studied;
3. informal and in-depth interviews, in which relatively small numbers of
individuals are interviewed at length, possibly on more than one occasion (in
contrast to questionnaire based surveys in which, usually, relatively large
numbers of people are interviewed in a limited, structured way);
4. group interviews or focus groups, where the informal/in-depth approach
is used with a group of people rather than with separate individuals.

Qualitative techniques stand in contrast to quantitative techniques. The
main difference between the two groups of techniques is that quanti-

ative techniques involve numbers – quantities – whereas qualitative techniques do not. With qualitative techniques generally the information collected does not lend itself to statistical analysis and conclusions are not based on such analysis. By contrast, with quantitative techniques, the data collected are susceptible to statistical analysis and the conclusions are based on such analysis.

In consequence there is a tendency for qualitative techniques to involve the gathering of large amounts of relatively rich information about relatively few people and for quantitative techniques to involve the gathering of relatively small amounts of data on relatively large numbers of people. It should be emphasised, however, that this is just a tendency. It is possible, for example, to have a piece of quantitative research which has collected 500 items of data on only 20 people and a qualitative piece of research involving relatively little information on 200 people. The difference lies in the type of information collected and the way it is analysed.

In what situations are qualitative techniques used? They tend to be used for the study of groups, where interaction between group members is of interest; when exploratory theory building rather than theory testing work is called for; when the focus of the research is on meanings and attitudes (although these can also be studied quantitatively); when the researcher accepts that the concepts, terms, and issues must be defined by the subjects and not by the researcher in advance. Qualitative techniques are not appropriate when the aim of the research is to make general statements about large populations, especially if such statements involve quantification.

Questionnaire based surveys

Questionnaire based surveys are probably the most common in leisure and tourism research, partly because the basic mechanics are relatively easily understood and mastered, but also because so much research does call for the sorts of general, quantified statement referred to above. Thus for example, governments want to know how many people engage in sport; managers want to know how many people are dissatisfied with a service and marketers want to know how many people are in a particular market segment. All these examples come from practical policy/management situations, which emphasises that most of the resources for empirical research come from the public or private sector of the leisure/tourism industries. Academic papers are very often a secondary spin-off from research which has been sponsored for specific, practical purposes.

Unlike qualitative techniques, where the researcher can begin data collection in a tentative way, can return to the subjects for additional information and can gradually build the data and concepts and explanation, questionnaire based surveys require researchers to be very specific about their data requirements from the beginning, since they must be translated into a questionnaire.

A further key feature of questionnaire based surveys is that they depend on respondents' own account of their behaviour, attitudes or intentions. In some situations – for example in the study of 'deviant' behaviour or in the study of activities which are socially approved (e.g. playing sport) or disapproved of (e.g. smoking or drinking), this can raise some questions about the validity of the technique.

Questionnaire based surveys come in a variety of forms and these are discussed in detail in Chapter 9. They include household-based face-to-face interview surveys, street interview surveys, telephone surveys, user/site surveys, and postal/mail surveys.

When are questionnaire based surveys used? They are used when quantified information is required concerning a specific population and when the individual's own account of behaviour and/or attitudes is acceptable as a source of information.

Other methods

The range of research methods, techniques and approaches available to the researcher are legion and it is not possible to give full weight to all possibilities in a text such as this. Mention is made here of a few additional techniques which arise in leisure and tourism research and an indication is given of how they relate to the pattern of this book.

Coupon surveys

In marketing research use is often made of information from the responses of the public to advertising coupons – that is where the public is invited in an advertisement to write or telephone for information on a product. This is a common practice in tourism research. The data can be used to indicate the level of interest in the product on offer (compared with other products or with the same product in previous years) and also to indicate the geographical spread of the interested public (Ronkainen and Woodside 1987).

En route surveys

In tourism research surveys of tourists while travelling, as opposed to home-based surveys, are sometimes referred to as 'en route' surveys (Hurst 1987). In this book this type of survey is considered to be a special case of site or user surveys, as discussed in Chapter 9.

Time-budget surveys

There is a long tradition in leisure studies of investigating people's allocation of time between such categories as paid work, domestic work, sleep and leisure. This approach to leisure research is basically a special case of the household survey and some reference is made to it in that context in Chapter 9.

Panels
Market research companies usually maintain 'panels' of individuals for some of their surveys. Panels are made up of a representative cross-section of the public who agree to be 'on call' for a series or a variety of surveys over a period of time. Often some financial reward is involved, but this is off-set by the cost savings in not having to select and contact new samples. While the management of such panels presents particular problems, the range of survey methods which can be used with panels – by telephone, by mail or by face-to-face interview – is the same as for normal one-off samples (LaPage 1987).

Longitudinal studies
Longitudinal studies involve studies of the same sample of individuals periodically over a number of years. Such studies are of course expensive because of the need to keep track of the sample over the years, but are ideal for studying social change and the combined effects of social change and ageing. While it is a recognised technique in the social sciences, there are few examples of it being used in leisure or tourism research.

Projective techniques
Projective techniques might be termed 'what if?' techniques, in that they involve measures to get subjects to respond to hypothetical – projected – situations. For example subjects might be asked to indicate how they might spend a particular sum of money if given a free choice, or how they might spend additional leisure time if it were made available. While the technique can become elaborate and specialised, in this book it is considered to be an extension of questionnaire based surveys and possibly of focus-group interviews.

Media surveys
Newspapers, magazines and radio and television stations often run opinion poll type surveys among their readers, listeners and viewers. At the local level the public's views on an issue may be canvassed by the inclusion of some sort of form in a newspaper, which readers may fill in and return, and radio and television stations often run 'phone in' polls on topical issues. The results of these exercises have entertainment value, but should not generally be taken seriously. This is mainly because there is no way of knowing whether either the original population (the readers/listeners/viewers who happen to read, hear or view the item) or the sample of respondents are representative of the population as a whole. In most cases they are decidedly unrepresentative, in that only those with pronounced views, one way or the other, are likely to become involved in the process.

Delphi technique
The Delphi technique (named after the classical Greek 'Delphic oracle'), is a procedure involving the gathering and analysing of infor-

mation from a panel of experts on future trends in a particular field of interest. The experts in the field (e.g. leisure or tourism) complete a questionnaire indicating their views on the likelihood of certain developments taking place in future; these views are then collated and circulated to panel members for further comment, a process which might be repeated a number of times before the final results are collated. The technique is used in some areas of business and technological forecasting, and has been used in leisure and tourism (Veal 1987, Moeller and Shafer 1987). In this book the technique is not examined explicitly, but to some extent it involves questionnaire design and analysis.

Further reading

For the methodological debate see Kelly (1980); Henderson (1990); Rojek (1989); Wilson et al. (1979), Borman et al. (1986), Krenz and Sax (1986).
For readings on particular techniques, see subsequent chapters.

5 Existing sources: the literature

The aim of this chapter is to explain the importance of reviewing previous research and writing on a topic as part of any research program, to indicate sources of literature and to set out the mechanics of compiling bibliographies and recording references to the literature.

An essential task

Reviewing previous research or writing – 'the literature' – on a topic is a vital step in the research process. As indicated in Chapter 3, the literature can serve a number of functions.

1. It may be the entire basis of the research.
2. It can be the source of ideas on topics for research.
3. It ensures that the research has not already been done.
4. It is a source of methodological or theoretical ideas.
5. It may be a source of comparison.
6. The information may be an integral or supportive part of the research.

Leisure and tourism studies are relatively new areas of academic enquiry and are wide-ranging and multi-disciplinary. Keeping track of literature and tracking down relevant literature is therefore a demanding task. It is nevertheless an essential one. Research is not so plentiful that we can afford to ignore work which has already been completed.

An important part of nearly all research is a 'review of the literature'. This involves a careful search for relevant published – and unpublished if necessary – work; obtaining copies of and *reading* relevant items; making a list of useful items – drawing up a 'bibliography' – and summarising salient aspects for the research proposal, research report or article.

The value of bibliographies

A great deal of useful work can be done in compiling bibliographies on specific topics; this can help consolidate the 'state of the art' and could save other researchers a great deal of time and trouble in searching out material.

Examples of such bibliographies are listed in the Further reading section at the end of the chapter and considerable scope exists for the development of similar bibliographies on other topics, for example: the recreational and tourist use of national parks; tourism impact studies; surveys of arts/cultural facilities; leisure centre studies; sports motivation; holiday decision-making; leisure needs of people with disabilities; leisure/tourism and the elderly; tourism demand forecasting; pricing and leisure services; market segmentation in the leisure industries.

Searching

Where can the researcher look for information on existing published research on a topic? In this section a number of sources is examined, including library catalogues, published bibliographies, indexes, general texts, reference lists and sources beyond leisure and tourism.

Library catalogues

Many modern libraries have computerised catalogues with key words which can be very helpful as a starting point in establishing a bibliography. But be warned! They can be very misleading to the researcher with a specialist interest.

Of course, if the words 'leisure', 'tourism', 'sport' or 'the arts', are entered the typical catalogue/computer will produce a large number of helpful references – but probably far too many! But if, for example, the word 'golf' is entered, the catalogue will probably produce very few references, and probably most of these will be concerned with how to play golf or with biographies of Greg Norman. But this does not mean that there is nothing in the library on golf. The key words in the catalogue are based only on the titles of catalogued items and on the keywords which the librarian decides to include.

Library catalogues generally do not contain references to:

- individual articles in journals;
- individual chapters in books which are collections of readings;
- individual papers in collections of conference papers.

Neither can a library catalogue indicate, for instance, whether a general report on 'sport' or 'recreation' or 'tourism' includes any reference to golf.

A library catalogue is therefore only a starting point, and chances are, for specialised needs, it will *only* be a starting point.

Published bibliographies

Reference has already been made to the value of bibliographies on particular topics. Libraries usually have a separate section for bibliographies and it may be worth 'browsing' in that section, especially when the topic of interest is interdisciplinary.

Indexes

The most extensive and well-established index of leisure and tourism publications is *Leisure, Recreation and Tourism Abstracts* (LRTA).

LRTA has been published quarterly for over a decade by CAB International of Oxford, England and is sponsored by the world Leisure and Recreation Association. It has very detailed subject indexes which make searching relatively easy. LRTA is also accessible by computer – the computer does the searching for you – this is available through libraries which subscribe to the appropriate tele-data services. Combinations of keywords can be specified and the computer will indicate the number of references available and,if requested, produce a printout of them.

LRTA has the advantage of drawing on a much wider data-base than most individual libraries and it includes individual journal articles and conference papers. However, it still suffers from some of the limitations of library catalogues in that it is only as good as the indexing or keywording system used. So again, for highly specialised needs, such searches may only be the starting point.

General texts

The researcher should be aware of general sources of information which contain information on specific activities or aspects of leisure or tourism. For example, in Chapter 6, national leisure participation and tourism surveys are discussed. These surveys contain information on as many as an hundred leisure activities, on tourism flows and a number of background items such as age and income. They are therefore often a source of at least some information on the topic of interest.

Many general texts on leisure or tourism, such as those by Torkildsen (1983), Kelly (1982), Clarke and Critcher (1985), Roberts (1978), Jackson and Burton (1989), Ritchie and Goeldner (1987), and Burkhart and Medlik (1981) may have something to say on the topic of interest.

Reference lists

Most importantly, the lists of references in the books and articles initially identified will generally lead to other material. The researcher interested in a particular topic should be constantly on the alert for sources of material on that topic in anything being read. Sometimes one comes across key items when least expecting them. The researcher should become a 'sniffer dog' obsessed with 'sniffing out' anything of relevance to the topic of interest. In a real-world research situation this process of identifying as much literature as possible can take months or even years. While a major effort should be made to identify material at the beginning of any research project, it will also be an on-going exercise, throughout the course of the project.

Beyond leisure and tourism

Lateral thinking is also an aid to this sort of exercise. The most useful information is not always found in the most obvious places. Some commentators have remarked on how many researchers fail to look beyond the immediate 'leisure' or 'tourism' material. Leisure and tourism are interdisciplinary areas of study, not disciplines in their own right – they do not have a set of research methods and theories uniquely their own. Much is to be gained from looking outside the immediate area of 'leisure or tourism studies'. For example, if the research involves measurement of attitudes then certain psychological literature will be of interest; if the research involves the study of leisure or tourism markets then marketing journals may be useful sources and if the research involves the leisure activities of the elderly then gerontology journals should be consulted.

Obtaining material

If material is not available in a particular library it can often be obtained through the 'inter-library loan' system. This is a system through which loans of material can be made between one library and another. In the case of articles the system usually involves the sending of a photocopy. In theory any item published in a particular country should be available through this system since it is connected with national copyright libraries where copies of all published items must be lodged by law. Practices vary from library to library; but in academic libraries the service is often available to undergraduate students only through a member of academic staff.

For researchers working in metropolitan areas the other obvious source of material is specialist libraries, particularly of government agencies. For example, in London, the Sports Council and English Tourist Board libraries are major resources for leisure and tourism researchers. In metropolitan areas and some other regions there is also often a cooperative arrangement between municipal reference libraries such that particular libraries adopt particular specialisms – so it can be useful to discover which municipal library service specialises in leisure and/or tourism.

Compiling and maintaining a bibliography

What should be done with the material once it has been identified? Firstly a record should be made of everything which appears to be of relevance. The researcher is strongly advised to start a card index of everything identified. This can be of use not only for the current research project but also for future references – a personal bibliography can be built up over the years. For those with access to computer facilities such record keeping can be done using a database program. This has the attraction that when there is a need to compile a bibliography in future a start can be made from the personal bibliography by getting the computer to copy designated items into a new file. In this way the researcher only ever needs to type out a reference once!

It only takes seconds to copy out the full details of a reference when it is first identified (it is sensible to have a stock of blank cards always at hand). If this practice is adopted hours of time and effort can be saved in not having to chase up details of references at a later date. Not only should the details be recorded accurately, as set out below, but a note should be made on the card or in the database about the availability of the material, e.g. the library catalogue reference, or the fact that the item is not in the library, or that a photocopy has been taken. People think they will remember these simple items in future but, unless they have exceptional memory powers, they will not!

Recording references

In what follows, the word 'text' refers to the main body of the research report or article. The general format recommended for recording references is as follows:

- For a book or report:
  Author(s), Initials (Year) <u>Title of Book or Report underlined</u>, Place of publication: Publisher.

- For an article from a periodical (journal/magazine/newspaper):
  Author(s), Initials (Year) 'Title of article', <u>Title of Periodical underlined</u>, Volume, Number, page numbers.

In some systems the date is put at the end, but when using the 'Author/date' or 'Harvard' system (see below) the date must follow the author name.

Note that the part which is underlined is the title which would be found in a library catalogue. Thus what is found in a library catalogue is the name of the periodical, not the title of the article. In the case of a chapter from a book, the title of the whole book is found in the catalogue, not the title of the chapter.

Underlining is the typing convention for what, in printed books, would be in italics: so if a word processor and printer which will produce italics is available then italics can be used rather than underlining.

Note that the publisher of a book is not the same as the printer; references do not need to refer to the printer. And note that it is not necessary to refer to the publisher in the case of periodicals.

Some examples are set out below to illustrate the principles:

1. A book:

   Iso-Ahola, S.E. (1980) The Social Psychology of Leisure and Recreation, Dubuque: Wm. C. Brown.

2. A chapter from the same book (note the page numbers);

   Iso-Ahola, S.E. (1980) 'Tools of social psychological inquiry' Chapter 3 of The Social Psychology of Leisure and Recreation Dubuque: Wm. C. Brown, pp 45–78.

3. An edited book of readings:

   Ritchie, J.R.B. and Goeldner, C.R. (eds) (1987) Travel, Tourism and Hospitality Research: A Handbook for Managers and Researchers, New York: John Wiley and Sons.

4. A paper from the same book (note the page numbers):

   Gunn, C.A. (1987) 'A perspective on the purpose and nature of tourism research methods', in Ritchie, J.R.B. and Goeldner, C.R. (eds) Travel, Tourism, and Hospitality Research: A Handbook for Managers and Researchers, New York: John Wiley and Sons, pp 3–12.

5. A number of references from the same book: when making a number of references to one collection such as the Ritchie and Goeldner collection referred to above, it is only necessary to write out the details of the book once. So if, for example, reference was made to four papers in the book, the list of references would contain five items as follows:

   Archer, B.H. (1987) 'Demand forecasting and estimation', in Ritchie and Goeldner, op.cit., pp 77–86.

   Gunn, C.A. (1987) 'A perspective on the purpose and nature of tourism research methods', in Ritchie and Goeldner, op.cit., pp 3–12.

   Peterson, K.I. (1987) 'Qualitative research methods for the travel and tourism industry', in Ritchie and Goeldner, op.cit., pp 433–438.

   Pizam, A. (1987) 'Planning a tourism research investigation', in Ritchie and Goeldner, op.cit., pp 63–76.

   Ritchie, J.R.B. and Goeldner, C.R. (eds) (1987) Travel, Tourism, and Hospitality Research: A Handbook for Managers and Researchers, New York: John Wiley and Sons.

The abbreviation op.cit. stands for the Latin *opere citato*, meaning 'in the work cited' – it is underlined because it is in a foreign language.

6. A conference report:

   Strellitz, Z. (ed.) (1979) Leisure and Family Diversity, Conference proceedings, Bedford College, London, March 30–31, LSA Conference papers No. 9 London: Leisure Studies Association.

Note that individual papers from the conference report would be treated the same way as the individual papers from the edited collection as shown in 4 and 5 above.

7.   A government agency report published by the agency concerned:

> **Sports Council (1982) <u>Sport in the Community: The Next Ten Years</u>, London: Sports Council.**

8.   A government report published by the Her Majesty's Stationery Office (HMSO):

> **Coopers and Lybrand Associates (1981) <u>Service Provision and Pricing in Local Government</u>, London: HMSO.**

9.   A journal article:

> **Oglethorpe, M. (1984) 'Tourism in Malta: a crisis of dependence', <u>Leisure Studies</u>, Vol. 3, No. 2, pp 147–162.**

(Note: Some systems suggest that the volume, number and page number details should be presented in the form 3, 2: 147 -162).

10. A newspaper article with author:

> **Walker, P. (1983) 'The way ahead for a better life for all', <u>News of the World</u>, Nov. 19.**

11. A newspaper item without an author:

> **<u>Sydney Morning Herald</u> (1987) 'Edelstein's court delay bid rejected', Nov. 17, p. 20.**

12. Many authors: if there are more than three authors you may use the first author's name and <u>et al</u>. The latter stands for the Latin <u>et alia</u>, meaning 'and the others', and is underlined because it is in a foreign language.

Referencing and referencing systems

What is the purpose of referencing? Firstly referencing is evidence of the writer's scholarship: it indicates that the particular report is related to the existing body of knowledge. This is not only of importance to teachers marking student assignments – it is part and parcel of the development of knowledge. Secondly references enable the reader either to verify the writer's interpretation of previous research or to follow up areas of interest.

There are two commonly used referencing systems: the 'author/date' system, sometimes referred to as the 'Harvard' system, and the 'footnote' or 'endnote' system.

The author/date or Harvard system

Basic features

This is the system in which references to an item of literature are made in the text by using the author's name and the year of publication; at the end of the paper or report, references are listed in alphabetical order. Thus, a sentence in a report might look something like this:

> **Research on women and leisure includes work in Britain (Deem 1986), in Canada (Bella 1989), in the United States (Bialeschki and Henderson 1986) and in Australia (Anderson 1975).**

Note that authors' initials are not used in these references (unless there happened to be two authors with the same surname).

At the end of the report, paper or book, a list of references is provided, arranged in alphabetical order:

References

Anderson, R. (1975) <u>Leisure: An Inappropriate Concept for Women?</u> Canberra: AGPS.

Bella, L. (1989) 'Women and leisure: beyond androcentrism', in E.L. Jackson and T.L. Burton (eds) <u>Understanding Leisure and Recreation</u>, State College, PA.: Venture, pp 151–180.

Bialeschki, M.D. and Henderson, K. (1986) 'Leisure in the common world of women', <u>Leisure Studies</u>, Vol. 5, No. 3, pp 299–308.

Deem, R. (1986) <u>All Work and No Play?</u> Milton Keynes: Open University Press.

Style variation

The style of presentation can be varied; for instance, the above statement could be made in the following alternative ways:

> **Interest in research on women and leisure has been widespread in the English speaking world, as work from authors in Britain, Canada, the United States and Australia indicates (Bella, 1989; Bialeschki and Henderson, 1986; Deem, 1986; Anderson, 1975).**

or, drawing more explicit attention to the authors:

> **Recent research on women and leisure has included Deem's (1986) work in Britain, Bella's (1980) work in Canada, the work of Bialeschki and Henderson (1986) in the United States and of Anderson (1975) in Australia.**

Specifics and quotations

When referring to specific points from a reference, rather than making a general reference to the whole article as above, page references should be given to the specific aspect of interest. For example:

> **At least one commentator has suggested that greater under-
> standing of leisure could be obtained by drawing on the
> Weberian concept of 'lifestyle' (Moorehouse 1989, p.31).**

When actually quoting:

> **Iso-Ahola makes the point that: 'To survive as an academic
> field, scholars must supply evidence that their methods of
> investigation are valid and reliable rather than 'soft"
> (1980, p. 49).**

A longer quotation would be indented in the page and handled like this:

> **Iso-Ahola argues the case for scientific research in the
> leisure area and states:**

> > **To survive as an academic field, scholars must supply
> > evidence to the effect that their methods of investigation
> > are valid and reliable rather than 'soft'. This becomes
> > increasingly important in obtaining grants from sources
> > inside and outside academic institutions.**
> > **(Iso-Ahola 1980, p.49).**

Advantages and disadvantages

The author/date system is an 'academic' style: the referencing is very
'upfront', even obtrusive, in the text. It is not an appropriate style for
some practically orientated reports and where the readership is not
academic. Large numbers of references, using this style, tend to
'clutter up' the text.

The author/date system also has the disadvantage that it cannot
accommodate footnotes and comments; but one view is that such
notes are undesirable anyway – that is, if something is worth saying it
is worth saying in the text. If notes and asides are considered necessary it is possible to establish a footnote system for this purpose in
addition to using the author/date system for references to the literature only. This of course becomes somewhat complex. If notes are
considered necessary then it is probably best to use the footnote style,
as discussed below, for everything.

The advantage of the author/date system is that it saves the effort
of keeping track of footnote numbers, it indicates the date of
publication to the reader, the details of any one item of literature has
to be written out only once and it results in a tidy, alphabetical list of
references at the end of the document.

Footnote or endnote system

Basic features

The 'footnote' style involves the use of numbered references in the
text and a list of corresponding numbered references at the end of the

report, paper or chapter. The term 'footnote' dates from the time when the notes were literally printed at the foot of each page – and this can be seen in older books. However, printing footnotes at the bottom of the page came to be viewed as too complex to organise and expensive to set up for printing, so it was generally abandoned in favour of providing the list of 'footnotes' at the end of each chapter or at the end of the document. Consequently the 'footnotes' are now often referred to as 'endnotes'. Ironically, the advent of word-processing has meant that placing footnotes at the bottom of the page can now be done automatically by computer – many word-processing packages provide this service, automatically making space for the appropriate number of footnotes on each page and keeping track of their numbering and so on. Publishers have, however, generally adhered to the practice of placing the notes all together at the end of the chapter or book.

The actual number reference in the text can be given in brackets: (1) or as a superscript: [1].

Using the footnote system, the paragraph given above would look like this:

Research on women and leisure has included Deem's (1) work in Britain, Bella's (2) work in Canada, Bialeschki and Henderson's (3) work in the United States and Anderson's (4) work in Australia.

The list of notes at the end of the report would then be in the numerical order in which they appear in the text:

Notes

1. **Deem, R. (1986) <u>All Work and No Play?</u> Milton Keynes: Open University Press.**
2. **Bella, L. (1989) 'Women and leisure: beyond androcentrism', in E.L. Jackson and T.L. Burton (eds) <u>Understanding Leisure and Recreation</u>, State College, PA: Venture, pp 151 -180.**
3. **Bialeschki, M.D. and Henderson, K. (1986) 'Leisure in the common world of women', <u>Leisure Studies</u>, Vol. 5, No. 3, pp. 299–308.**
4. **Anderson, R. (1975) <u>Leisure: An Inappropriate Concept for Women?</u> Canberra: AGPS**

It can be seen that this format is less obtrusive in the text than the author/date system. In fact it can be made even less obtrusive by using only one footnote, as follows:

Research on women's leisure has included work by researchers in Britain, Canada, the United States and Australia (1).

At the end of the report the reference list could look something like this:

Notes

1. **In Britain:**
   Deem, R. (1986) <u>All Work and No Play</u>? Milton Keynes: Open University Press.
   In Canada:
   Bella, L. (1989) 'Women and leisure: beyond androcentrism' in E.L. Jackson and T.L. Burton (eds) <u>Understanding Leisure and Recreation</u>, State College, PA.: Venture, pp 151–180.
   In the United States:
   Bialeschki, M.D. and Henderson, K. (1986) 'Leisure in the common world of women', <u>Leisure Studies</u>, Vol. 5, No. 3, pp 299–308.
   In Australia
   Anderson, R. (1975) <u>Leisure: An Inappropriate Concept for Women?</u> Canberra: AGPS.

Multiple references

It should never be necessary to write a reference out in full more than once in a document. Additional references to a work already cited can be made using <u>op.cit.</u>, or references back to previous footnotes. For example, the above paragraph of text might be followed by:

> **Deem pioneered the study of women and leisure in Britain (2).**

The footnote would then say:

> **2. Deem, <u>op. cit.</u>**

or: **2. See footnote 1.**

Specifics, quotations, page references

Page references for specific references or quotations are given in the footnote rather than the text. So the Iso-Ahola quotation given above would look like this:

> **Iso-Ahola makes the point that: 'To survive as an academic field, scholars must supply evidence to the effect that their methods of investigation are valid and reliable rather than 'soft'' (4).**

The footnote would then say:

> **4. Iso-Ahola, S.E. (1980) 'Tools of social psychological inquiry', Chapter 3 of <u>The Social Psychology of Leisure and Recreation</u>, Dubuque: Wm. C. Brown, p. 49.**

Further quotations from the same work might have footnotes as follows:

7. Iso-Ahola, op.cit. p. 167.

Note the page number.

Advantages and disadvantages

One of the advantages of the footnote system is that it can accommodate notes other than references to the literature, as discussed above.

A disadvantage of the footnote style is that it does not result in a tidy, alphabetical list of references. This diminishes the convenience of the report as a source of references for others. Some writers therefore resort to producing a *bibliography* in addition to the list of references. This results in extra work since it means that references have to be written out a second time (but see 'The best of both worlds' below).

The best of both worlds

One way of combining the advantages of both systems is for the list of notes to consist of author/date references and then have an alphabetical list as in the author/date system proper. So the list of footnotes for the above paragraph would then look like this:

Notes
1. Deem, 1986.
2. Bella, 1989.
3. Bialeschki and Henderson, 1986.
4. Anderson, 1975.

An alphabetical bibliography would then follow which would be the same as for the author/date system. This system is particularly useful when making several references to the same document.

Second hand references

Occasionally you want to refer to an item which you yourself have not read but which is referred to in something you have read. It is misleading to give a full reference to the original if you have not read it yourself! You should give the reference to where you obtained the material, even if it is a quotation. For example:

> Kerlinger characterises research as 'systematic controlled, empirical, and critical investigation of hypothetical propositions about the presumed relations among natural phenomena' (quoted in Iso-Ahola 1980, p. 48).

In this instance the writer has not read Kerlinger in the original but is relying on Iso-Ahola's quotation from Kerlinger.

Reading, abstracting, summarising, keywording

How a piece of literature should be read and what should be distilled from it depends very much on the purpose of the study in hand. The item may be of key importance, in which case all of it is relevant; in other cases only a small part of the item is relevant to current needs. It may even be the case that the item contains nothing of relevance, but attention should still be drawn to it – for instance in a study of holiday-taking it might be relevant to note that an important national survey fails to say how many people go away on holiday each year.

Another device is the use of 'keywords'. These are often seen listed at the beginning of academic articles and they are used in literature indexes and in library catalogue systems. Again these can be very useful in tracking down information, but you should always bear in mind that keywords generally attempt to indicate the contents of, possibly whole books, using only three or four words. They should therefore be used with caution.

Further reading

Examples of bibliographies: Veal 1990, 1991, Knight and Parker 1978, Baretje 1964, Goeldner and Dicke 1980.
Style manuals: American Psychological Association 1983.

6 Existing sources: secondary data

In this chapter the use of existing sources of data is examined, as opposed to the collection of new data which is the subject of most of the rest of the book. Chapter 5 dealt with published research – the 'literature'; this chapter examines mainly statistical sources, such as the census and national surveys.

Introduction

In doing research it is obviously sensible to use existing information where possible, rather than embarking on new information collection exercises. One aspect of this has already been examined in Chapter 5 on the literature. In searching the literature the researcher may come across references to statistical or other data which may not have been fully analysed or exploited by the original collectors of the data – because of their particular interests, or lack of time and money. In other cases information may exist which was not collected for research purposes in the first place, for example the records of an organisation, but which can provide the basis for research.

Data are referred to either as *primary* data – that is new data specifically collected in the current research project (the researcher is the primary user) – or *secondary* data - that is data which already exists and was collected for some other (primary) purpose but can be used a second time in the current project (the researcher is the secondary user). Further analysis of data in addition to the analysis carried out by the original researchers is referred to as *secondary analysis*.

As with the literature, secondary data can play a variety of roles in a research project from being the whole basis of the research to being a vital or incidental point of comparison.

National leisure surveys

In most developed countries surveys of leisure participation are conducted by government departments or agencies on a regular basis. In the USA such surveys have been conducted since the early 1960s, particularly on outdoor recreation. In Britain the General Household Survey (GHS), commissioned by government agencies and conducted by the Office of Population Censuses and Surveys (OPCS), has provided such information every two or three years since 1973. In Australia the Commonwealth government commissioned the first National Recreation Participation Survey (NRPS) in 1985/86.

While such surveys have been carried out in a number of countries over the last two decades, since each country has adopted different design principles, the findings are not comparable, as a number of attempts at international comparisons indicate (Kamphorst and Roberts 1989, Hantrais and Kamphorst 1987).

National surveys, and their regional equivalents, are the main source of information available to researchers on overall participation levels in a range of leisure activities. A number of issues arise in the use of these important data bases.

Validity and reliability

The surveys suffer from the limitation of all interview surveys in that they are dependent on respondents' own reports of their leisure participation. How sure can we be, therefore, that the resultant data are accurate? We cannot be absolutely sure, as discussed in Chapter 9, however, a number of features of surveys such as the GHS lend credence to their reliability and value as sources of data.

Firstly organisations such as the OPCS have an enviable reputation for excellence and professionalism in their work. Secondly, in the case of the GHS, the fact that there has been little dramatic variation in the findings of the various surveys over the years is reassuring (Veal 1991), erratic and unexplainable fluctuations in reported levels of participation would have led to suspicions that the surveys are unreliable, but this has not happened. Other reasons for placing some faith in the surveys are the sample sizes and the form of the questions used, as discussed below.

Sample size

As discussed in Chapter 11, it is generally the case that the larger the sample size the more reliable and precise are the survey findings. The GHS is based on a large sample of around 20,000 interviews, divided into four quarterly samples of 5 000 each. The Australian NRPS of 1985/86 was based on four quarterly samples of 2 500. These surveys are therefore large and subject to only minimal 'statistical error' – a term explained in Chapter 11.

Main question – time period covered

The main question asked in the GHS is what leisure activities people have engaged in during their leisure time in the previous four weeks. In contrast American surveys have tended to ask people what they have done in the previous year. This has the advantage of covering all seasons of the year and picking up more of the infrequent participants, but has the disadvantage of introducing possible errors in people's recall of their activities. The GHS avoids this by limiting the time period over which people are asked to recall to one month. Seasonal variations are covered by interviewing at different times of the year. The Australian survey is even more restrictive, covering just one week.

As a result of this methodological approach, it is important to note that the surveys do not indicate the total number of people who take part in an activity, but rather the number that take part in an average month or week. This affects different activities differently. For example most people who visit zoos at all do so very rarely, perhaps once in two or three years: so the reported number of people visiting in a month or a week, while it may be accurate, includes only a small proportion of total number of people in the community who visit zoos. By contrast someone who plays football is quite likely to do so at least once a week, so the people playing football in any one month or week are likely to represent most football players.

This illustrates an important point about data in general: the meaning of information and the uses to which it can be put depend vitally on the way the data were collected.

Age range

In addition to its restriction to participation in a month, the GHS is also restricted in term of age range: it covers only those aged 16 and over. Most surveys of this sort are limited in this way: some go down as far as 12 year-olds, some cover only those aged 18 and over. The reasons for this restriction are two-fold. Firstly it may be difficult to obtain accurate information from young children, and it may even be considered ethically unacceptable to subject children to the sort of questioning which adults can freely choose to face or not. Secondly there is a question as to when children actually engage in their own independent leisure activities as opposed to being under the control of parents.

The lower age limit affects the results, in that for some activities – for example swimming or cycling – young teenagers may be a significant proportion of the participants. For other activities – for example gardening or going to the opera – the age limit may be inconsequential. When using data from surveys such as the GHS it is therefore important to bear in mind that under-16 year-olds are excluded.

Activities

The GHS covers a wide range of home-based, indoor, outdoor, sporting and cultural activities, as indicated in Appendix 6.1. Respondents in the survey are asked whether they have been away on holiday in the previous month, and then they are asked what activities they have engaged in during their leisure time in the past month, and, for each activity, how many times.

The results are reported as percentages, either averaged over the year, or in four quarters or seasons (OPCS Annual, Veal 1984). As can be seen from the summary of results in Appendix 6.1, for many activities, the percentage participation level is small. However, even one per cent of the adult population in Britain is almost half a million people! But, although the sample size of the GHS is large, one per cent of 20,000 is only 200 and for the seasonal samples of 5000 this falls to just 50, so the scope for detailed analysis of participants in individual activities is limited. A further limitation of the sample size is that the survey cannot be subdivided to give detailed results for regions of the country.

Social characteristics

In addition to the basic information on participation the GHS also contains a large range of background information on the people interviewed, including:

Sex	Occupation
Age	Education level reached
Size of family unit	Country of birth

The importance of participation surveys

Surveys such as the GHS, despite their limitations, are the main source of information, not only on overall levels of participation but also on differences in participation between different groups in the community, such as the young and the old, men and women, different occupational groups and so on. Any leisure professional should therefore be fully familiar with such key data sources.

Tourism surveys

In the case of domestic tourism there is also reliance on interview surveys for basic statistical information. In the case of international tourism some data are available from government international arrivals and departures statistics which are compiled by immigration authorities at ports of entry. The advantage of this source of information is that it lends itself to a certain degree of international comparison, a task which is undertaken by the OECD (OECD Annual). However, the information on each traveller is limited, so recourse must also be had to surveys for much of the data on tourists.

In Britain the main source of information on domestic tourism is the British Home Tourism Survey, commissioned each year since 1971 by the English Tourist Board. This is a home-based survey with a substantial monthly sample size, which records origins and destinations of trips with at least one overnight stay in the previous two months.

Information on visitors to Britain and British trips overseas is collected by the International Visitor Survey, conducted each year by OPCS. It records such information as destinations, length of trip and expenditure.

Economic surveys

In most developed countries surveys of household expenditure are conducted on a regular basis. In Britain this survey is an annual one and is called the 'Family Expenditure Survey' (FES). The Family Expenditure Survey collects information from a cross-section of families throughout Great Britain on their weekly expenditure on scores of items, many of which relate to leisure, including the following:

Alcoholic Drink	Magazines
Arts and crafts	Musical instruments
Audio	Newspapers
Books	Pets
Cinema	Photography
DIY	Records and tapes
Eating out	Sports
Gambling	Television
Gardening	Toys and games
Holidays	Video
Home computers	

The other form of economic data available relate to employment in the leisure and tourism industries. Data are available from the Department of Employment, at national and regional level, on employment in such industry sectors as:

Public houses
Sport and recreation
Betting and gambling
Clubs
Restaurants
Catering contractors
Hotels
Cinema, theatre, radio.

The population census

The population census is an important source of information in any country and any aspiring recreation or tourism manager should be fully aware of its content and its potential. A complete census of the population is taken in Britain by the Office of Population Censuses and

Surveys (OPCS) every 10 years; the latest was 1991, and before that 1981, 1971 and so on. As in most countries it is a statutory requirement for householders (and hoteliers) to fill out a census form on 'census night', indicating the number of people, including visitors, in the building, their ages and so on. Some people escape the net, for instance people sleeping rough, or illegal immigrants, but generally the information is believed to be reliable and comprehensive.

Data are available at the following levels:

National
Regions
Counties
Local government areas
Parliamentary constituencies
Enumeration districts (EDs)

EDs are small areas, with populations of around 250 to 500 and are the areas which a single census collection officer deals with on census night.

Content

An enormous amount of information is available on each of these areas including:

Resident population.
Number of males/females.
Number/per cent in five-year age-groups (and single years for under 20s).
Number of people:
• in different religions;
• born in UK and other countries;
• speaking different languages;
• with parents born in UK and other countries.
Number of families:
• of different sizes;
• with different numbers of dependent children;
• which are single parent families;
• with various numbers of vehicles.
Numbers of people:
• who left school at various ages;
• with different educational/technical qualifications;
• in different occupational groups;
• unemployed;
• living in different types of dwelling.

Relevance

It can be seen that none of the census information is concerned directly with leisure or tourism. So why should the census be of interest to the leisure professional?

Firstly many leisure managers have responsibility for a particular geographical area, whether that be a whole country, a local government area or the catchment area of a particular facility or service. One of the cardinal rules of the manager/marketer is to 'know the market or customer'. This applies as much in public sector agencies as in commercial agencies. The census provides valuable information about the numbers and characteristics of customers or potential customers in a geographical area.

The census can put the particular leisure or tourism operation into perspective. For example, if the facility or enterprise is intended to serve a particular geographical area and is aimed at teenagers, the census will indicate how many teenagers live in that area. If 5000 teenagers live in the area and the facility has 500 teenage customers then it is reaching 10 per cent of the potential market. This may be good or bad, depending on the level of competition and how specialised the 'product' is.

In a more general sense the census can be used to produce a 'profile' of an area, so that the manager has an overall view of the nature of the community. Nearly all the items of information listed above can be relevant to such a profile.

More sophisticated uses of the census involve feeding a large range of data into computers in order to classify areas into 'types'. Residential areas can be classified, for example, into retirement areas, working class family areas, affluent areas, and so on. In Britain 'ACORN' (A Classification of Residential Neighbourhoods) has been developed to do this classification and it has been found that residents of different area 'types' have markedly different leisure participation patterns (Shaw 1984). This is related to the ideas of 'lifestyle' and 'psychographics', which were referred to in Chapter 1.

Using secondary data

Some useful analysis can be done using these secondary sources of data – in fact there are certain forms of analysis which can only be done with these data. Two case studies are given here by way of illustration.

Case study 6.1: Demand for cinema

The problem
Suppose a developer or local council is considering whether to build a cinema on a particular site as part of a multi-purpose leisure complex. The town has a population of 100,000 and already has two 400-seat cinemas. The developer wants to know what demand exists in the area for such a facility. There is a range of approaches which could be considered to investigate this question.

Possibilities
One approach to the problem would be to examine existing cinemas in the area to see whether they are over-used or under-used, that is whether demand is already being adequately met by existing facilities. This however may not give the full answer, since it might be found that some well managed, well located cinemas were well used while others, poorly managed and poorly located, or

with restricted access, were poorly used. It might also be difficult to obtain commercially sensitive data from potential competitors.

Another approach might be to conduct an interview survey of local residents to ask them whether they would like to go to the cinema but do not do so at present because of lack of suitable facilities. Even if the time and money were available to conduct such a survey, the results could not be relied on as the main piece of information on which to base the decision because, while people's honesty and accuracy in recalling activities might be relied on in relation to activities which they have actually taken part in, asking them to predict their behaviour in hypothetical future situations is very risky.

A third approach would be to examine communities of similar population size and type to see what levels of cinema provision they have and how well they are used. Again this may be a time-consuming process and somewhat 'hit-and-miss' because it is not easy to find comparable communities and because some of the data required, being commercially 'sensitive', may not be readily available.

A fourth approach would be to use secondary data, namely the appropriate national survey (NS) and the census, to provide an approximate estimate of likely demand for cinema seats in the area. The aim is to provide an estimate of the level of demand which a community of the size of the study area is likely to generate and compare that with the level of demand already catered for by existing cinemas, to see whether or not there is a surplus of demand over supply.

Suppose the census gives the population of the town as 100,000, and the population aged 16 and over as 80,000.

The particular NS deals only with people aged 16 and over and obviously children under that age do go to the cinema; but it may be that there is sufficient demand for an additional cinema even without taking account of the under 16s; so the under 16s can be ignored for the moment, only returning to them if necessary.

One of the features of cinema attendance is that it varies considerably by age. Cinema is attended more by young people than by older people. If the study town contains a higher than average proportion of young people, for example, it would be expected that it would produce a higher than average cinema attendance, and vice versa. The NS gives information on the percentage of people of different ages who go to the cinema, as shown in Table 6.1. It can be seen that teenagers are almost six times as likely to attend the cinema as the over 60s.

In Table 6.2 the age structure of the national population aged 16 and over, is compared with that of the study town. Clearly the town has a much younger age profile than the national average with only just over half the proportion of

Table 6.1   Cinema attendance by age (hypothetical)

Age group	Percentage of age-group who go to the cinema in an average week
14–19	14.9
20–24	11.5
25–29	7.4
30–39	5.2
40–49	4.8
50–59	3.5
60+	2.5
Total/average	6.6

Table 6.2 Study town and national age structures compared

National (not UK)		Study town	
Age group	%	No.	%
14–19	12.5	15600	19.5
20–24	11.9	15200	19.0
25–29	10.6	11360	14.2
30–39	20.1	16880	21.1
40–49	14.2	7200	9.0
50–59	11.8	6160	7.7
60+	18.9	7600	9.5
Total	100.0	80000	100.0

Table 6.3 Estimating demand

Age group	Percentage of age group participating (NS) (A)		Town Population (Census) (B)		Estimated number participating (AxB/100)
14–19	14.9%	of	15600	=	2324
20–24	11.5		15200		1748
25–29	7.4		11360		841
30–39	5.2		16880		878
40–49	4.8		7200		346
50–59	3.5		6160		216
60+	2.5		7600		190
Total	8.2		80000		6543

over 55s and correspondingly larger proportions in the young age-groups. So it is clearly advisable to give consideration to the question of age structure.

Table 6.3 indicates how demand for cinema attendance would be estimated: attendances are estimated for each age group and summed to give a total of 6543 attendances per week.

If a typical 400 seat cinema auditorium requires, say, 1500 ticket sales a week to be viable (this is entirely hypothetical – in a real situation this information would be checked out with experts), then the town could, it is estimated, support four such cinemas. Since two cinemas already exist, then it is estimated that there is demand for two more, bearing in mind that there is also children's demand to be taken into account.

This exercise is not predicting demand precisely – it merely indicates a 'ball park' demand figure. A well managed and programmed cinema might draw far more demand than is estimated – the NS attendance rates relate to average attendances across the country, so clearly there are places where higher attendance rates occur as well as places where lower rates occur. What the exercise indicates is that, on the basis of data to hand, 6500 cinema attendances a week seem reasonably likely. This seems a very simple and crude calculation, but quite often investors – in the public and private sector – fail to carry out even this sort of simple calculation to check on 'ball park' demand figures; investments are made on the basis of personal hunch, and then surprise is expressed when demand fails to materialise.

Forecasting note
To provide a simple forecast of future demand, for, say, the year 2001, it would be necessary merely to insert population forecasts for the year 2001 into column B of Table 6.3 and rework the calculations.

Case study 6.2: tourism trend analysis

Typically tourism statistics are produced on a quarterly basis, as in Table 6.4 (column A). Each quarterly figure of tourist arrivals reflects two factors: seasonal variation and longer-term trends. One way of examining the trend without the distraction of the seasonal variation is to produce a 'smoothed' series by calculating a 'moving average' (column B). The moving average consists of the average of the previous four quarters' figures - so, for example, the first average for Oct-Dec 1986, is the average of the four figures for 1986, and the figure for Jan-Mar 1987 is the average of the figures from Apr-Jun 1986 to Jan-Mar 1987 (note the calculations can be done very easily with a spreadsheet program). The effect is to present a 'smoothed' trend series, as shown graphically in Figure 6.1.

Table 6.4 Tourism arrivals 1986–1990 (hypothetical)

Quarter		No. of arrivals millions A	Moving average B
1986	Jan-Mar	1.1	—
	Apr-Jun	2.5	—
	Jul-Sep	4.5	—
	Oct-Dec	3.3	2.9
1987	Jan-Mar	1.3	2.9
	Apr-Jun	2.8	3.0
	Jul-Sep	4.9	3.1
	Oct-Dec	3.9	3.2
1988	Jan-Mar	1.6	3.3
	Apr-Jun	3.0	3.3
	Jul-Sep	5.5	3.5
	Oct-Dec	4.3	3.6
1989	Jan-Mar	1.8	3.7
	Apr-Jun	3.0	3.7
	Jul-Sep	5.2	3.6
	Oct-Dec	3.1	3.3
1990	Jan-Mar	1.7	3.3
	Apr-Jun	2.8	3.2
	Jul-Sep	4.8	3.1
	Oct-Dec	3.0	3.1

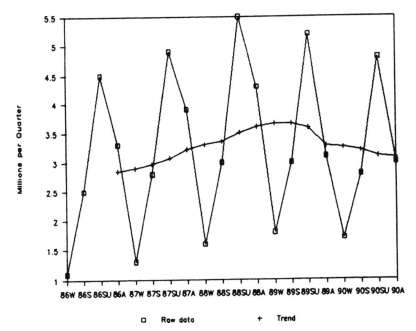

Figure 6.1 Tourism trends

Further reading

On the GHS: Office of Population Censuses and Surveys (Annual), Veal 1984.

On employment statistics: Corley 1982.

On economic data: Martin and Mason (Annual), Henley Centre for Forecasting (Quarterly).

On tourism data sources: Burkart and Medlik 1981, Part III.

On international comparisons: Kamphorst and Roberts 1989, Hantrais and Kamphorst 1987.

On sport: Duffield *et al.* 1983.

Appendix 6.1   Leisure participation in Great Britain 1977–1986

	participating in 4 weeks prior to interview Annual average rate – persons aged 16 & over			
	1977	*1980*	*1983*	*1986*
Amateur drama/music	3	3	3	4
Athletics (incl. jogging)	1	1	2	3
Badminton	2	2	2	2
Bowls	1	1	1	1
Bowls/tenpin	1	1	1	2
Camping/caravanning	1	1	1	1
Cinema/film clubs	10	10	7	8
Cricket	1	1	1	1
Cycling	1	1	2	2
Dancing	15	14	11	11
Darts	9	7	7	6
DIY	35	37	36	39
Exhibitions/shows	2	2	2	3
Fairs/arcades/fêtes/carnivals	4	4	2	4
Fishing	2	2	2	2
Football	3	3	3	3
Gardening	42	43	44	43
Going out for a drink	}64	54	54	55
Going out for a meal	}	40	40	47
Golf	2	2	2	3
Gymnastics/athletics	*	1	1	1
Historic buildings/sites/towns	8	9	8	9
Horse riding	1	1	1	1
Keep fit/yoga	1	2	3	3
Listen to records/tapes	62	64	63	67
Museums/art galleries	4	3	3	4
Outings by car/ motorbike/boat	2	2	1	4
Read books	54	57	56	59
Sewing/knitting	29	28	27	27
Snooker/billiards/pool	6	7	8	9
Squash	2	2	3	2
Swimming (indoor pool)	5	6	7	9
Swimming (sea, outdoor pools)	2	2	3	2
Table tennis	2	2	1	1
Tennis	1	2	1	1
Theatre/ballet/opera	5	5	4	5
Visits to countryside	5	4	3	3
Visits to parks	4	4	4	4
Visits to seaside	7	7	7	7
Walking (2 miles or more)	17	19	19	19
Zoos	1	2	1	1
Sample size	23,171	22,594	19,050	19,209

*Less than 0.5 per cent
Source: General Household Surveys/OPCS

7 Observation

The aim of this chapter is to draw attention to the importance of *looking* in research and to introduce some of the specific approaches of observational research. It examines situations in which observation is particularly appropriate and outlines the main steps which should be taken in an observation based project.

The nature and purpose of observational research

Observation is a neglected technique in leisure and tourism research. While it is rarely possible to base a whole research project on observation, the technique has a vital role to play in most research.

Observation involves *looking*. The results can be recorded and analysed qualitatively or quantitatively. The looking can be done with the naked eye or with the help of sophisticated equipment. For example, time-lapse photography can be used to photograph a given area automatically at set periods; aerial photography can be used to gain a picture of a whole recreation area; and video can also be used. These more sophisticated techniques are considered later in the chapter, but first the more simple approaches are examined.

Possibilities

A number of types of situation where observation is appropriate or necessary can be identified:

- children's play;
- the use of informal leisure areas;
- spatial use of sites;
- deviant behaviour;
- consumer testing;
- complementary research;
- everyday life;
- development of theory.

These situations are discussed in turn below.

Children's play

There is some research which can only be tackled by means of observation. One example is children's play. Research on children's play is often concerned with discovering play patterns. What types of equipment do children of different ages prefer? Do boys have a different pattern of play from girls? Is there any difference in play patterns between children from different ethnic backgrounds? And so on. It is fairly clear that answers to such questions could not be found by interviewing children, particularly very young children. The obvious way to find out is to observe children at play and record their behaviour.

Use of informal recreation areas

A second example of the use of observation is in estimating the level of use of informal recreation areas such as beaches, urban parks or tourist sites where there is no admission charge. Since there is no charge for entry to this type of area managers and planners can only obtain estimates of their levels of use by observation.

An indication of the level of use of sites may be required for a variety of reasons. For instance, a public agency could decide that it would be useful, politically or for public relations, to be able to state the total number of people or visitors which a facility serves in a week or a year – to justify the taxpayer's money being spent on maintaining it. In management terms it is often useful to be able to relate the *costs* of maintaining a site to the number of visits which it attracts as an input to decisions on how much money should be spent on different sites. A single site manager might be interested to compare levels of use over time to assess the impact of various management measures.

In order to obtain an estimate of use levels it is necessary to observe and count the number of users.

Where the bulk of users arrive by private car it may be possible to install automatic vehicle counters to count the number of vehicles entering and leaving the site to give an approximation of use levels. In this case the help of a mechanical device is enlisted to do the counting.

However, vehicle counts provide information on the number of *vehicles* using a site but not the number of *people*. To obtain estimates of the numbers of people it is necessary to supplement these data by observation – to ascertain the average number of persons in each vehicle and, at some sites, to estimate the numbers arriving by foot or bicycle, who would not be recorded by the mechanical counting device.

Spatial use of sites

Observation is useful not only for gathering information on the number of users of a site but also on the way people make use of a site. This is particularly important in relation to the design and layout of leisure spaces and their capacity. For instance if people tend to crowd close to entrances and parking areas then the places where those entrances and areas are positioned will affect the pattern of use of the site and this can be used as a management tool. Figure 7.1 illustrates the point. Similarly if, as has been found, people tend to locate themselves along 'edges' – such as fences, banks, areas of trees and shrubs, etc. – then this tendency can be used to influence the pattern of use of a site (Ruddell and Hammitt 1987). While this applies particularly to outdoor natural areas, it can also have some relevance in built up areas, such as shopping malls, and in buildings such as museums. Public buildings and public open spaces are often designed with either little or no consideration of how people will actually use them, or on the basis of untested assumptions about how they will be used. In reality it is often found that people do not actually behave as anticipated: that some spaces are underused while some are over-crowded, or that spaces are not designed or equipped for the activities which they are accommodating. Observation is the means by which these aspects of space utilisation can be discovered.

Deviant behaviour

Deviant behaviour is a situation where observation is likely to be more fruitful than interviews. People are unlikely to tell an interviewer about their litter dropping habits, their lack of adherence to the rules in a

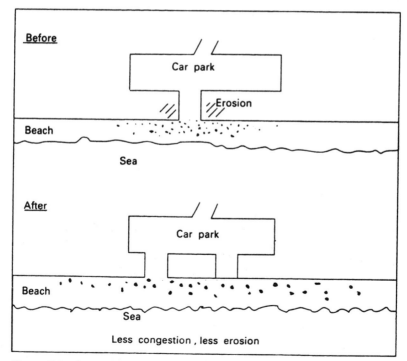

Figure 7.1 Site use and management

park, or their beer can throwing habits at a football match. Finding out about such things requires observation... covert observation! This then raises ethical issues, which are considered under the heading of participant observation in Chapter 8.

Consumer testing

Consumer testing is another potentially fruitful but underexploited use of observation. While interviews are one way of obtaining information on the quality of the experience offered by a leisure or tourism facility or product, an additional means is to use an incognito user/customer/observer. Such an observer would have a checklist of features to observe – cleanliness, information, staff performance, etc. – and would make a report after using the facility or product.

Complementary research

Observation can be a necessary complement to interview surveys to correct for variation in sampling rates. For instance in a typical urban park or beauty spot two interviewers, working at a steady rate, may be able to interview virtually all users in the less busy periods in the early morning but only manage to interview a small proportion of the users during the busy lunch hour and afternoon. The final sample will therefore over-represent early morning users and under-represent mid-day and afternoon users and, if these two groups are different, this may have a biasing effect on, for example, the balance of views expressed by the users. Counts of the hourly levels of use can provide data to give an extra 'weight' to the mid-day and afternoon users. The process of weighting is described in more detail in Chapter 11.

Everyday life

The idea of simply observing everyday life as an approach to studying social life is associated with Britain's Mass Observation anthropological study of the British way of life in the 1930s and 1940s and with the work of Irving Goffman (1959). An anthology of Mass Observation sketches published in 1984 (Calder and Sheridan 1984) includes descriptions of everyday events in pubs, on the Blackpool promenade and in the wartime blitz in London. Goffman's work was more theoretical and concerned the ways individuals use space and interact in public and private places. An anthology of work in the Goffman style (Birenbaum and Sagarin 1973) includes observational studies of such leisure activities as pinball, bars, card games and restaurants.

Development of theory

Observation has been used in sociological research to develop ideas and theories about human behaviour, as in the research of Fiske (1983) and Grant (1984) on the use of beaches, Cunneen and Lynch's (1988) work on the riots at the Australian Motor Cycle Grand Prix and Marsh and his colleagues' (1978) research on soccer fans. These researchers use an interactive, inductive process to build explanations of social behaviour from what they observe. Very often a key feature of such studies is to contrast what the researcher observes with what has apparently been observed by others, particularly those with influence or authority such as officials, police, and the media. Observational research can challenge existing stereotypical interpretations of events.

Participant observation

The specific technique of participant observation is not dealt with here since it is covered in Chapter 8 on qualitative methods.

Main elements of observational research

Observation is essentially a simple research method so there is not a great deal of 'technique' to consider. What is often required is precision, painstaking attention to detail, and patience. In general the main tasks in devising an observational project are:

1. choice of site(s);
2. choice of observation point(s) within or outside the site;
3. choice of time period to cover;
4. decision on whether to observe continuously or to undertake spot counts/observations;
5. if sampling, decision on number and length of sampling periods;
6. decision on what to observe – numbers, behaviour, etc.;
7. where spatial behaviour is involved decision on the areas into which the site is to be divided and preparation of site maps;
8. design of a recording sheet.

As with the 'steps in the research process' outlined in Chapter 3, it is difficult to produce a list of steps which will cover all eventualities. In particular, if the approach is not quantitative but qualitative, then a number of the steps above concerning counting will be redundant.

Stage 1: choice of site(s)

In the case of consultancies the sites to be studied may be fixed; where there is some element of choice some time should be devoted to inspecting and choosing sites which will offer the appropriate leisure/tourism behaviour but also provide suitable conditions for observation.

Stage 2: choice of observation point(s)

Choice of observation points within a site is clearly important and needs to be done with care.

Stage 3: choice of time period

The choice of time period is important because of variations in use of a facility, either by time of the year, day of the week or time of day. Observation to cover all time periods may be very demanding in terms of resources, so some form of sampling may be necessary.

Stage 4: continuous observation or spot counts?

The question of continuous observation or spot counts is related to the resources available and the nature of the site and is particularly important if one of the aims of the research is to obtain an accurate estimate of the number of visitors. For instance it could be very expensive to place observers at the numerous gates of a large urban park for as much as 100 hours in a week to estimate the number of users. A sampling approach will usually have to be adopted.

Having decided to sample it is of course necessary to decide how often to do this. This is discussed further below.

There is also a decision to be made on whether to count the number of people entering during specified periods or the number of people present at particular points in time. Counting the number of people present at particular points in time is probably easier since it can be done by one person regardless of the number of entrances and can provide information on the spatial use of the site at the same time. Thus one person, at specified times, makes a circuit of the park or beach and records the numbers of people in designated zones.

When qualitative rather than quantitative observation is being undertaken it is more likely that continuous observation will be adopted since the aim will generally be to observe the dynamics of events and behaviour at the site. However, the question of *when* to undertake such observation in order to cover all aspects of the use of the site still needs careful consideration.

Stage 5: count frequency

How often should such counts be undertaken? This will depend to a large extent on the rate of change in the level of use of the site. For example, the four counts in Figure 7.2 are clearly insufficient since the unbroken line is the pattern of use observed but the broken line *could* be the actual pattern and it will have been missed by the counts actually undertaken.

There is little advice that can be given to overcome this problem, except to sample frequently at the beginning of a project until the basic patterns of peaks and troughs have been established; subsequently it may be possible to sample less often.

But how should the counts be interpreted to obtain an overall

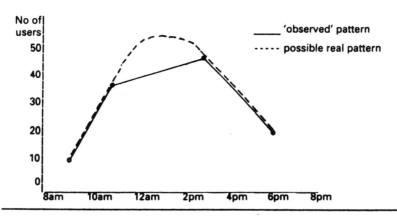

Figure 7.2   Counts of park use – 1

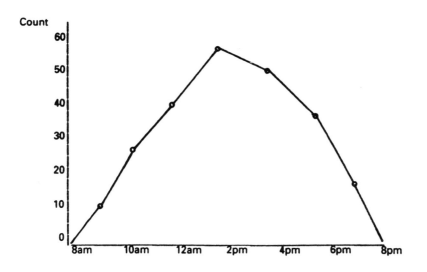

Figure 7.3   Counts of park use – 2

estimate of use? Consider the following set of counts of the numbers of people present in a park, which opens at 8 am and closes at 8 pm:

8 am	0	4 pm	50
9 am	10	5 pm	35
10 am	25	7 pm	15
12 am	40	8 pm	0
2 pm	55		

This pattern is illustrated in Figure 7.3

By interpolating for the missing hours, the following estimates could be made of the number of users present at hourly intervals (figures in

Time	No. of people present	Time	No. of people present
8 am	0	2 pm	50
9 am	10	3 pm	55
10 am	25	4 pm	55
11 am	*32*	5 pm	35
12 am	40	*6 pm*	*25*
1 pm	*47*	7 pm	15
		8 pm	0
		Total	389
		Average	32.4

italics are interpolated – that is, they are averages of the two adjacent observed figures).

It is therefore estimated that there is an average of 32.4 people in the park at any one time, over a twelve hour period, giving a total of 389 'person-hours'. The person-hour or user-hour or visitor-hour is a perfectly valid measure of use in its own right and could be used to compare different sites or the performance of the same site over time.

If, however, an estimate of the number of *users* over the day is required, additional information on the length of stay will be necessary. The minimum possible number of users is 55 – what we could have been observing is one crowd of people building up to a peak by 2 pm and then beginning to drift away. But if instead there was a certain amount of coming and going and if each visitor stayed, say, exactly half an hour the number of users would be estimated at twice the number of person-hours – 778. If the average user stayed two hours, the number of users would be 194 or 195. In other words the number of users is equal to the number of person-hours divided by the average length of stay. The length of stay would have to be obtained either by detailed observation of a sample of groups or by an interview survey.

Stages 6 and 7: what to observe – characteristics and spatial behaviour

To observe the spatial behaviour of users within a facility it is necessary either to record people's positions directly onto a map as indicated in Figure 7.4, or to divide the site into areas or zones and record the number of people and their activities within those zones. The zones should be determined primarily by management concerns – for example, how many use the children's playground? But they should also be designed for ease of counting; ideally zones should be such that they can be observed from one spot and should be clearly demarcated by natural or man-made features. Figure 7.5 is an example of a counting sheet designed for an area with six zones and the possibility of a variety of activities. The data collected using such a

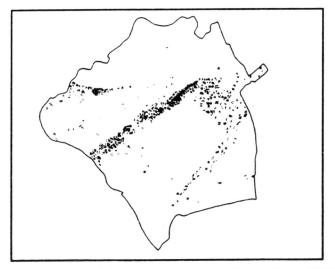

Figure 7.4   Recording of observations using a map — (Source: Glyptis, 1991)

SITE: _____   DATE: _____

NAME OF OBSERVER: _____   START TIME: _____

ACTIVITY	ZONE						
	A	B	C	D	E	F	Total
Walking							
Sitting							
Playing sport							
Children playing							
Eat/drinking in cafe							
Total							

Figure 7.5   Example of a count recording sheet

form is ideal for storage, manipulation and presentation in graphic form using a spreadsheet computer program such as LOTUS123. An example of a graphical presentation of count data is shown in Figure

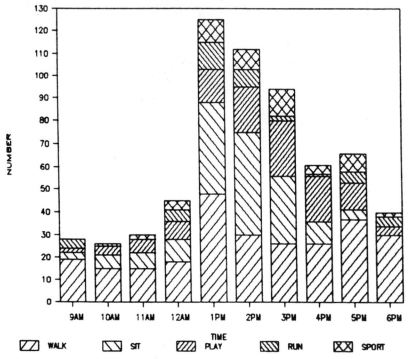

Figure 7.6 Graphic display of count data

7.6 – this relates to a whole site and not to a site divided into zones, but similar graphics could be produced for each zone.

In addition to observing activity it is possible to observe user characteristics of a limited kind. For instance men and women could be separately identified and it is possible to distinguish between children and adults, although if more than one counter is involved care will need to be taken over the dividing line between child and young adult or teenager. Similarly, with care, it should be possible to distinguish senior citizens and also some ethnic minorities. It is also possible, again with care, to observe the size of parties using a site, especially if they are observed arriving or leaving at a car park. This additional information would of course complicate the recording sheet and symbols would be necessary to record the data on a map.

Care needs to be taken not to make the data collection so complicated that it becomes too difficult for the observers and leads to inaccuracies. This is one of those situations where it is necessary to consider carefully why the data are being collected and not to get carried away with data collection for its own sake.

Recording of user characteristics can be used as a check on the accuracy of sampling in interview surveys and may be used to 'weight' the results so that the final result is a better reflection of the characteristics of the users of the facility. This is similar to the 'time of day' correction discussed above, but relates to the personal characteristics of users directly, rather than their time of use of the facility. For instance, if it was found by observation that half the users of a site were women but in an interview survey only a third of those interviewed were women, the women in the sample could be given a greater weighting in the analysis so that their views and attitudes would receive due emphasis. The details of weighting are described more fully in Chapter 11.

In addition to observing people statically, or arriving at an entrance, it is also possible to observe users' movement through a site. Of course care must be taken not to give offence by letting users become aware that they are being 'followed', but routes taken by users can be revealing for management.

Car registration numbers can be a useful source of information. Firstly they can provide information on where people have travelled from. Secondly number plates can be used to trace the movement of vehicles in an area – for instance within a national park with a number of stopping points.

Photography

Aerial photography

The use of aerial photography is well developed in geography and geology where a whole sub-discipline of 'remote sensing' has developed using a variety of techniques. It can also be an effective technique in leisure and tourism studies. Where large areas are concerned – such as coastlines and estuaries – where access is difficult and recreational use of the site is very scattered, aerial photography may be the only way of obtaining estimates of levels and patterns of use. In harbours and estuaries it is probably the best means of obtaining estimates of numbers of craft using the area since, as they are generally moving, it can be difficult to count manually on a crowded waterway. Needless to say a good quality camera is needed for such work. Generally slides are the best medium because they can easily be projected on a large screen for the subsequent laborious task of counting.

Photography

The value of ordinary, land-based, photography as an adjunct to quantitative observation should not be overlooked. The level of crowding of a site, its nature and atmosphere can be conveyed to the reader of a report with the aid of photographs. Particular problems, for instance of erosion, or design faults, can be conveyed better visually than verbally – a picture speaks a thousand words.

Just looking

Finally we should also not forget how important it is to use our eyes even if the research project does not involve systematic observational data collection. Familiarity with a leisure activity or site helps to design a good research project and interpret the results. Many studies have been based just on informal, but careful, observation. All useful information is not in the form of numbers. Careful observation of what is happening in a particular leisure situation, at a particular facility or type of facility or among a particular group can be a more appropriate research approach than the use of questionnaires or even informal interviews. The good researcher is all eyes.

Further reading

General/methodological: Burch 1981, Ely 1981, Tyre and Siderelis 1978, TRRU 1983, Heberlein and Dunwiddie 1979, Peine 1984.

Examples of studies using observation: Child 1983, Cunneen and Lynch 1988, Fiske 1983, Glyptis 1981a, 1981b (see also Patmore 1983, p. 146), Gold 1972, Grant 1984, Marsh *et al.* 1978, van der Zande 1985, Birenbaum and Sagarin 1978.

8 Qualitative methods

In this chapter methods of data collection which result in qualitative information rather than numbers are reviewed. The chapter discusses the advantages and features of qualitative methods, their role in market research, the range of methods available and, in turn, in-depth interviews, group interviews/focus groups, participant observation, and ethnographic approaches.

Introduction

The term 'qualitative' is used to describe research methods and techniques which use and give rise to qualitative rather than quantitative information. In general the approach is to collect a great deal of 'rich' information about relatively few people rather than more limited information about a large number of people.

It is however possible to envisage qualitative research which actually deals with large numbers of people – for example, a research project on sports spectators, involving observation, participation in spectator activity, and possibly a small number of informal interviews with fans, could involve information relating to tens of thousands of people.

Qualitative methods can be used for pragmatic reasons, in situations where formal, quantified research is not necessary, is not possible, or is inappropriate. But there are also theoretical reasons for using qualitative methods. For example it may be felt that structured research imposes too much of the researcher's view on the situation, that it is not appropriate for the researcher to be the only one to decide which are the important issues and which questions are to be asked and to determine the whole framework within which the discourse of the research will be conducted.

Much qualitative research is based on the belief that the people personally involved in a particular (leisure or tourism) situation are best placed to analyse and describe it in their own words – that they should be allowed to speak without the intermediary of the researcher – a sort of 'cinema verite' or 'vox pop' style of research.

Merits of qualitative methods

Kelly (1980), in making a plea for more qualitative leisure research a decade ago, argued that qualitative research had been neglected in the field of leisure during the 1960s and 1970s, particularly in the United States. He suggested that qualitative research has the following advantages over quantitative research.

1. The method corresponds with the nature of the phenomenon being studied – that is, leisure is a qualitative experience.
2. The method 'brings people back in' to leisure research – by contrast, quantitative methods tend to be very impersonal – real people with names and unique personalities do not feature.
3. The results are much more understandable to people who are not statistically trained.
4. The method is better able to encompass change over time – by contrast much quantitative research tends to look only at current behaviour as related to current social, economic and environmental circumstances, ignoring the fact that most people's behaviour is heavily influenced by their life history and experience.
5. Reflecting the first point, Kelly argues that leisure itself involves a great deal of face-to-face interaction between people – symbols, gestures, etc. – and qualitative research is much better at investigating this.
6. Although some researchers in the psychological field might disagree with him, Kelly argues that qualitative techniques are better at understanding people's needs and aspirations.

Purposes in market research

Peterson (1987), speaking from a market researcher's perspective, lists the potential *purposes* of qualitative research as:

1. to develop hypotheses concerning relevant behaviour and attitudes;
2. to identify the full range of issues, views and attitudes which should be pursued in large-scale research;
3. to suggest methods for quantitative enquiry – for example in terms of deciding who should be included in interview surveys;
4. to identify language used to address relevant issues (to avoid the use of jargon in questionnaires);
5. to understand how a buying decision is made – questionnaire surveys are not very good at exploring processes;
6. to develop new product, service or marketing strategy ideas – the free play of attitudes and opinions can be a rich source of ideas for the marketer;
7. to provide an initial screening of new product, service or strategy ideas;
8. to learn how communications are received – what is understood and how – particularly related to advertising.

The range of methods

The range of qualitative techniques available to the leisure researcher and discussed in more detail in this chapter is as follows.

In-depth interviews	Interviews are conducted, usually with a relatively small number of subjects, with the interview being guided by a checklist of issues/questions rather than by formal, set questions in the form of a questionnaire. Very often such interviews are tape recorded and a word for word transcription prepared. In some research respondents are interviewed on two or more occasions.
Group interviews/focus groups	Similar to in-depth interviews but conducted with a group rather than an individual, so that interaction between the subjects takes place as well as interaction between interviewer and subject.
Participant observation	Where the researcher gathers information by being an actual participant with the subjects being studied. The researcher may be known by the subjects as a researcher or may be 'incognito'.
Ethnography	Ethnography is a type of research which utilises a number of the above techniques rather than being a single technique in itself. The word derives from the Greek *ethnos* meaning 'people', and therefore means the study of people. It is borrowed from anthropology – anthropologists essentially study groups of people and attempt, by a variety of data collection methods, to understand how a community works and what makes it 'tick'.

In-depth interviews

Purposes

In-depth interviews tend to be used for three basic reasons. Firstly the subjects of the research may be relatively few in number so a questionnaire based, quantitative style of research would be inappropriate. Secondly the information likely to be obtained from each subject would be expected to vary considerably. An example would be interviews with the management staff of a recreation or tourism department of a local council, or interviews with the coaches of national teams for a number of sports. Each of these interviews would be different and would be a 'story' in its own right. In reporting the research it would be the nature and structure of these 'stories' which would be of interest – the question of 'what percentage of respondents said what' would not be relevant.

Thirdly in-depth interviews can be used to explore a topic as a preliminary stage in planning a more formal questionnaire based survey.

Conducting a good in-depth interview could be said to require the skills of a good investigative journalist. As Dean and his colleagues put it:

> Many people feel that a newspaper reporter is a far cry from a social scientist. Yet many of the data of social science today are gathered by interviewing and observation techniques that resemble those of a skilled newspaper man at work on the study of, say, a union strike or a political convention. It makes little sense for us to belittle these less rigorous methods as 'unscientific'. We will do better to study them and the techniques they involve so that we can make better use of them in producing scientific information.
> (Dean, Eichhorn and Dean, quoted in Mccall and Simmons 1969, p. 1)

Checklist

Rather than a formal questionnaire the 'instrument' used in in-depth interviews is usually a checklist of topics to be raised. For example, a formal questionnaire might ask a question: 'Up to the age of 15, which of the following sports did you take part in, in your leisure time?' The informal interview checklist would probably simply include the words 'childhood sport'. The interviewer would shape the question according to the circumstances.

If the interviewer is interested, for example, in the influence of child-hood sport experiences on current participation, it may be necessary to ask a specific question such as: 'What sports did you play in your childhood?' In other cases it might not be necessary to ask the question explicitly because the interviewee will already have discussed childhood activity in great detail in response to the interviewer's initial question: 'What are the main influences on your current sports participation?' In other words, in-depth interviews vary from interview to interview; they take on a life of their own. The skill on the part of the interviewer is to ensure that all appropriate topics are covered – even though they may be covered in different orders and in different ways in different interviews. An example of a checklist is included as Appendix 8.1.

Interviewing

An important skill in interviewing is to avoid becoming so taken up in the conversational style of the interview that the interviewee is 'led' by the interviewer. The interviewer should avoid *agreeing* - or disagreeing - with the interviewee or *suggesting* answers. This is more difficult than it sounds because in normal conversation we tend to make friendly noises and contribute to the discussion – in the in-depth interview we are torn between the need to maintain a friendly conversational atmosphere and the need *not* to influence the interviewee.

Some of the carefully planned sequencing of questions which is built into formal questionnaires must be achieved by the interviewer being very sensitive and quick thinking. For example, having discovered that the respondent does not go to the theatre, the interviewer should not say, 'Is this because it is too expensive?' Rather the interviewee should be asked something like, 'Why is that?' If the interviewee does not mention cost but cost is of particular interest, then a question such as, 'What about seat prices?' might be asked, but only *after* the interviewee has given his or her own explanation of why they do not attend the theatre.

Whyte (1982) lists a sort of 'hierarchy' in interviewer responses which vary in their degree of intervention in the interview. Whyte also sees this as the interviewer exercising varying degrees of control over the interview. Beginning with the least intrusive style of intervention, Whyte's list is as follows.

1. 'Uh-huh'   a non-verbal response which merely indicates that the interviewer is still listening and interested.
2. 'That's interesting'   encourages the subject to keep talking or expand on the current topic.
3. Reflection   repeating the last statement as a question - eg. 'So you don't like sport?'
4. Probe   inviting explanations of statements, e.g. 'Why don't you like sport?'
5. Back tracking   Remembering something the subject said earlier and inviting further information, e.g. 'Let's go back to what you were saying about your school days'.
6. New topic   e.g. 'Can we talk about other leisure activities – what about entertainment?'

It should be noted that, except for 6, the interviewer is essentially drawing on what the subject has already said and is inviting them to expand on it.

An important skill in interviewing of this sort is not to be afraid of silence. Some questions do puzzle respondents and they need time to think. The interviewer does not have to fill the space with noise under the guise of 'helping' the interviewee. They should be allowed time to ponder. The initiative can be left with the respondent to ask if they do not understand a question. While it is pleasant to engender a conversational atmosphere in these situations, the in-depth interview is in fact different from a conversation. The interviewer is meant to *listen* and *encourage* the respondent to talk – not to engage in debate with them!

Recording

Tape-recording of in-depth interviews is common, although in some cases it might be felt that such a procedure could inhibit respondents. Obviously if tape-recording is not possible then notes must be taken, at the time or immediately afterwards.

There can be great value in producing complete verbatim transcripts of interviews. This is a laborious process, one hour of interview taking as much as six hours to transcribe. Such transcripts can however be used to analyse the results of interviews in a methodical manner.

Analysis

There are various ways of going about the analysis of interview transcripts or notes. The essence of any analysis procedures must be to return to the terms of reference, statement of objectives, or hypotheses of the research and begin to sort and evaluate the information gathered in relation to the questions posed and the concepts identified. In qualitative research however, those original ideas may be very fluid; data gathering and hypothesis formulation and even the identification of concepts is a two-way process. Ideas are refined and revised in the light of the information gathered.

Lofland and Lofland (1984) provide a list of eleven 'thinking units' which can be useful in designing research and conducting interviews, but would appear to be particularly relevant to the analysis process. The thinking units are as follows:

1. Meanings – subjects' beliefs and attitudes and the significance they attach to 2–11.
2. Practices – routine behaviour patterns.
3. Episodes – notable events.
4. Encounters – episodic interactions between individuals.
5. Roles – ascribed, informal, and occupational roles, 'social types', 'social psychological types' and the articulation and tactics associated with roles.
6. Relationships – on-going relationships between individuals and groups.
7. Groups – informal groupings of people.
8. Organisations – formal groupings.
9. Settlements – ranging from the block or neighbourhood through to the city.
10. Social worlds – for example occupational 'worlds', sub-cultures.
11. Lifestyles – ways of life.

Lofland and Lofland suggest that the questions which might be asked about these 'units', in interviewing and in analysis concern the unit's type, structure, frequency of occurrence, causes, processes and consequences.

In addition to the problem of ordering and summarising the data conceptually, the researcher is faced with practical problems of how to approach the pile of interview notes or transcripts. Again Lofland and

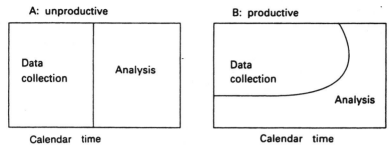

Figure 8.1 Data collection and analysis (Source: Lofland and Lofland, 1984)

Lofland offer sound advice when they contrast the two approaches to data collection and analysis shown in Figure 8.1 and, in recommending approach B, state:

> In this format, analysis and data collection run concurrently for most of the time expended on the project, and the final stage of analysis (after data collection has ceased) becomes a period for bringing final order to previously developed ideas.
>
> (Lofland and Lofland, 1984, p. 131)

Barton and Lazarsfield (1969) outline four types of analytical procedure in qualitative research:

1. Analysis of single observations – particularly the surprising, unusual or unexpected. The analyst proceeds to attempt to explain the unexpected observation.
2. Construction of descriptive systems – where the analyst attempts to put some order into a mass of material by devising systems of 'types', taxonomies, etc.
3. Qualitative data suggesting relationships – where the analyst looks for 'possible relationships, causes, effects, and even dynamic processes' in the data.
4. Matrix formulations – where the analyst, faced with a mass of information, manages to come up with 'a descriptive concept on a higher level which manages to embrace and sum up a great wealth of particular observations in a single formula'.

There is little guidance in the literature on how to generate the 'flashes of brilliance' which solutions like this fourth one of Barton and Lazarsfield seem to call for. It would seem that the creative leap comes from more hum-drum, painstaking analysis which at least develops in the researcher an in-depth familiarity with the data. The initial steps in analysis therefore involve fairly methodical procedures to classify and organise the data.

In a very practical way, it is sensible to ensure that the transcripts have wide margins so that they can be annotated or 'flagged' with key words for analytical purposes. This is necessary not only to identify topics across a number of interviews but also because very often the same topic is covered several times in the same interview so some sort of flagging is necessary for analysis. Also, a particular line of analysis may not be related to substantive topics raised in the interview but may relate, for example, to attitudes expressed by interviewees, which might arise at any time in an interview.

Alternatively a card index of topics can be created on which references can be recorded, e.g. School sport: interview 5 page 12/ paragraph 34.

The collection of papers edited by Burgess (1982) gives some ideas which are useful, even though much of the material in that collection relates to more traditional anthropological/ethnographic research. Little guidance is apparent from the written up results of qualitative research, although there are some exceptions. The nature of the material is such that it is difficult for researchers to explain in detail how they have used the interview material to arrive at their conclusions.

More recently a variety of computer packages have become available to analyse interview transcripts (Fielding and Lee, 1991). At a simple level a word-processing package can of course be used to search text for particular words or phrases, but the specialist packages enable the researcher to classify and 'flag' the text as discussed above and thus to speed up the process of transcript analysis.

Of course detailed analysis may be less important when the purpose of the in-depth or informal interviews is to provide input into the design of a formal questionnaire. In that case the interviewer might make a series of notes arising from the interview which might be of relevance to the questionnaire design process and will provide input from memory as long as the questionnaire design work is undertaken fairly soon after the interviews.

Group interviews/focus groups

The idea of interviewing groups of people together rather than individually is becoming increasingly popular in market research. In this technique the interviewer becomes the facilitator of a discussion rather than an interviewer as such. The aim of the process is much the same as in an in-depth interview, but in this case the 'subjects' interact with each other as well as with the researcher.

A group will usually comprise between 5 and 12 people. They may be chosen from a 'panel' of people who make themselves available to market researchers for this sort of exercise, or they may be chosen because they are members of a particular group of interest to the research, for instance local residents in a particular area, members of sports clubs, or members of particular ethnic groups. The members of the group may or may not be known to one another.

The usual procedure is to tape-record the discussion and for the researcher to produce a summary from the recording.

Many of the same considerations apply here as in the in-depth interview situation: the process is informal but the interviewer still has a role in guiding the discussion and ensuring that all the aspects of the topic are covered. In addition, in the group interview, the interviewer has the task of ensuring that everyone in the group has their say and that the discussion is not dominated by one or two vociferous members of the group.

Participant observation

In participant observation the researcher becomes a participant in the social process being studied. The classic study of this type is Whyte's *Street Corner Society* (1955), in which the researcher spent several years living with an inner city US Italian community. Smith's (1985) study of pubs in England is a direct leisure example as is Wynne's (1986) study of community involvement with recreation facilities.

In leisure and tourism elements of 'participant observation' are common in many types of research. For instance, a researcher involved in studying the use of a park or resort can easily spend periods as a user of the facility. This is however a very minimalist view of participant observation. Traditionally the process has involved much more interaction of the researcher with the people being researched. In many cases some sort of participant observation is the only way of researching particular phenomena – for instance it would be difficult to study what really goes on in a drug sub-culture or in some youth sub-cultures using a questionnaire and clip-board. Becoming part of the group is the obvious way of studying the group.

Participant observation raises a number of practical/tactical problems. For example, in some cases actually gaining admittance to the social setting of interest may be a problem – for instance where close-knit groups are involved. Having gained admittance to the setting, the question arises as to whether to pose as a 'typical' member of the group, whether to adopt a plausible 'disguise' (e.g. a 'journalist' or 'writer') or whether to admit to being a researcher.

Selection of informants is an issue to be addressed by the participant observer in the same way that sampling must be considered by the survey researcher. The members of the study group who are most friendly and talkative may give a biased picture of the views and behaviour of the group.

In addition there are practical problems to be faced over how to record information. When the researcher's identity has not been revealed, the taking of notes or the use of a tape-recorder may be impossible. Even when the researcher has identified her or himself as such, or has a plausible 'identity', the use of such devices may interfere with the sort of natural relationship which the researcher is trying to establish.

Ethics

Ethical considerations arise in a number of research methods, relating particularly to questions of privacy and confidentiality. They are, however, particularly pronounced in the case of participant observation. To what extent is it ethical for researchers to disguise their identity from the people they are interacting with and studying – in effect to lie about their identity? To what extent is it ethical for researchers, in writing up their research, to reveal confidences when these have been unwittingly shared? While fictitious names of places and people may be used, for those in the know, the places and the people may be all too easily identifiable. When researchers are involved with groups engaging in illegal and/or anti-social activities, where do their loyalties lie?

In a celebrated case in recreation research, Moeller and his colleagues (1980a) used incognito interviewers, posing as campers, to investigate campers' attitudes to pricing (and discovered different results from those collected by formal, identified interviewers). The ethics of this practice raised considerable controversy in the *Journal of Leisure Research* (Christensen 1980; Moeller et al. 1980b, LaPage 1981).

Ethnography

The ethnographic style of research is not one technique but an approach drawing on a variety of techniques. Generally, as applied to leisure and tourism research, it seeks to see the world through the eyes of those being researched, allowing them to speak for themselves, often through extensive direct quotations. Often also, the aim is to debunk conventional, 'common sense' views of 'social problems', 'deviants', sexual and ethnic stereotypes, and so on. In leisure studies the approach has become particularly associated with 'cultural studies', for example of youth subcultures and ethnic groups.

It is better to read the material than read about it – for example, Griffin et al. (1982) on women and leisure, Hollands (1985) on unemployed youth and Hall and Jefferson (1976) on youth sub-cultures.

Further reading

Methodological: Lofland and Lofland 1984, Burgess 1982.
Informal/in-depth interviews: Moeller et al. 1980a, Rapoport and Rapoport 1975.
Participant observation: Campbell 1970, Glancy 1986.
Focus groups:Calder 1977, Krueger 1988, Reynolds and Johnson 1978.
Examples: Cunneen and Lynch 1988, Griffin *et al.* 1982, Hollands 1985, Marsh *et al.* 1978, Walker 1988, Wynne 1986.
Ethics: Bulmer 1982, Moeller *et al.* 1980a, 1980b, Christensen 1980, LaPage 1981.

This is part of a checklist devised in connection with a study of people's use of leisure time and attitudes towards leisure.

Appendix 8.1 Example of a checklist for in-depth interviewing

Current activities		How often?	Home
		Why?	
Explore each one		Where?	Away from home
– compare		Who with?	
		Meaning/importance	
		Type of involvement	
Activities would *like* to do		Why not?	
Meaning of 'leisure' to you			
Home	Family roles		Being a woman/man
	Constraints		Being a parent
Past activities	School		
	College		Why changes?
	Family		
Money	Costs		
Car/transport			
Facilities	Locally	Favourite	
	City	Use/non-use	Why?
	Region	Access	
Clubs/associations			
Personality			
Work time/energy/colleagues			
Skills			
Dislikes		Aspirations	

---

9 Questionnaire surveys

This chapter presents an overview of the range of types of questionnaire survey, including interviewer versus self-completion, the household questionnaire survey, the street survey, the telephone survey, the postal or mail survey, on-site or user surveys, and captive groups surveys.

Introduction

Questionnaire surveys involve the gathering of information from individuals using a formally designed schedule of questions called a *questionnaire* or *interview schedule*.

Questionnaire surveys are usually conducted using only a proportion, or sample, of the population in which the researcher is interested. For example the national surveys discussed in Chapter 6 involve samples of only a few thousand to represent tens of millions of people. How such samples are chosen, how the size of the sample is decided and the implications of relying on a sample, are discussed in Chapter 11.

Compared with the qualitative techniques discussed in Chapter 8, questionnaire surveys usually involve quantification – the production of results in numerical terms. This has implications for the way the data are collected, analysed and interpreted. It should be stressed at the outset that the fact that questionnaire surveys are more formalised, are generally conducted on a substantial scale and have more space devoted to them in text books such as this, does not mean that they are in some way superior to other forms of research. As discussed in Chapter 4, research methods should be chosen to suit the task in hand – 'horses for courses'. Questionnaire surveys have a role to play when the research questions indicate the need for fairly structured data and generally when data are required from samples which are explicitly representative of a defined wider population.

Questionnaire surveys rely on information from respondents, and what respondents say depends on their own powers of recall, on their honesty and, fundamentally, on the questions included in the questionnaire. There has been very little research on the validity or accuracy of questionnaire data in leisure and tourism studies; however, one such study, by Chase and Godbey (1983), discovered that in a survey of tennis participation, respondents exaggerated their levels of participation by as much as one hundred per cent. This suggests that the researcher and the user of research results should always bear in mind the nature and source of the data and not fall into the trap of believing that, because information is presented in numerical form and is based on large numbers, it represents immutable 'truth'.

Questionnaire surveys usually involve substantial numbers of 'subjects' (the people being surveyed), ranging from perhaps 50 or 60 to many thousands. This, together with the complexity of some forms of quantitative analysis, means that computers are invariably used to analyse the results. The practical implications of this are considered in Chapter 10 which deals with questionnaire design.

Interviewer-completion or self-completion?

Questionnaire surveys can take one of two forms: they can be interviewer-completed or self-completed. When it is interviewer-completed the questionnaire provides the 'script' for an interview: an interviewer reads the questions out to the respondent and records the respondent's answer on the questionnaire. When the questionnaire is self-completed respondents read and fill out the questionnaire themselves.

Interviewer-completed surveys are more expensive in terms of interviewers' time (which usually has to be paid for) but the use of an interviewer usually ensures a more accurate and complete response.

Self-completion can be cheaper and quicker but often results in low response rates, which can introduce bias in the results because the people who choose not to respond or are unable to respond because of perhaps language or literacy difficulties, may differ from those who do respond. When designing a questionnaire for self-completion, greater care must be paid to layout and presentation since it must be read and completed by 'untrained' people. In terms of design, self-completion questionnaires should consist primarily of 'closed' questions – that is questions which can be answered by ticking boxes. 'Open-ended' questions, where respondents have to write out their answers, should be avoided, since they invariably achieve only a low response. For example, in an interview, respondents will often give expansive answers to questions such as 'Do you have any comments to make on the overall management of this facility?' But they will not as readily write down such answers in a self-completion questionnaire.

There may, however, be cases when self-completion is to be preferred, or is the only practicable approach, for example when the people to be surveyed are widely scattered geographically, which would make face-to-face interviews impossibly expensive and a postal survey an obvious choice, or when it is felt that, on sensitive matters, respondents might prefer the anonymity of the self-completed questionnaire. Some of the issues connected with self-completion questionnaires are discussed more fully in the section on postal surveys.

Types of questionnaire survey

Questionnaire surveys in the leisure and tourism field can be divided into six types.

1. Household or home based   People are selected on the basis of where they live and are interviewed in their home.
2. Street   People are selected by stopping them in street, in shopping malls, etc.
3. Telephone   Interviews are conducted by telephone.
4. Postal/mail   Questionnaires are sent and returned by post.
5. Site/user   Users of a leisure or tourism facility or site are surveyed on-site.
6. Captive group   Members of groups such as classes of school children, members of a club or employees of an organisation are surveyed.

Each of these is discussed in more detail below and some of their basic characteristics are summarised in Figure 9.1

The household questionnaire survey

The household questionnaire is perhaps the 'standard' research vehicle in leisure and tourism research: most of the quantified data in the field come from this type of research. The advantage of the household questionnaire is that it is generally representative of the community;

Type	Self- or Interviewer Completion	Cost	Sample	Possible length	Response rate
Household	Either	Dear	Whole population	Long	High
Street	Interviewer	Medium	Most population	Short	Medium
Telephone	Interviewer	Medium	People with telephone	Short	High
Postal	Self	Cheap	General or special	Varies	Low
On-site	Either	Medium	Users only	Medium	High
Captive Group	Self	Cheap	Group only	Medium	High

Figure 9.1   Types of questionaire survey – characteristics

the samples drawn tend to include all age and occupational groups and represent a complete geographical area, whether that be a country, a region, a local government area or a neighbourhood. Household surveys therefore provide information on the reported leisure or tourism behaviour of the community as a whole.

While some household leisure/tourism questionnaire surveys are specialised, they are often broad ranging in their coverage. That is, they tend to ask, among other things, about participation in a wide range of leisure activities, holiday-taking patterns or buying habits. This facilitates exploration of a wide range of issues which other types of survey cannot tackle.

Being home-based this sort of survey can involve quite lengthy questionnaires and interviews. By contrast, in the street, at a leisure or tourism facility, or over the telephone, it can be difficult to conduct a lengthy interview. Leisure participation surveys in particular, with their huge range of possible activities, often involve a very complex looking questionnaire which is difficult to administer 'on the run'. With the home-based interview it is usually possible to pursue issues at greater length. An interview of one hour's duration is not out of the question and 20–30 minutes is quite common.

While considering household surveys mention should be made of the *omnibus* survey. Omnibus surveys are single surveys conducted by a market research or survey organisation for several clients who each contribute their own particular questions to the questionnaire. The main cost of household interviews lies in sampling and contacting respondents, and in an omnibus survey these costs are shared by a number of clients. In addition, it is found that most household survey questionnaires include a fairly standard set of demographic and socio-economic information, such as age, sex, family structure, occupation, income and so on; in an omnibus survey the cost of collecting this information is shared among the clients. The British General Household Survey is an omnibus survey of 20,000 people run by the government Office of Population Censuses and Surveys, the clients being government departments and agencies. In the years when leisure questions are included the clients for those questions are the various national leisure/recreation agencies, such as the Sports Council and the Countryside Commission. In Australia the National Recreation Participation Survey and the annual Domestic Tourism Monitor use a commercially run omnibus survey, the AGB: McNair Market Monitor.

Normally household questionnaire surveys are interviewer-completed but it is possible for questionnaires to be left at the respondent's home for self-completion and later collection. The field-worker then has the responsibility of checking that questionnaires have been fully completed and perhaps conducting an interview in those situations where respondents have been unable to fill in the questionnaire, either because they have been too busy, have forgotten, or have lost the questionnaire, or because of literacy or language problems or infirmity.

A variation on the standard household questionnaire interview survey is to combine interviewer-completed and self-completed elements. This often happens with leisure surveys: the interviewer conducts an interview with one member of the household about the household – how many people live there, whether the dwelling is owned or rented, perhaps information on recreational equipment, or anything to do with the household as a whole. Then an individual questionnaire is left for each member of the household to complete, concerning their own leisure behaviour. The interviewer calls back later to collect these individual questionnaires.

The potential length of interviews, the problems of contacting representative samples, and on occasions the wide geographical spread of the study area, mean that household surveys are usually the most expensive to conduct, per interview. Costs of the order of £15 or £20 per interview are typical, depending on the amount of analysis included in the price. When samples of several thousands are involved, it can be seen that the costs can be substantial. In the case of omnibus surveys many of the procedures, such as sampling and data processing, have become routinised, and interviewers are in place throughout the country already trained and familiar with the type of questionnaire and the requirements of the market research company – these factors can reduce costs significantly.

The street survey

The street survey can be conducted, as the name implies, on the street – usually a shopping street or tourist area – or in squares or shopping malls, where a cross-section of the community or of visitors to an area might be expected to be found. Stopping people in such environments for an interview places certain limitations on the interview process.

Firstly an interview conducted in the street cannot generally be as long as one held at someone's home – especially when the interviewee is in a hurry. Of course there are some household interviews which are very short because the interviewee is in a hurry or is a reluctant respondent and there are street interviews which are lengthy because the respondent has plenty of time – but as a general rule the street interview must be shorter. Both in the home and street interview situation potential respondents often ask, 'How long will it take?' before committing themselves to an interview. In the home-based situation a reply of '15–20 minutes' is generally acceptable but in the street situation anything more than '5 minutes' would generally lead to a marked reduction in the number of people prepared to cooperate. The range of topics/issues/activities which can be covered is therefore restricted and this must be taken into account in designing the questionnaire.

The second limitation is the problem of contacting a representative sample of the population. Certain types of people might not frequent shopping areas at all, or only infrequently – for instance people who are housebound for various reasons or people who have other people to do their shopping. Some types of tourist – for example business tourists or those visiting friends or relatives – may not be found in the popular tourist areas. Such individuals might be of particular importance in some leisure and tourism research, so their ommission can significantly compromise the results. There is little that can be done to overcome this limitation; it has to be accepted as a limitation of the method. The other side of this coin is that certain groups will be over-represented in shopping streets – notably full-time housewives and the retired in suburban shopping areas, or office workers in business areas. It might also be the case that certain areas are frequented more by, for example, young people than old people or by men rather than women, so any sample would be representative of the users of the area, but not of the local population or visitor population as a whole.

The means used to attempt to overcome the problem of unrepresentative samples is the technique of *quota sampling* in which the interviewer is given a 'quota' of different types of people – by age, sex, occupation, etc. – to interview. The proportions in each category are determined by reference to the Census or other appropriate information sources. When the survey is complete, if the sample is still not representative with regard to the key characteristics, further adjustments can be achieved through the process of 'weighting', discussed in Chapter 11.

The telephone survey

The telephone survey is particularly popular with political pollsters because of its speed and the ease with which a widespread sample of the community can be contacted. It is also used extensively in market and academic research for the same reasons.

The obvious limitation of the technique is that it excludes non-telephone subscribers – generally low income groups and some mobile sections of the population. With telephones in the great majority of homes in developed countries this is not now as serious a problem as it was in the past. In the case of fairly simple surveys like political opinion polls, where the researcher has access to previous survey results using telephone and face-to-face interviews, this problem may be overcome by the use of a correction factor; for instance it might be known that non-telephone subscribers always add x per cent to the Labour vote. In certain kinds of market research the absence of the poorer parts of the community from the survey may be unimportant because they do not form a significant part of the market. For some public policy and academic research however, this can be a significant limitation.

Length of interview can be a limitation of telephone surveys, but not as serious as in the case of street interviews; telephone interviews of 10 or 15 minutes are acceptable.

The technique has its own unique set of problems in relation to sampling. Generally the numbers to be called are selected at random from the telephone directory; many market research companies have equipment which will automatically dial random telephone numbers as required. If a representative cross-section of the community is to be included then it is necessary for this type of interviewing to be done in the evening and/or at weekends if those who have paid jobs are to be included.

A further limitation of the telephone interview is that respondents cannot be shown such things as lists. This is particularly relevant to leisure and tourism surveys. In leisure participation surveys respondents are frequently shown lists of activities and asked if they have participated in them. Such lists can include 20 or 30 items, which could be tedious to read out over the telephone. Similarly in tourism studies respondents may be shown a list of places and asked which they have visited. Surveys which involve long checklists – for example of attitude dimensions – are not easily conducted by telephone.

It can be argued that telephones have an advantage over face-to-face interviews in that respondents feel that they are more anonymous and therefore are more forthcoming in their opinions. But it could also be argued that the face-to-face interview has other advantages in terms of eye-contact and body language which enable the skilled interviewer to conduct a better interview than is possible over the telephone.

The main advantage of the telephone survey is that it is quick and relatively cheap to conduct. A further advantage is that, because the interviewer is office-based, arrangements can be made for the interviewer to key answers directly into a computer, so dispensing with the printed questionnaire. This speeds up the analysis process considerably and cuts down the possibility of error in transcribing results from questionnaire to computer. It explains how the results of overnight political opinion polls can be published in the newspapers the next morning.

The postal or mail survey

There are certain situations where the postal method is the only practical survey technique to use. The commonest example is where members or customers of some national organisation are to be surveyed. The costs of conducting face-to-face interviews with even a sample of the members or customers would be substantial – a postal survey is the obvious answer. The postal survey has the advantage that a large sample can be included. In the case of a membership organisation, there may be advantages in surveying the whole membership, even though this may not be necessary in statistical terms. It can however be very helpful in terms of the internal politics of the organisation in that all members can be given the opportunity to participate in the survey and to 'have their say'.

The most notorious problem of postal surveys is low response rates.

In many cases as few as 25 or 30 per cent of those sent a question-naire bother to reply. There are even notorious instances, for example in community surveys on local government planning strategies, of only 3 or 4 per cent responses. What affects the response rate? Seven different factors can be identified.

1. The interest of the respondent in the survey topic

A survey of a local community about a proposal to route a six-lane highway through the neighbourhood would probably result in a high response rate, but a survey of the same community on general patterns of leisure behaviour would probably result in a low response rate. Variation among the population in the level of interest in the topic can result in a biased, that is unrepresentative, response. For example a survey on sports facility provision might evoke a high response rate among those interested in sport and a low response rate among those not interested – giving a false impression of community enthusiasm for sports facility provision. To some extent this can be corrected by weighting (see Chapter 11) if the bias corresponds with certain known characteristics of the population. For example, if there was a high response rate from young people and a low response rate from older people, information from the Census on the actual proportion of different age groups in the community could be used to weight the results.

2. Length of the questionnaire

It might be expected that a long questionnaire would discourage potential respondents. It can however be argued that other factors, such as the topic and the presentation of the questionnaire, are more important than the length of the questionnaire – that is if the topic is interesting to the respondent and is well presented then length is not an issue.

3. Questionnaire design/presentation/complexity

More care must be taken in design and physical presentation with any self-completed questionnaire. Type-setting, colour coding of pages, graphics and so on may be necessary. Leisure and tourism surveys often present awesome lists of activities which can make a question-naire look very complicated and demanding to complete.

4. The accompanying letter

The letter from the sponsor or researcher which accompanies the questionnaire may have an influence on people's willingness to respond. Does it give a good reason for the survey? Is it from someone, or the type of organisation, whom the respondent trusts or respects?

5. Postage-paid reply envelope

It is usual to include a postage-paid envelope for the return of the questionnaire. Some believe that an envelope with a real stamp on it will produce a better response rate than a business-reply-paid envelope. Providing reply envelopes with real stamps is more expensive because, apart from the time spent in sticking stamps on envelopes, stamps are provided for both respondents and non-respondents.

6. Rewards

The question of rewards for taking part in a survey can arise in relation to any sort of survey but it is a device used most often in postal surveys. One approach is to send every respondent some small reward, such as a voucher for a firm's or agency's product or service, or even money. A more common approach is to enter all respondents in a draw for a prize. Even a fairly costly prize may be money well spent if it results in a substantial increase in the response rate. When the cost of the alternative household surveys involving face-to-face interviews are considered, a substantial prize which results in a significant increase in responses may be considered good value.

It could however be argued that the introduction of rewards causes certain people to respond for the wrong reasons and that it introduces a potential source of bias in responses. It might also be considered that the inclusion of a prize or reward 'lowers the tone' of the survey and places it in the same category as other, commercial, junk mail that comes through people's letter boxes every day.

7. Reminders/follow-ups

Sensible reminders and follow-up procedures are perhaps the most significant tool available to the researcher. Typically, a post-card reminder might be sent one week or ten days after the initial mailing. After two weeks a letter accompanied by a second copy of the questionnaire ('in case the first has been mislaid') should be sent. A final reminder card can be sent a week or so after that. The effects of these reminders and follow-ups can be seen in Figure 9.2, which relates to a survey of residents' recreational use of an estuary. It can be seen that the level of responses peaked after only 3 days and looked likely to cease after about 16 days, giving a potential response rate of just 40 per cent. The surges in responses following the sending of the post-card and the second copy of the questionnaire can be seen and the net result was a 75 per cent response rate, which is very good for this type of survey.

Of course the sending out of reminders means that it must be

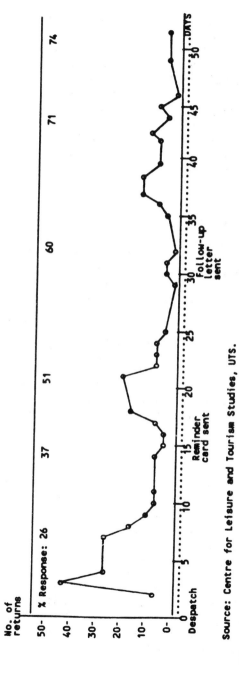

Figure 9.2 Pattern of response to postal/mail survey

Source: Centre for Leisure and Tourism Studies, UTS.

possible to identify returned questionnaires, so that reminders are not sent to those who have replied. This means that questionnaires or envelopes must have an identifying number which can be matched with the mailing list. Some respondents resent this potential breach of confidentiality but it cannot be avoided if only non-respondents are to be followed up. There is often a further advantage to being able to identify responses; they can be used to check the representativeness of the response. For instance, the questionnaire may not include res-pondents' addresses, but the geographical spread of the responses can be examined if the identity of the responses is known, and any necessary weighting can be carried out.

The need for follow-ups must be considered when budgeting for a postal survey, since postage and printing costs are often the most significant items in such budgets.

On-site or user surveys

The on-site survey, site survey, user survey or visitor survey (referred to in the rest of this chapter as 'site survey') is perhaps the most common type of survey used by managers in leisure and tourism. Surveys of tourists and local users are carried out at particular recreation or leisure facilities and surveys of tourists are carried out at hotels and en route on various types of transport, particularly international air trips. General surveys of visitors to a tourist area often take the form of street surveys – visitors are interviewed in the street, in squares/plazas or in seafront areas, anywhere where tourists are known to congregate. In this case the 'facility' is the tourist town or area, so the 'street survey' and the 'site survey' overlap and consideration must be given to the features of both types of survey. In general the site survey is more controlled than the street survey: those conducting the survey are seen to be part of the management of the facility and usually the opportunity is taken to interview users at a convenient time when they are not 'in a rush', as they may be in the street or shopping mall.

Site surveys can be conducted by interviewer or by self-completion. Unless carefully supervised, self-completion methods can lead to a poor standard in the completion of questionnaires and a low response level. And as with all low response levels this can be a source of serious bias in that those who reply may be unrepresentative of the users or visitors as a whole.

The usual self-completion survey involves handing users a question-naire on their arrival and collecting them on their departure, or con-ducting the whole procedure upon departure. Where self-completion is thought to be desirable or necessary then sufficient staff should be employed to check all users leaving the site, to ask for the completed questionnaires, to provide replacements for questionnaires which have been mislaid, and to assist in completing questionnaires, including completion by interview if necessary.

Conducting site surveys by interview is generally preferable to self-completion for the reasons discussed earlier in this chapter. The use of interviewers obviously has a cost disadvantage, but, provided the length of the interview is reasonable, costs per interview are usually comparatively low. Typically a site-survey interview will take about 5 minutes. Given the need to check through questionnaires, the gaps in user traffic and the need for interviewers to take breaks, it is reasonable to expect interviewers in such situations to complete about six interviews in an hour. Such estimates are of course necessary when considering budgets and timetables.

The survey methods considered so far have been fairly multi-purpose – they could be used for market research for a range of products or services, by public agencies for a variety of policy orientated purposes, or for academic research. Site surveys are a little more specific. While academics might want to use site surveys as a convenient way of gathering data on a particular leisure or tourism activity, the more usual use of such surveys is for policy, planning or management purposes. Site surveys are the type of survey which readers of this book are most likely to be involved with; they are the most convenient for students to 'cut their teeth' on and they are the most common surveys for individual managers – who tend to be site managers – to become involved in. For these reasons the roles of site surveys are considered in some detail below.

The uses of site surveys

What can site surveys be used for? The most obvious use is to provide direct feedback to management on a range of issues, including the following.

Catchment area
What is the catchment or market area of the facility or service? That is, what geographical area do most of the users come from? This can be important in terms of advertising policy. Management can concentrate on its existing catchment area and focus its advertising and marketing accordingly or it can take conscious decisions to use marketing to attempt to extend its catchment area.

User profile
What is the socio-economic/demographic profile of the users? It might be thought that a management capable of observation would be able to make this assessment without the need for a survey. This depends on the type of facility, the extent to which management is in continuous contact with users and the variability of the user profile. For example, a restaurant, hotel or resort manager might be very well informed on this but the managers of beaches, urban parks, national/state parks or theatres might, for various reasons, be less well informed, or even mis-informed.

Profile information can be used in a number of ways. Similarly to the data on catchment area, it can be used to *concentrate* or *extend* the market. Very often the commercial operator will opt to concentrate – to focus on a particular client group and maximise the market share of that group. In the case of a public sector facility the remit is usually to attract as wide a cross-section of the community as possible, so the data would be used to highlight those sections of the community not being catered for and therefore requiring marketing attention.

User opinions

What are the opinions of users? These data are invariably collected in site surveys and are usually of great interest to managers, but the interpretation of such data is not without its difficulties (Veal 1988). If management is looking for pertinent *criticisms* current users may be the wrong group to consult. Those who are most critical are likely to no longer be using the facility. Those using the facility may be reluctant to be very critical because it undermines their own situation – if the place is so poor why are they there? Those who are prepared to be critical may not be the sorts of clients for whom the facility is designed. As Lucas has said:

> It seems misleading to give equal weight to evaluations by people who are seeking a different type of area or experience. By analogy, a Chinese restaurant would do well to ignore the opinion about the food by someone who ate there by mistake while seeking an Italian restaurant .
> (Lucas 1970, p. 5)

In some situations people have little choice between facilities so criticisms are perhaps more easily interpreted. For example, parents' comments about the suitability of a local park for children's play can be particularly pertinent when it is the only play area available.

When opinion data have been collected it is often difficult to know precisely what to do with the results. Very often the largest group of users has no complaint to make – either because they cannot be bothered to think of anything in the interview situation or because of the 'self selection' process referred to above. Often the most common complaint is only raised by as few as 10 per cent of users. If this is the most common complaint, then logically something ought to be done about it by the management – but it could also be said that 90 per cent of the users are not concerned about that issue so perhaps there is no need to do anything about it! Very often therefore, management can use survey results to suit their own needs. If they want to do something about X, they can say that X was complained about by more users than anything else: if they do not want to do anything about X they can say that 90 per cent of users are satisfied with X the way it is.

Managers mostly want to enhance and maximise the quality of the experience enjoyed by their visitors: it may not be criticism of specific features that is important but users' overall evaluation of the experience. Thus users can be asked to rate a facility or area using a scale such as: very good/good/fair/poor/very poor or very satisfied/satisfied/dissatisfied/very dissatisfied. The results of such an evaluation can be used to compare users' evaluation of one facility with another – for example in a system of parks – or to examine the same facility at different times to see if satisfaction has increased or declined. This can be important in evaluation research of the sort discussed by Hatry and Dunn (1971) and discussed in Chapter 3.

Non-users
Site surveys by definition involve only current users of a facility or current visitors to an area. This is often cited as a limitation of such surveys, the implication being that non-users may be of more interest than users if the aim of management is to increase the number of users or visitors.

Caution should however be exercised in moving to consider research on non-users. For a start the number of non-users or non-visitors is usually very large. For example, in a city of a million population, a facility which has 5000 users has 995,000 non-users! In a country with a population of 50 million, a tourist area which attracts a million visitors a year has 49 million non-visitors, and if management is interested in international visitors, they have around five billion non-visitors! The idea that all non-users are potential users is therefore somewhat naive.

The user survey can assist in focusing any research which is to be conducted on non-users. For example, in the case of a local recreation facility the user survey defines the catchment area and, unless there is some reason for believing that the catchment area can or should be extended, the non-users to be studied are those who live within that area. Similarly the user profile indicates the type of person currently using the facility, and again, unless there is a conscious decision to attempt to change that profile, the non-users to be studied are the ones with that profile living within the defined catchment area. Comparison between the user profile and the profile of the population of the catchment area, as revealed by Census data, will indicate the numbers and characteristics of non-users in the area. Thus user surveys can reveal something about non-users!

Conclusion
The message from this brief discussion of the site survey is that, as with all research, careful consideration needs to be given to *why* data are being collected and *how* data are to be used.

Captive group surveys
The 'captive group' survey is not referred to in other research methods texts. It refers to the situation where the people to be included in the

survey comprise the membership of some group where access can be negotiated *en bloc*. Such groups include school children, adult education groups, clubs of various kinds and groups of employees, although all have their various unique characteristics.

A roomful of cooperative people can provide a number of self-completed questionnaires very quickly. Self-completion is less problematic in 'captive' situations than in less controlled situations because it is possible to take the group through the questionnaire question by question and therefore ensure good standards of completion.

The most common example of a captive group is school children: the easiest way to contact children under school leaving age is via schools. The method may, however, appear simpler than it is in practice. Research on children for education purposes has become so common that education authorities are cautious about permitting access to children for surveys. Very often permission for any survey work must be obtained from the central education authority – the permission of the class teacher or head teacher is not sufficient.

The most economical use of this technique therefore involves using a self-completion questionnaire, but interview methods can also be used. The essential feature is that access to members of the group is facilitated by their membership of that group and the fact that they are gathered together in one place at one time. It is important to be aware of the criteria for membership of the group and to compare those with the needs of the research. In some cases an apparent match can be misleading. For example membership of a retired people's club does not include all retired people – it excludes 'non-joiners' and the housebound. While schools include all young people, care must be taken over their catchment areas, compared with the study area of the research, and with the mix of public and private schools.

The pilot survey

Pilot surveys are small-scale 'trial runs' of a larger survey. As such they are not a unique type of survey, but relate to all the survey types discussed in this chapter. It is advisable always to carry out one or more pilot surveys before embarking on the main data collection exercise. Pilot surveys have a number of functions:

1. to try out the wording of questions in a questionnaire, to ensure that it is understood by respondents;
2. to test the sequencing of questions in the questionnaire;
3. to test the layout of the questionnaire in terms of convenience of use by interviewers or self-completion respondents;
4. to gain some familiarity with respondents and their views, etc., which may lead to some modification of questionnaire content;
5. to try out field-work management arrangements;
6. to train and test interviewers;
7. to gain a preliminary estimate of the likely response rate;

8. to obtain an estimate of the time taken to complete a questionnaire/interview and the overall rate at which interviewing can be completed;

9. to try out analysis procedures (especially when the main sample is planned to be very large).

In general at least some of the pilot interviews should be carried out by the researcher, or at least by experienced interviewers, since the interviewers will be required to report back on the pilot survey experience and contribute to discussions on any revisions to the questionnaire or fieldwork arrangements which might subsequently be made. The debriefing session following a pilot survey is very important and should take place as soon as possible after the completion of the exercise.

Further reading

See reading list for Chapter 6 for details of large-scale, national household surveys.

Surveys generally: Hudson 1988, Hoinville and Jowell 1978, Frank Small and Associates 1988, Marriott 1987, Veal 1988, Tourism and Recreation Research Unit 1983, Williamson et al 1982.

Telephone surveys: Lavrakas 1987.

Postal surveys: Hoinville and Jowell 1978.

10 Questionnaire design

In this chapter the aim is to review in detail the factors which must be considered in designing questionnaires for leisure and tourism studies. The chapter considers firstly the relationship between research problems and information requirements. It then goes on to consider the types of information typically included in leisure/tourism questionnaires (including respondent characteristics, activities, and attitudes/motivations), the wording of questions, coding of questionnaires for computer analysis, the ordering and layout of questions and the problem of validity. Finally some consideration is given to the special requirements of time-budget studies.

Research problems and information requirements

The important principle in designing questionnaires is to take it slowly and carefully and to remember why the research is being done. Very often people go too quickly into 'questionnaire design mode' and begin listing all the things 'it would be interesting to ask'. In many organisations a draft questionnaire is circulated for comment and everyone in the organisation joins in – the process begins to resemble Christmas tree decorating – nobody must be left out and everybody must be allowed to contribute their favourite bauble. This is not the way to proceed!

The decision to conduct a questionnaire survey should itself be the culmination of a careful process of thought and discussion, involving consideration of all possible techniques, as discussed in Chapter 3. The concepts and variables involved, and the relationships being investigated, possibly in the form of hypotheses, theories, models or evaluative frameworks – should be clear and should guide the questionnaire design process.

It is not advisable to begin with a list of questions to be included in the questionnaire. The starting point should be an examination of the management, planning, policy or theoretical questions to be addressed, followed by the drawing up of a list of information required to address the problems.

Case study 10.1: leisure centres in London

In the early 1980s the then Greater London Council (GLC) decided to assist the poorer inner London councils by, among other things, giving them grants to help meet the running costs of six large indoor leisure centres. Since local leisure provision was normally the responsibility of the local councils, in order to justify the grants the GLC needed to demonstrate that these centres were helping to implement GLC inner city policies. A research project was commissioned to assess the extent to which this was so – as such it was an example of a piece of *evaluative* research. The existing GLC policies which formed the basis of the justification for the grants were:

1. provision of greater than local services, that is serving more than one local council area;
2. provision for women;
3. provision for ethnic minorities;
4. provision for the unemployed, especially young unemployed.

No clear guidelines were given on what would be acceptable levels of non-local use, or use by women, ethnic minorities or unemployed, although implicit in the research brief was the idea that, as far as the three latter groups was concerned, the proportion of users from among these groups should ideally be at least equal to their proportion in the community and, in the case of the unemployed, somewhat higher.

Before the questionnaire design stage, these requirements were examined more fully.

1. Local versus non-local – clearly this required the research team to find out the extent to which users came from outside the local council area in which the centre was located. But did this mean where users *lived* or where they had *travelled from*? In inner city areas it was likely that many users would travel from their place of work. It was decided to find out both pieces of information. It was envisaged that it would be useful, in the report to the GLC, to illustrate where users came from on maps, so fairly detailed information on where users lived and travelled from would be required.

2. Women – the GLC wanted to see that the leisure centres were attracting female users because of their overall policy to promote sexual equality, so obviously the sex of users would need to be recorded. But it is possible that simple information on the number of women attending the centres would be misleading if women attended in order to accompany children, spouses or partners, and were not taking an active part. It was therefore necessary also to know what activity users came to the centre to do.

3. Ethnic minorities – in the London context this meant mainly users of, either Afro-Carribean or Indo/Pakistani descent. Clearly it would be necessary to establish the ethnic group of all users. Whether the centres were attracting satisfactory proportions of these groups could only be assessed in the light of information on the sizes of ethnic groups in the community. This is difficult information to obtain because, while the UK Census provides information on country of birth and even parents' country of birth, it does not provide information on third and fourth generation black people. Some local councils have however produced their own studies of the ethnic composition of their populations, which could be used for comparison purposes. This illustrates the point that survey information is often only meaningful when compared with information from other sources.

Youth – youth were defined as being under 18 years old, and the young unemployed as those who described themselves as unemployed. Again the 'performance' of the centres could only be assessed in the light of information from other sources on the number of young people and the number of young unemployed in the catchment areas of the centres.

Other issues also arose when thinking about the use of the centres by these target groups. For instance, it might be important to distinguish between frequent users and infrequent or once-only users, since the value of such centres should lie in the incorporation of recreation activity into the user's lifestyle. The target groups might be using the centres but were they *regular* users?

This review produced the following list of information requirements:

1. Home location
   Where travelled from to use the centre
2. Sex
   Activity at the centre
3. Ethnic group
4. Age
   Economic status, i.e. employed or unemployed
+ Frequency of attendance.

Other data sources

- Census re age, sex
- Unemployment statistics
- Local council studies of ethnic minority populations.

The design of the questionnaire and other data collection were based on the above list of information requirements. The results of the study were reported in Griffiths and Veal (1985).

In the case-study the survey arose from policy issues and the concepts involved were fairly straightforward. Surveys can of course also arise from academic/theoretical requirements when very often the concepts involved are more complex. Even something as apparently simple as participation in a leisure activity can be complex – do we mean *regular* participation, if so how often? Does the length of time spent doing the activity or the 'seriousness' of involvement (e.g. casual scratch game of cricket on the beach versus membership of a permanent team) matter?

It is therefore recommended that, preparatory to designing a questionnaire, a table be drawn up with the following headings:

1. Theoretical/management issues
2. Information requirements
3. Information source

Questions should only be included in the questionnaire if they relate to the requirements listed above, which means that every question included must be linked back to the original research or management issues or questions, which should be set out in the terms of reference or objectives of the research, as discussed in Chapter 3.

It goes without saying that in designing a questionnaire, the researcher should have sought out as much previous research on the topic or related topics as possible. This can have an effect on the overall design of a project as discussed in Chapter 3. More specifically, if it is decided that the study in hand should have points of comparison with other studies then data will need to be collected on a similar basis. Questionnaires from previous studies therefore become part of the input into the questionnaire design process.

Introductory remarks

Should a questionnaire include introductory remarks, for example, explaining the purpose of the survey and asking for the respondent's assistance?

In the case of a postal survey such material is of course included in the covering letter. In the case of other forms of self-completion questionnaire such a note is also advisable, unless the field-workers handing out the questionnaires have sufficient time to provide the necessary introduction and explanation. In the case of interviewer-administered questionnaires the remarks can be printed on the top of each questionnaire or can be included in the interviewers' written instructions.

In fact interviewers are unlikely to approach potential interviewees and actually read from a script. When seeking cooperation of a potential interviewee it is usually necessary to maintain eye contact, so the interviewers must know in advance what they want to say. In the case of household surveys potential interviewees may require a considerable amount of information and proof of identity from the interviewer before agreeing to be interviewed. But in the case of site interviews respondents are generally more interested in knowing how long the interview will take and 'what sort of questions' they will be asked, so only minimal opening remarks are necessary – for example: 'Excuse me, we are conducting a survey of visitors to the area; would you mind answering a few questions?'

It is usually necessary for an interviewer to indicate what organisation they represent, and this can be reinforced by an identity badge. In the case of market research or consultancy companies, they have the advantage of being able to instruct interviewers to indicate only that they represent the company and not the client. This can ensure that unbiased opinions are obtained, although in some cases it can raise ethical considerations if it is felt that respondents have a right to know what organisation will be using the information gathered.

One function of opening remarks can be to ensure the respondent of confidentiality. In the case of site surveys where names and addresses are not collected confidentiality is easy to maintain. In the case of household and some postal surveys respondents can be identified. One way of ensuring that confidentiality is maintained is to arrange for names and addresses to be kept separate from the actual questionnaires and for questionnaires to include only an identifying number.

Types of information

Introduction

Generally the information to be gathered from questionnaire surveys can be divided into three groups:

1. Respondent characteristics   Who?
2. Activities   What?
3. Attitudes/motivations   Why?

In this section a broad overview of these types of information is presented. Each item is examined in more detail in the section on the wording of questions. The items covered are of course necessarily general in nature and do not cover all the specialised types of information which can be collected by questionnaire surveys.

Characteristics

The most common characteristics of people which are addressed in leisure/tourism questionnaire surveys are the following:

- Sex
- Age
- Economic status
- Occupation/social class (own or 'head of household')
- Income (own or household)
- Education/qualifications
- Marital/family status
- Household type/family size
- Life-cycle
- Ethnic group/country of birth
- Residential location
- Dwelling type/tenure
- Mobility – driving licence, access to private transport
- Party/group size/type (site/visitor surveys).

Activity

Differences between site or visitor surveys and household surveys are considered to illustrate how the type of survey affects the type of activity information which can be collected.

In *site/visitor surveys* activity information collected includes:

- Activities while on site or in the area
- Use of site attractions/facilities
- Frequency of visit
- Time spent on site
- Expenditure per head – amounts and purposes.

An important form of activity associated with leisure, and particularly with tourism, is travel. Information on travel generally collected in user/visitor surveys includes:

- Trip origin (where travelled from)
- Trip purpose
- Home address (see also under characteristics)
- Travel mode
- Travel time
- Accommodation type used.

In *household surveys* a wide range of information can be collected, including:

- Activities (including holidays) – what, where, how often, time spent, when, who with
- Use of particular facilities
- Travel mode to out-of-home leisure
- Expenditure
- Past activities (personal leisure histories).

In both types of survey respondents may be asked about their media use.

Attitudes/motivation

In *site/visitor surveys* typical attitudinal and movitational information collected includes:

- Reasons for choice of site/area
- Meaning/importance/values
- Satisfaction/evaluation of experience/services
- Comments on facility
- Future intentions.

In *household surveys* a similar range of information can be collected, including:

- Leisure/travel aspirations/needs
- Evaluation of services/facilities available
- Psychological meaning of activities/satisfactions
- Reactions to development/provision proposals
- Values – re environment etc.

Pre-coded versus open-ended questions

An *open-ended* question is one where the interviewer asks a question without any prompting of the range of answers to be expected, and writes down the respondent's reply verbatim. In a self-completed questionnaire a line or space is left for the respondent to write their answer.

A *closed or pre-coded* question is one where the respondent is offered a range of answers to choose from, either verbally or from a show card or, in the case of a self-completed questionnaire, having the range of answers set out in the questionnaire and (usually) being asked to tick boxes. The following are examples of the two approaches:

Open-ended:
What is the main constraint on your use of leisure time?

Closed/pre-coded:
Which of the items listed on the card is the main constraint on your use of leisure time? (show card)

A.	My job	1
B.	Child care	2
C.	Spouse/partner	3
D.	Money	4
E.	Energy	5
F.	Other	6

The interviewer circles the appropriate code (details of coding in next section).

Card shown to respondent:

```
┌─────────────────────────┐
│ A. My job               │
│ B. Child care           │
│ C. Spouse/partner       │
│ D. Money                │
│ E. Energy               │
│ F. Other                │
└─────────────────────────┘
```

In the open-ended case there is no prior list. In the closed/pre-coded case there is a list which is shown to the respondent. A third possibility is the combination of the two, where the question is asked in an open-ended manner, and no card is shown to the respondent. The questionnaire however, includes a pre-coded list where the answer is recorded. If respondents answer 'other' (F in the list above) it is usual to write in what the 'other' is.

The advantage of the open-ended question is that the respondent's answer is not influenced unduly by the interviewer or the questionnaire and the verbatim replies from respondents can provide a rich source of varied material which might have been hidden by categories on a pre-coded list. Figure 10.1 gives an example of the range of responses which can result from an open-ended question.

Open-ended questions have two major disadvantages. Firstly analysis of verbatim answers for computer analysis is laborious and may result in a final set of categories which are of no more value than a well constructed *a priori* list. Secondly, in the case of self-completed questionnaires, response rates to open-ended questions can be very low – people are often too lazy or busy to write out free-form answers. When to use open-ended or closed questions is therefore a matter of judgement.

Wording of questions: principles

In wording the questions for a questionnaire the researcher should:

- Avoid jargon
- Simplify wherever possible
- Avoid ambiguity
- Avoid leading questions
- Ask only one question at a time (i.e. avoid multi-purpose questions).

Question: Do you have any complaints about this (beach/picnic) area? (located in a national park) (Number of responses in brackets)

Sand bars (22)
Parking (5)
Wild car driving
Lack of beach area
Too few shops
Too few picnic tables (4)
No timber for barbecue (2)
Need more picnic space (3)
Need boat hire facilities
Need active recreation facilities
Litter/pollution (74)
Need more food places
Having to pay for entry (6)
Houses along waterfront (2)
Unpleasant smell (drain) (2)
Sales people
Ethnic groups (6)
Dogs (21)
No access to coast
Park rangers not operating in
    interest of the public
Behaviour of others (20)
Access – long indirect road
Remove huts (2)
Need more shops (2)
Navigation marks unclear
Need more taps
Need more swings
Can't live on boat
Need powered caravan sites
Allow dogs
Private beach areas
Lack of restaurant
Need rain shelters
Can't spear fish
Infrequent ferry
Remove rocks from swim areas
Dangerous boat ramp
Water too shallow
No first-aid facilities
Uncontrolled camping

Uncontrolled boats (23)
Jet skis (39)
Surveys
Should be kept for locals
Seaweed (3)
Need showers
Administration of national park
Maintenance and policing of park
Trucks on beach (2)
Anglers
Crowds/tourists (26)
Urban sprawl
Need more wharf fishing access
Lack of info. on walking trails
Not enough facilities (3)
Slow barbecues (2)
Closure of ferry service
Lack/poor toilets (9)
Amenities too far from camp site
Harassment by NPWS re hut and
    environment
(Speed) boats (44)
Too much development (4)
Need more trees for shade
Yobos drinking beer on beach
Spear fishermen
Water skiers (2)
Against nudism (3)
Music
Dumped cars
Traffic
Poor roads
Sand flies
More barbecues
Shells/oysters
Need outdoor cafés
Should allow only non-pollutant
    activities
No road shoulders for cyclists
Need electric barbecues

Source: Robertson and Veal, 1987.

Figure 10.1 Example of range of replies which can result from an open-ended question

Below are comments on the wording and format of the more usual questions included in leisure/tourism questionnaires.

Characteristics – sex

In an interviewer-completed survey it is of course normal to observe the sex of the respondent rather than ask!

Characteristics – age

Two approaches can be adopted: open-ended or pre-coded.

Open-ended:
What was your age last birthday?

The age is recorded in the space provided.

Pre-coded:
Which of these age groups do you fall into (Show card)

A	0–14	1
B	15–19	2
C	20–24	3
D	25–39	4
E	40–59	5
F	60 +	6

Card shown to respondent

0–14	A
15–19	B
20–24	C
25–39	D
40–59	E
60 +	F

Note that it is important not to have overlapping age-categories, e.g.:

0–14	A	
14–19	B	WRONG!

Note that to ensure comparability with census data the age groups should be defined as above (i.e. 15–19, 20–24, 25–29, etc., not 16–20, 21–25, 26–30 etc.).

The advantage of the open-ended approach in the case of age (or when any numerical data are required) is that recording the actual number rather than a code for a group permits the option of grouping categories in a variety of ways when carrying out the analysis. Also it enables averages and other measures to be calculated and facilitates a range of statistical analysis. The pre-coded approach has the advantage of convenience and saving any embarrassment respondents may have about divulging their precise age. The show card system is deemed to be the least embarrassing and is believed to reduce the instances of refusal.

Characteristics – economic status

Open-ended:
What do you do for a living?

Pre-coded:
Which of the groups on the card best describes your situation?

Categories: Full-time paid work (30+ hrs/wk) 1
Part-time paid work 2
Full-time home/child care 3
Full-time education 4
Retired 5
Looking for work/unemployed 6
Other 7

An appropriate show-card would be used.

Characteristics – occupation

This question is generally asked of those identified from the economic status question as being in paid work. The retired or unemployed are sometimes asked what their last paid job was and others may be asked what the occupation of the 'main breadwinner' of the household is. Such questions can, however become complex because of full-time students living independently, single parents living on social security and so on. In a household survey it may be possible to pursue these matters, but in other situations it may not be appropriate.

For those in paid work the sorts of question asked are:

- What is your occupation?
- What sort of work do you do?
- Which of the groups on this card best describes your occupation?

Sufficient information should be obtained to enable respondents to be classified into an appropriate category. Market researchers tend to use the following classification:

- AB Managerial, administrative, professional (at senior or intermediate level)
- C1 Supervisory or clerical (i.e. white collar) and junior managerial, administrative or professional
- C2 Skilled manual.
- DE Semi-skilled, unskilled and casual workers and those entirely dependent on state pensions.

An alternative classification is used by official bodies, such as OPCS:

- Professional
- Employers, managers
- Other self-employed
- Skilled workers and foremen
- Non-manual
- Service, semi-skilled and agricultural
- Armed forces
- Unskilled.

Because people can be vague in response to an open-ended question on occupation it is wise to include a supplementary question to draw out a full description. For example 'local government worker', 'engineer' or 'self-employed' are not adequate answers because they can cover such a wide variety of grades of occupation. A supplementary question could be, 'What sort of work is that?' In a household survey it may be possible to ask additional questions to be absolutely sure of the respondent's occupation. Such questions would check on the industry involved and the number of staff supervised by the respondent (Hoinville and Jowell 1978, p. 172).

Characteristics – income

A typical wording would be:

- What is your own personal gross income from all sources before taxes? or
- Which of the groups on the card does your own personal gross income from all sources fall into?

One of the problems with income is that *personal* income is not a particularly useful measure for those who are not income earners/receivers or who are not the main income earners/receivers of the household. This can be overcome if all members of the household are being interviewed or if the respondent is asked about the 'main income earner' in the household. However, many teenage children, for example, do not know their parents' income and it might be seen as improper to ask.

Income is a sensitive issue and, in view of the limitations discussed above, is often excluded in site/visitor surveys.

Characteristics – educational qualifications

Many questionnaires include questions about education and/or qualifications. One possible wording is:

What was the last level you completed in your formal education?

- Primary school
- Secondary school to age 16
- Secondary school to 17/18
- Some university or other tertiary education
- University or other tertiary graduate.

Asking about qualifications is less common and is probably best done by using a show card.

Characteristics – marital status

Since legal marital status fails to indicate the domestic situation of increasing numbers of people the usefulness of this variable is perhaps declining. Usual categories are:

- Married
- Single – never married
- Widowed/divorced/separated.

Respondents who are not married but living in a *de facto* relationship can then decide for themselves how they want to be classified, or a separate category can be created.

Characteristics – household type

Household type is a useful item of information for many leisure/tourism studies but, except in the household interview situation, the data may be difficult to collect, because a number of items of information are required.

In a household interview it is possible to ask, 'Who lives here?' A simplified version would be to ask just about the number of children of various ages in the household. A form to enter full household information might look like Figure 10.2.

Relationship to respondent	M/F	Age	Economic status
1. Respondent			
2.			
3.			
4.			
5. etc.			

Figure 10.2 Example of household information form

Classifying the information into 'household type' must be done subsequently. Typical categories are:

A. Single parent and 1 dependent child
B. Single parent and 2 or more dependent children
C. Couple and 1 dependent child
D. Couple and 2 or more dependent children
E. Couple, no children
F. Related adults only
G. Unrelated adults only
H. Single
I. Other.

In the case of user/site surveys it is more usual to ask about the size of the party or group and its composition. Typical categories might be:

Group type:

- Youngest member aged 0–4
- Youngest member aged 5–15
- Lone adult
- Two adults (under 60)
- Older couple (60 and over)
- 3–5 adults
- 6 and over adults.

Characteristics – life-cycle

As with household type life-cycle is not based on a single question but built up from a number of items of information, including age, economic status and marital/family status. A possible classification is:

- Young single – dependent (on parents)
- Young single – independent
- Young married/partnered – no children
- Parent – dependent children
- Parent – children now independent
- Retired – up to 70
- Retired – over 70.

Characteristics – ethnic group

A common approach to ethnicity in the past was to ask the respondent's country of birth. But this of course does not identify members of ethnic minority groups born in Britain. Parents' place of birth would identify the second generation of migrant groups but not third and subsequent generations. Country of birth has therefore become less and less useful as an indicator of ethnic group membership.

Observation is an obvious solution but is not reliable for many groups. The solution is to *ask* people what ethnic group they consider they belong to. While this may cause offence to some, it is the most satisfactory approach overall.

Characteristics – residential location/trip origin

In the case of a household survey the residential location would be known by the interviewer and some sort of code – for street, suburb, local government area, county, as appropriate – can be recorded on the questionnaire.

In the case of site/visitor surveys it is necessary to ask people where they live or have travelled from and record the details. One form of wording could be:

a. Where did you travel from to visit here today?

　　Home
　　Work
　　School/college
　　Hotel etc.
　　Other

b. Where is that?
c. If *not* from home: Where do you live?

How much detail is required? In some surveys the suburb/town is sufficient. In other cases it is necessary to know the street. The number of the dwelling in the street is rarely necessary. For overseas visitors the country is usually adequate information. (Market research firms, however, often take down full addresses and/or telephone numbers in order to undertake subsequent quality checks, to ensure that the respondents have in fact been interviewed.)

Characteristics – dwelling type

Information on the type of dwelling in which respondents live is usually collected in household surveys because it can easily be done by observation. The information is clearly relevant in leisure research because of the implications in terms of access to private recreational space. Typical categories are:

- Separate house
- Semi-detached house
- Row/terrace house
- Flat/maisonette
- Caravan etc. in park
- Other caravan, houseboat etc.
- Other.

Characteristics – housing tenure

Whether or not people own their own house is an important socio-economic variable. Typical categories are:

- Owned outright
- Being purchased
- Rented
- Other.

Characteristics – transport

Because mobility is such an important factor in leisure behaviour, leisure questionnaires often include questions on ownership of and access to vehicles. In household survey questionnaires information of the following type might be collected:

Own car/motorbike – exclusive use
                 – primary user
                 – secondary/occasional user.
No access to private transport.

People are sometimes asked if they possess a current driver's licence.

In the case of site surveys, the mode of transport used to travel to the site is often asked:

How did you travel here today?

- Walk only
- Train
- Ferry
- Taxi

- Car as driver
- Car as passenger
- Motor bike
- Bicycle.

If people claim to have used two modes of transport, the two modes can be recorded or they can be asked to indicate the one on which they travelled the furthest.

Activities

Leisure

The problem of devising questions to gather information on leisure activities in household leisure participation surveys is a difficult one. The difficulties centre on two main issues:

- whether to use an open-ended or pre-coded format, and
- the time period for participation.

An open-ended format question could simply ask respondents to list the activities they have engaged in in leisure time or free time over a specified period. Without any prompting of the range of activities intended to be included respondents might have difficulty in recalling all their activities, and in any case may not understand the full scope of the word 'leisure' or 'free time'. The word 'leisure' has different connotations for different people. Without explanation, some people might assume that having a cup of coffee and chatting with a friend was not leisure, or that knitting or gardening was not leisure. Using the word 'free time' might help a little, but it is still open to variation in interpretation.

Although providing people with checklists of activities to choose from may be unwieldy, it at least ensures that all respondents consider the same range of options. The disadvantage of the checklist is that, in the case of self-completion or if a show card is used, the length of the list may be daunting to some respondents, particularly the less literate. In the case of an interviewer-completed questionnaire the main problem may be the time it takes to read out the list and the problem of patience and tedium which it may entail. The General Household Survey compromises by offering a checklist of about a dozen 'types' of leisure activity, such as home-based activities, outdoor recreation, arts and entertainment, as an *aide memoir* for the respondent.

The time period for recalling activities is crucial to the nature of the findings. Figure 10.3 shows the results from an Australian study in which respondents were asked about participation in sporting and entertainment/arts activities in the previous week, but if they had not participated in the previous week they were asked when they had *last* participated. The results are plain to see. The relative popularity of

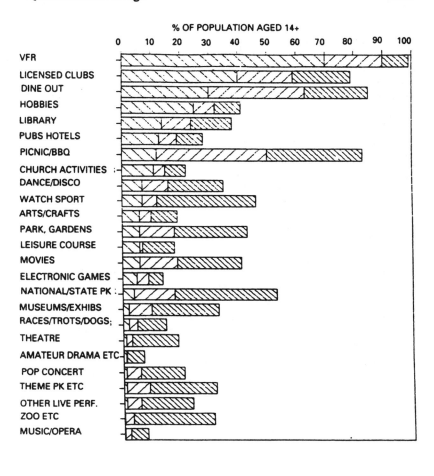

% OF POPULATION AGED 14+

IN LAST 7 DAYS   2–4 WEEKS AGO   1–12 months

Source: Centre for Leisure and Tourism Studies, UTS

Figure 10.3 Effect of time-period on participation levels

activities depends on the time period used to measure participation. The shorter the time period used the more accurate the results are likely to be, but the shorter time period excludes large proportions of participants in those activities which are engaged in relatively infrequently.

In addition to asking whether they have participated in an activity respondents can also be asked how often they have participated and how much time was spent on the activity. In some surveys a particular leisure occasion, say the last trip to the countryside, is explored in more detail – where the respondent went, who with, what day of the week and what time of day, what specific activities were engaged in, and so on. This relates to the various measures of leisure ad tourism activity as discussed in Chapter 3.

In local surveys or surveys with an interest in specific policy areas, it may be of interest to explore the use of specific leisure facilities – for example visits to national parks or to sports centres.

In the case of site/user surveys there is usually little problem in asking about activities. Many leisure sites offer opportunity for more than one activity – e.g. swimming, picnicking, sunbathing, at the beach – so it is usual to ask people what activities they plan to engage in or have engaged in. Specific activities, such as use of refreshment facilities, may also be explored.

Tourism

In the case of household tourism questionnaires, the 'activity' question concerns trips taken over a specified time period. As with local leisure activities, a major consideration is the recall time period. For major holidays a one-year recall period is not out of the question, but for short breaks that length of time may lead to inaccuracies in recall, so a shorter time period of, say three months may be adopted.

A second time period issue concerns the definition of tourist 'trip'. The definition used in a survey may follow an accepted definition of tourism, for example a trip involving a stay away from home of one night or more. However, in some local studies day-trips may also be of interest.

In addition to indicating trips taken, household tourism questionnaires also generally ask where the respondent has been on the trip, how long for, their travel mode and the type of accommodation stayed in. Tourism surveys are usually much more concerned with economic matters than leisure surveys, so questions on the cost of the trip and categories of expenditure are often included.

For site or 'en route' surveys the activity questions asked of tourists and locals will generally be identical.

Media use

Questionnaires often include questions on media use because such information can be used when considering advertising policy. To obtain accurate information in this area would require a considerable number of questions on frequency of reading/viewing/listening and, in the case of electronic media, the type of programmes favoured. When the research is concerned with small-scale local facilities or services television advertising is out of the question because of cost, so information on television watching need not be gathered. Similar considerations may apply to magazine and national newspaper reading. For many surveys therefore, two questions are involved:

What (local) newspapers do you read regularly?
What (local) radio stations do you listen to regularly?

Show cards would usually be used.

Attitudes/opinions

Attitudes and opinions are more complex aspects of questionnaire design. A range of techniques exists to explore people's opinions and attitudes. These include:

- open-ended/direct questions;
- ranking;
- scales;
- attitude statements.

Open-ended/direct question

A simple open-ended question could be of the form:

What attracted you to visit this area?
The response is written down verbatim – or as nearly verbatim as possible.

Checklist

Respondents are given a range of possible answers to choose from, usually shown to them on a card, for example:

Of the items on the card, which was the most important to you in choosing to visit this area?

Card shown to respondent:

A. Low entry charge
B. Good facilities
C. Uncrowded
D. Beauty of area
E. Easy parking
F. Recommended in guidebook

Ranking

If ranking is required the question asked is as above, but instead of respondents being asked to choose one factor, they are asked to rank the six factors in order of importance.

Scales

Scaling techniques are sometimes known as 'Likert scales' after the psychologist who developed their use and analysis. In this technique respondents are asked to indicate their agreement or disagreement with a proposition or the importance they attach to a factor, using a standard set of responses. One of the advantages of this approach is that the responses can be quantified, as discussed below under coding. An example:

Looking at the items on the card, please say how important each was to you in deciding to visit this area; was it:

Very important
Quite important
Not very important
Not at all important.

	Very imp.	Quite imp.	Not Very imp.	Not at all imp.
Low entry charge	☐	☐	☐	☐
Good facilities	☐	☐	☐	☐
Uncrowded	☐	☐	☐	☐
Beauty of area	☐	☐	☐	☐
Easy parking	☐	☐	☐	☐
Recommended in guidebook	☐	☐	☐	☐

Attitude statements

Attitude statements are a means of exploring respondents' attitudes towards a wide range of issues, including questions of a philosophical or political nature. Respondents are shown a series of statements and asked to indicate, using a Likert type scale, the extent to which they agree or disagree with them. For example:

Please read the following statements and say whether you:

Agree strongly
Agree
Have no opinion
Disagree
Disagree strongly.

	Agree strongly	Agree	No opinion	Disagree	Disagree strongly
Marijuana should be legalised	☐	☐	☐	☐	☐
Tobacco sponsorship of sport should be banned	☐	☐	☐	☐	☐

Responses to both scaled questions and attitude statements can be scored, as indicated in the discussion of coding below. For example, 'agree strongly' could be given a score of 5, 'agree' a score of 4, and so on to 'disagree strongly' with a score of 1. Scores can then be averaged across a number of respondents. So, for example, a group of

people who either 'agreed' or 'agreed strongly' with a st
would produce an average score between 4 and 5, whereas
who 'disagreed' or 'disagreed strongly' would produce a low
between 1 and 2. Such scores enable the strength of agreement with
different statements to be compared, and the opinions of different
groups of people to be compared.

Interviewing

The general approach to interviewing using a questionnaire is that the
interviewer should be instructed to stick precisely to the wording on
the questionnaire. If the respondent does not understand the question
the question should simply be repeated exactly as before; if the
respondent still does not understand then the interviewer should move
on to the next question. If this procedure is to be adhered to then the
importance of question-wording and the testing of such wording in
one or more pilot surveys is clear.

The above procedure is clearly important in relation to attitude
questions. Any word of explanation or elaboration could influence, and
therefore bias, the response. In relation to factual questions, however,
it may be less important – a word of explanation from the interviewer
may be acceptable if it results in obtaining accurate information.

It is important to convey these rules and the reasons for them
to interviewers, in induction/training sessions and in written instructions.

Coding

Introduction

Most questionnaire data are now analysed by computer. This means
that the information in the questionnaire must be *coded* – that is
converted into numerical codes and organised in a systematic,
'machine-readable', manner. Different procedures apply to pre-coded
and open-ended questions and these are discussed in turn below.

Pre-coded questions

The principle for coding of pre-coded questions is best shown by an
example:

When was your last visit here?

Within the last week	1
8–14 days ago	2
15–30 days ago	3
More than 30 days ago	4
This is my first visit	5
Don't know.	6

The 'code' is the number against the answer. Only one answer is possible, so only one 'code' is recorded as the answer to this question – in this example this would be indicated by circling the appropriate number/code.

If there are more than nine possible answers then a two-digit code must be used. For example:

What do you most enjoy about visiting this area?

Relaxation	01
A sense of escape	02
Communing with nature	03
Fresh air	04
Being with friends	05
Learning something	06
Physical exercise	07
Refreshment for work	08
Meet new people	09
Fun	10
Other	11

Where the answer is a number already, there is no need to code the answer because the numerical answer can be handled by the computer. For example:

How many times have you visited here
in the last year, including today?...

Scaled answers readily lend themselves to coding. For instance, the example given above could be coded as follows:

	Very imp.	Quite imp.	Not very imp.	Not at all imp.
Low entry charge	1	2	3	4
Good facilities	1	2	3	4
Uncrowded	1	2	3	4
Beauty of area	1	2	3	4
Easy parking	1	2	3	4
Recommended in guide	1	2	3	4

Open-ended questions

In the case of completely open-ended questions quite an elaborate procedure must be followed to devise a coding system. As already suggested, the answers to open-ended questions can be copied from the questionnaires and presented in a report 'raw', as in Figure 10.1. If this is all that is required from the open-ended questions then there is no point in spending the considerable labour necessary to code the information for computer analysis: the computer will merely reproduce what can be more easily achieved manually.

The computer comes into its own if it is intended to analyse the results in more detail – for example comparing the opinions of two or more groups. But if such comparisons are to be made it will usually be difficult to do so with, say, 50 or 60 different responses to compare, especially if many of the responses are only given by one or two respondents. The aim is to devise a coding system which groups the responses into a manageable number of categories.

If a large sample is involved, it is advisable to select a representative sample of the responses, say 50 or 100, and write out the responses, noting, as in Figure 10.1, the number of occurrences of each answer. Then give individual codes for the most frequent responses and group the others into meaningful categories – this is a matter of judgement. The aim is not to leave too many in the 'other' category. A coding system for the responses in Figure 10.1 might turn out as follows:

National park management practices	1
Picnic/barbecue facilities complaints	2
Other users' behaviour	3
Specific services (shops, first aid etc.)	4
Access/transport/roads	5
Environmental	6
Other	7

Columns

Computer analysis involves providing a guide so that the data can be keyed into a computer file in correct format. This is best illustrated by an example – a completed questionnaire is set out in Figure 10.4.

Note that the questionnaire is laid out for self-completion by the respondent, so it is made fairly simple by providing boxes to be ticked and the codes for the answers are discretely printed beside the boxes. An 'office use' column is provided into which the coded information is transferred ready for keying into the computer. This layout might be different for an interviewer-completed questionnaire, as discussed in the section on layout.

The numbers in brackets are 'column numbers' and relate to the following layout, which shows that, when transferred to the computer, the information from one questionnaire would become a string of digits – in this case 20 digits.

Column

(1	2	3)	(4)	(5)	(6)	(7)	(8)	(9)	(10)	(11	12)	(13	14)	(15	16	17)	(18	19	20)
0	0	1	1	1	1	0	0	1	5	0	4	0	7	0	0	2	2	3	1

Question're 1   Q 2a Q 2b Q 2c Q 2d Q 2e Q 3   Q4   Q5   Q6
number

	Office use
Student Leisure survey	I 0 I 0 I 1 I
	(1 – 3)

1. What course are you registered for? (tick the appropriate box)

Undergraduate leisure studies	[x]₁	I 1 I (4)
Undergraduate tourism studies	[ ]₂	
Undergraduate sports studies	[ ]₃	
Post-graduate leisure studies	[ ]₄	
Post-graduate tourism studies	[ ]₅	
Post-graduate sports studies	[ ]₆	

2. Have you visited any of the following in the last month?

a. National park	[x]₁	I 1 I (5)
b. Museum	[x]₁	I 1 I (6)
c. Zoo	[ ]₁	I_I (7)
d. Nightclub	[ ]₁	I_I (8)
e. Beach	[x]₁	I 1 I (9)

3. Given a choice, over the next 24 hours, which *one* of these facilities would you *most* like to visit?

National park	[ ]₁	I 5 I (10)
Museum	[ ]₂	
Zoo	[ ]₃	
Nightclub	[ ]₄	
Beach	[x]₅	

4. What do you think you would most enjoy about such a visit?

Fresh air　　　　*Exercise*

	I 0 I 4 I
	(11–12)
	I 0 I 7 I
	(13–14)

5. How much would you expect to spend, for yourself, on such a visit (excluding travel cost)?

£　2

I 0 I 0 I 2 I
(15–17)

6. Please indicate how important the following are to you in choosing leisure activities.

	Very important	Moderately important	Not important	
Cost	[ ]₁	[x]₂	[ ]₃	I 2 I (18)
Distance	[ ]₁	[ ]₂	[x]₃	I 3 I (19)
Friends' wishes	[x]₁	[ ]₂	[ ]₃	I 1 I (20)

Figure 10.4　Sample questionnaire – self completion

The data from this particular completed questionnaire are therefore:

0 0 1 1 1 1 0 0 1 5 0 4 0 7 0 0 2 2 3 1

Data from five questionnaires would appear as follows:

0 0 1 1 1 1 0 0 1 5 0 4 0 7 0 0 2 2 3 1
0 0 2 2 0 0 1 1 0 4 1 0   0 2 0 2 2 1
0 0 3 5 1 0 0 1 1 1 1 1   0 0 5 1 1 1
0 0 4 6 1 1 0 0 0 5 0 1   0 0 0 3 3 1
0 0 5 6 0 0 0 0 1 0 3 0 2 0 0 4 1 2 3

Questionnaire number, in columns 1–3, is an identifier so that a link can be made between data in the computer and actual questionnaires. It is a three-figure number, so it needs three 'columns' – the example questionnaire is number 001. A survey involving a sample of 99 responses or less would require only a two-digit questionnaire number, and a survey with 1000 responses or more would require a four-digit number.

Question 2 requires five columns because respondents can tick up to *five* boxes, but question 3 requires only one column because only *one* box can be ticked.

Question 4 is an open-ended question which could have a coding system as follows:

Relaxation	01
A sense of escape	02
Communing with nature	03
Fresh air	04
Being with friends	05
Learning something	06
Physical exercise	07
Refreshment for work	08
Meet new people	09
Fun	10
Other	11

It is envisaged that respondents might give more than one answer to question 4, so coding space has been reserved for *two* two-digit coded answers (columns 11–12 and 13–14) – if required space could be reserved for more answers.

Question 5 the actual amount of expenditure is entered in the boxes in the 'office use' column, with leading zeros if necessary.

Question 6 requires three columns to record the answers for the three items.

Ordering of questions and layout of questionnaires

Ordering

It is important that a questionnaire and the interview based on the questionnaire flow in a logical and comfortable manner. A number of principles should be borne in mind.

1. Start with easy questions.
2. Start with 'relevant' questions – for example if the respondent has been told that the survey is about leisure, begin with some questions about leisure.
3. Personal questions, dealing with such things as age or income, are generally best left to near the end: while they do not generally cause problems, and respondents need not answer those personal questions if they object, they are less likely to cause offence if asked later in the interview when a rapport has been established between interviewer and respondent. Similar principles apply in relation to self-completion questionnaires.

Layout

A questionnaire must be laid out and printed in such a way that the person who must read it, whether interviewer or interviewee, can follow all the instructions easily and answer all the questions that they are meant to answer.

Layout becomes particularly important when a questionnaire contains *filters* – that is when whether or not respondents have to answer certain questions depends on their answer to a prior question. For example in a survey of park users respondents might be asked:

(a)   Have you visited the park cafe?   Yes   ☐
                                          No   ☐

       If yes

(b)   Did you think the prices charged were: Too high   ☐
                                                 Average   ☐
                                                 Low   ☐

In some cases there can be many additional questions for the 'yes' respondents to answer and so clear instructions must be provided for those who have answered 'no' – for example: if no go to question 13. A possible layout is as follows:

(a)   Have you visited the park cafe?   Yes   ☐   Go to (b)
                                          No   ☐   Go to q.13

In the case of self-completion questionnaires extra care must be taken because it can be very difficult to rectify faults 'in the field'. Clarity of layout, and the overall impression given by the questionnaire can be all-important in obtaining a good response.

Postal surveys, where the researcher does not have direct contact with the respondent, are the most demanding. A professionally laid out, type-set and printed questionnaire will pay dividends in terms of level, accuracy and completeness of response, insofar as the length of a questionnaire can affect the response rate in a postal survey, a type-set format can reduce the number of pages considerably.

Even where interviewers are used there are advantages in keeping the questionnaire as compact as possible for ease of handling. A two-column format – relatively easily achieved with modern word-processing packages – is worth exploring.

Student Leisure Survey

|⌞⌟⌞⌟⌞⌟|
(1 – 3)

1. What course are you registered for?

Undergraduate leisure studies	1
Undergraduate tourism studies	2
Undergraduate sports studies	3
Post-graduate leisure studies	4
Post-graduate tourism studies	5
Post-graduate sports studies	6

(4)

2. Have you visited any of the following in the last month?

a. National park	1	(5)
b. Museum	1	(6)
c. Zoo	1	(7)
d. Nightclub	1	(8)
e. Beach	1	(9)

3. Given a choice, over the next 24 hours, which *one* of these facilities would you *most* like to visit?

National park	1	(10)
Museum	2	
Zoo	3	
Nightclub	4	
Beach	5	

4. What would you most enjoy about such a visit?

_____

|⌞⌟⌞⌟|
(11–12)
|⌞⌟⌞⌟|
(13–14)

5. How much would you expect to spend, for youself, on such a visit (including travel cost)?

£ _____

|⌞⌟⌞⌟⌞⌟|
(15–17)

6. Please indicate how important the following are to you in choosing leisure activities.

	Very important	Moderately important	Not important	
Cost	1	2	3	(18)
Distance	1	2	3	(19)
Friends' wishes	1	2	3	(20)

Figure 10.5   Sample questionnaire – Interviewer completion

The example questionnaire shown in Figure 10.4 was designed for self-completion and the layout therefore involved boxes for the respondent to tick. This is ideal for self-completion. Boxes are however laborious to type/layout. Where an interviewer is being used, rather than ticking boxes, the interviewer can circle codes, as shown in Figure 10.5, and the 'office use' column is not necessary. This type of layout can be used for self-completion in some situations – for example in some 'captive group' situations or where respondents are known to be highly literate and are unlikely to be deterred by the apparent technicalities of the layout.

Validity

Questionnaires gather information from individuals about their characteristics, behaviour and attitudes. The interview situation is not always conducive to careful, thoughtful responses. Respondents may tend to exaggerate answers to some questions and understate answers to other questions. They may also have problems in recalling some information accurately. Respondents may tend to give answers which they believe will please the interviewer. Thus the validity of questionnaire based data – the extent to which they accurately reflect what they are meant to reflect – is a constant source of concern. To some extent the researcher must simply live with these limitations of the survey method and hope that they are not too significant and that some of them cancel each other out. There are however some measures which can be taken to check on the presence of this type of problem.

One approach is to include 'dummy' categories in some questions. For example, in a survey of recreation managers in Britain in the early 1980s respondents were asked to indicate, from a list, what books and reports they had heard of and had read. Included in the list was one plausible, but non-existent title. A significant proportion of respondents indicated that they had heard of the report and a small proportion claimed to have read it! Such a response does not necessarily mean that respondents were lying – they may simply have been confused about the titles of particular reports. But it does provide cautionary information to the researcher on the degree of error in responses to such questions, since it suggests that responses to the genuine titles may also include a measure of inaccuracy.

A similar approach is to include two or more questions in different parts of the questionnaire, which essentially ask the same thing. For example an early question could ask respondents to rank a list of activities or holiday areas in order of preference. Later in the questionnaire, in the context of asking some detailed questions, respondents could be asked to indicate their favourite activity or holiday area. In the analysis, the responses could be tested for consistency.

One possibility is that the interview experience itself may cause respondents to change their opinion, because it causes them to think through in detail something which they might previously have only considered superficially. Similar questions at the beginning and end of the interview may detect this. In an Australian survey of gambling behaviour and attitudes towards a proposed casino development Grichting and Caltabiano (1986) asked, at the beginning of the interview: 'What do you think about the casino coming to Townsville? Are you for it or against it?' At the end of the interview they asked: 'Taking everything you have said into consideration, what do you think now

Day: _____

Start/finish Time	Activity	Where done?	Who with?

Etc.

Figure 10.6 Example of time-budget study layout

about the casino coming to Townsville? Are you for it or against it?' It was found that about 'one in six respondents changed their attitude towards the casino during the course of the interview'.

Time-budget studies

Time-budget studies are designed to collect information on people's use of time. Such information is usually collected as part of a household survey, but in addition to answering a questionnaire, respondents are asked to complete a diary, typically over a period of between two and four days. Respondents are asked to record their activities during their waking hours, including starting and stopping times, together with information on where the activity was done, who with, and possibly whether the respondent considered it to be paid work, domestic work or leisure. A typical layout might be as shown in Figure 10.6.

Coding and analysis of such data presents a considerable challenge, since every possible type of activity must be given a code and information processed for, say, 60 or 70 quarter hour periods each day. Space does not permit a detailed treatment of this specialised topic here, but it can be followed up in the literature indicated in the Further reading section.

Next, the computer

The procedures necessary to transfer the information from the coded questionnaires to a computer for analysis are discussed in Chapter 12.

Further reading

Questionnaire design: Hoinville and Jowell 1978, Kidder 1981, Oppenheim 1966.
Time-budget diaries: Burton 1971, BBC 1978, Australian Bureau of Statistics 1988, Cities Commission 1975.
Life-cycle: Rapoport and Rapoport 1975, O'Brien and Ford 1988.

11 Sampling

This chapter is an introduction to the principles of sampling rather than a complete guide. It addresses the idea of sampling; samples and populations; representativeness and random sampling; sample sizes and their consequences in terms of 'confidence intervals'; and weighting.

The idea of sampling

In most survey research and some observational research it is necessary to *sample*. Mainly because of costs, it is not usually possible to interview all the people who are the focus of the research. For example, if the aim of a research project was to study the leisure patterns or holiday-making behaviour of the adult population of Britain, no-one has the resources to conduct interviews with 50 million people! The only time when the whole population is interviewed is every 10 years, when the OPCS conducts the Census of Population – and the cost of collecting and analysing the data runs into tens of millions of pounds.

At a more modest level, it would be virtually impossible to conduct face-to-face interviews with all users of an urban park or busy tourist area since, in busy periods, many hundreds might enter the site and leave in a short space of time. It might be possible to hand self-completion questionnaires to all users but, as discussed in Chapter 9, this approach has disadvantages in terms of quality and level of response. The usual procedure is to interview a sample – a proportion – of the users.

In Chapter 7, on observation, the problems of continuous counting of numbers of users of recreation sites were discussed and it was noted that often available resources demand that sample counts be undertaken – that is the numbers entering the site or present at the site are counted on a sample of occasions.

Samples and populations

One item of terminology should be clarified initially. The *total* category of subjects which is the focus of attention in a particular research project is known as the *population*. A *sample* is selected from the population. The use of the term 'population' makes sense when dealing with communities of people – for instances the adult population of Britain or the population of London. But the term also applies in other instances; for example the visitors to a resort over the period of a year constitutes the *population* of resort visitors; and the users of a sports facility are the *population* of users.

The term population can also be applied to non-human phenomena, for example, if a study of the physical characteristics of Australia's beaches found that there were 10,000 beaches in all, from which 100 were to be selected for study, then the 10,000 beaches would be referred to as the population of beaches and the 100 selected for study would be the sample. In some texts the word *universe* is used instead of population.

If a sample is to be selected for study then two questions arise:

1. What procedures must be followed to ensure that the sample is *representative* of the population?
2. How *large* should the sample be?

These two questions are related, since the larger the sample, the more chance it has of being representative.

Representativeness

A sample which is not representative of the population is described as biased. The whole process of sample selection must be aimed at minimising bias in the sample.

Representativeness is achieved by the process of *random* sampling. This is not the most helpful term since it implies that the process is not methodical. This is far from the case – random does not mean haphazard! The meaning of random sampling is as follows:

> In random sampling all members of the population have an equal chance of inclusion in the sample.

For example, if a sample of 1000 people is to be selected from a population of 10,000 then every member of the population must have a 1 in 10 chance of being selected. In practice most sampling methods involving human beings can only approximate this rule. The problems of achieving random sampling vary with the type of survey.

Household surveys

The problem of achieving randomness can be examined in the case of a household survey of the adult residents of a country. If the adult population of the country is, say, 40 million and we wish to interview 1000, then every member of the adult population should have a 1 in 40,000 chance of being included in the sample. How would this be achieved? Ideally there should be a complete list of all 40 million of the country's adults – their names should be written on slips of paper and placed in a revolving drum, as in a Lotto draw, and 1000 names should be drawn out. Each time a choice is made everyone has a one in 40 million chance of selection – since this happens 1000 times, each person has a total 1000 in 40 million or one in 40,000 chance of selection.

This would be a very laborious process. Surely a close approximation would be to forget the slips of paper and the drum and choose every 40,000th name on the list. But where should the starting point be? It should be some random point between 1 and 40,000. There are such things as 'tables of random numbers', which can also be produced from computers, which can be used for this purpose. Strictly speaking the whole sample should be chosen using random numbers, since this would approximate most closely to the 'names in a drum' procedure.

But in practice such a list of the population being studied rarely exists. The nearest thing to it would be the electoral registers of all the constituencies in the country. Electoral registers are fairly comprehensive because adults are required by law to register, but they are not perfect. Highly mobile/homeless people are often not included; many who live in multioccupied premises are omitted. The physical task of selecting the names from such a list would be immense, but there is another disadvantage with this approach. If every 40,000th voter on the registers were selected the sample would be scattered throughout the country. The cost of visiting every one of those selected for a face-to-face interview would be very high.

In practice therefore, organisations conducting national surveys compromise by employing 'multi-stage' sampling and 'clustered' sampling.

Multi-stage means that sampling is not done directly but by stages. For example if the country had, say, four states or regions the proposed sample would be sub-divided in proportion to the populations of the regions, for example:

Region A:	Population	10	million	Sub-sample size	250
Region B:	Population	5	million	Sub-sample size	125
Region C:	Population	20	million	Sub-sample size	500
Region D:	Population	5	million	Sub-sample size	125

Within each region local government areas would then be divided into rural and urban and, say four urban and two rural areas would be selected at random – with the intention of selecting appropriate sub-samples, of perhaps 25, 40 or 50 from each area. These sub-samples would be selected from electoral registers or streets could be selected and individuals contacted by calling on, say, every fifth house in the street. In any one street interviewers may be instructed to interview, say, 10 or 15 people. By interviewing 'clusters' of people in this way costs are minimised. But care must be taken not to reduce the number of clusters too much since then the full range of population and area types would not be included (Hoinville and Jowell 1978).

Site/visitor surveys

Conditions at leisure/tourism sites or facilities vary enormously, depending on the type and size of facility, the season, day of the week, the time of day or the weather. This discussion can only therefore be in general terms.

To ensure randomness, and therefore representativeness, it is necessary for interviewers to adhere to strict rules. Site interviewers operate in two ways. Firstly the interviewer can be stationary and the users mobile – for instance when the interviewer is located near the entrance and interviews people as they enter or leave. Alternatively the user may be stationary and the interviewer mobile – for instance when interviewing beach users or users of a picnic site.

In the case of stationary interviewers, the instructions they should follow should be something like:

> When one interview is complete, check through the questionnaire for completeness and legibility. When you are ready with a new questionnaire stop the *next* person to enter the gate. Stick strictly to this rule and *do not* select interviewees on any other basis.

The important thing is that interviewers should not *avoid* certain types of user by picking and choosing whom to interview. Ideally there should be some rule such as interviewing *every* fifth person to come through the door/gate but, since users will enter at a varying rate and interviews vary in length, this is rarely possible.

In the case of stationary users and a mobile interviewer, the interviewer should be given a certain route to follow on the site and be instructed to interview, say, every fifth group they pass.

Where interviewers are employed, the success of the process will depend on the training given to the interviewers and this could involve observation of them at work to ensure that they are following the rules.

As indicated in Chapter 9, sampling in site/visitor surveys leads inevitably to variation in the proportion of users interviewed at different times of the day. Where users tend to stay for long periods, as in the case of beaches, this may not matter, but where people stay for shorter periods and where the type of user may vary during the course of the day or week, the sample will probably be unrepresentative, that is, biased. This should be corrected by weighting as indicated below.

When surveys involve the handing out of questionnaires for self-completion – as for example, in a number of tourist en route/hotel surveys – it can now be seen that, unless field staff are available to encourage their completion and return, respondents will be self-selected. Busy hotel or leisure facility receptionists can rarely be relied upon to do a thorough job in handing out and collecting in questionnaires, unless the survey is a priority of the management and therefore closely supervised. Normally a significant proportion of the 'population' will fail to return the questionnaire, but it is unlikely that this self-selection process will be random. For example, people with difficulties in reading or writing English, or people who are in a hurry, may fail to return their questionnaires; those with 'something to say', whether positive or negative, are more likely to return their questionnaires than people who are apathetic or just content with the service, thus giving a misleading impression of the proportion of users who have strong opinions. Thus it can be seen that this type of survey is at risk of introducing serious bias into the sample. This sort of 'uncontrolled' survey should therefore be avoided if at all possible.

Street surveys and quota sampling

Although the technique of *quota* sampling can be used in other situations, it is most common in street surveys. The street survey is usually seen as a means of contacting a representative sample of the community but in fact it can also be seen as a sort of 'site survey', the site being a shopping area. As such a street survey which involved a random sample of the users of the street would be representative of the users of the shopping area rather than of the community as a whole – in a suburban shopping centre it would for instance have a high proportion of full-time housewives.

If the aim is in fact to obtain a representative sample of the whole community, then to achieve this interviewers are given 'quotas' of people of different types to contact, the quotas being based on information about the community which is available from the census. For example, if the census indicates that 12 per cent of the population is retired then interviewers would be required to include 12 retired people in every 100 interviewed. Once interviewers have filled their quota in certain age/sex groups, they are required to become more selective in whom they approach in other to fill the gaps in their quotas.

The quota method can only be used when background information on the target population is known, as with community surveys. In most user surveys this information is not known so the strict following of random sampling procedures must be relied upon.

Postal surveys

The initial list of people to whom the questionnaire is sent in a postal survey may be the whole population or a sample. If a sample is selected it can usually be done completely randomly because the mailing list for the whole population is usually available.

The respondents to a postal survey form a sample, but it is not randomly selected but self-selected. This introduces sources of bias similar to those in the uncontrolled self-completion site surveys discussed above. There is little that can be done about this except to make every effort to achieve a high response rate. In some cases information may be available on the population which can be used to weight the sample to correct for certain sources of bias, for example, in the case of a national survey the sample could be weighted to correct for any geographical bias in response because the geographical distribution of the population would be known. If, for example, the survey is of an occupational association and the proportion of members in various grades is known from records, then this can be used for weighting purposes. But ultimately, postal surveys suffer from an unknown and uncorrectable element of bias caused by non-response. All surveys experience non-response of course, but the problem is greater with postal surveys.

Sample size

There is a popular misconception that the size of a sample should be decided on the basis of its relationship to the size of the population, for example that a sample should be 5 per cent or 10 per cent of the population. *This is not so.* What is important is the *absolute* size of the sample, regardless of the size of the population. For example, a sample size of 1000, is equally valid, provided proper sampling procedures have been followed, whether it is a sample of British adults (population 50 million), the residents of London (population 7 million), the residents of Brighton (population 100,000) or the students of a University (population, say, 10,000).

It is worth repeating that: *it is the absolute size of the sample which is important, not its size relative to the population.*

On what criteria therefore should a sample size be determined? The criteria are basically threefold:

1. the required level of precision in the results;
2. the level of detail in the proposed analysis;
3. the available budget.

The idea of the level of precision can be explained as follows. The question is to what extent the findings from a sample precisely reflect the population. For example, if a survey was designed to investigate holiday-making and it was found that 50 per cent of a sample of 500 people took a holiday in the previous year, how sure can we be that this finding – this 'statistic' – is true of the population as a whole? How sure can we be, despite all efforts taken to choose a representative sample, that the sample is not in fact *un*representative, and that the real percentage of holiday-taking in the population is in fact, say, 70 per cent or 30 per cent?

If the true value is around 50 per cent then, with random sampling, the chances of drawing a sample where no-one had been on holiday would be remote – almost impossible one might say. On the other hand the chances of coming up with say 48 or 49 or 51 or 52 per cent would, one would think, be pretty high. The chances of coming up with 70 or 30 per cent would be somewhere in between.

Statisticians are clever people and they have come up with the finding that, when a sample is randomly drawn, the *sample* value of a statistic is highly likely to be within a certain range either side of the *real* value of the statistic. That range is plus or minus 1.86 times the 'standard error' of the statistic. The size of the standard error depends on the size of the sample and is unrelated to the size of the population. A properly drawn sample has a 95 per cent chance of producing a value within 1.86 standard errors of the true, population, value so there is a 95 per cent chance that the true population value is within 1.86 standard errors of the sample value.

This range is referred to as the '95 per cent confidence interval' of a statistic. Tables have been drawn up by statisticians which give the confidence intervals for various statistics for various sample sizes. For a statistic of 50 per cent – that is, as in the example above, a result from the survey that 50 per cent of the sample have some characteristic – the confidence intervals are as follows :

Sample size	95% confidence interval for a finding of 50%	Sample size	95% confidence interval for a finding of 50%
30	±19.6%	800	±3.5%
50	±14.9%	1000	±3.2%
100	±10.3%	2000	±2.2%
200	± 7.2%	2500	±2.1%
300	± 5.8%	3000	±1.8%
400	± 5.0%	4000	±1.6%
500	± 4.5%	10000	±1.0%

For the hypothetical survey referred to above, with a sample size of 500, it can be seen that the 'confidence interval' for the finding on holiday-taking is plus or minus 4.5 per cent. This means that there is a 95 per cent chance that the population value lies in the interval 45.5 per cent to 54.5 per cent. This is true provided that the sample has been randomly selected and is true regardless of the population size.

An important point should be noted about these confidence intervals: to halve the confidence interval it is necessary to quadruple the sample size. In the example above, a sample of 2000 people (four times the original sample) would give a confidence interval of plus or minus 2.2 per cent (half the original confidence interval).

Note that for smaller samples the confidence intervals become very large, for instances, for a sample of 50 the interval is ±14.9, meaning that a finding of 50 per cent can only be estimated to be within the range 35.1 to 64.9 per cent. The implications of the first criterion for deciding sample size now become clear. A sample size of, say 1000, would give a confidence interval for a finding of 50 per cent of ± 3.2 per cent. If that margin of error was not considered acceptable then a larger sample size would be necessary. Whether or not it is considered acceptable would depend on the uses to which the data were to be put and is related to the type of analysis to be done, as discussed below.

We have dealt so far only with a 'finding' or 'statistic' of 50 per cent as an example. The confidence interval however varies, depending on the statistic involved. For instance, with a sample of 2500, if it was found that 10 per cent of the sample had some characteristic, the confidence interval would be ± 1.2 per cent compared with ± 2.0 per cent for the 50 per cent statistic. The various confidence intervals for a sample of 2500 are as follows:

Percentage found from sample	*95% confidence interval for sample of 2500*
50	±2.1
40 or 60	±2.1
30 or 70	±1.9
20 or 80	±1.7
10 or 90	±1.2

Why '40 or 60', '30 or 70' and so on? Because if it is found that 40 per cent of the sample have a certain characteristic then it has also been found that 60 per cent do *not* have the characteristic (e.g. if 40 per cent have been on holiday then 60 per cent have *not* been on holiday). The two statistics therefore have the same confidence interval.

To complete the picture we need a matrix showing the different statistics and the varying sample sizes. This is given in Table 11.1. Note that for some statistics for the smaller sample sizes the confidence intervals are not calculable because the total margin of error is larger than the original statistic.

Table 11.1 Confidence intervals and sample size

| Sample size | *Percentages found from samples* | | | | |
| | 50 | 40/60 | 30/70 | 20/80 | 10/90 |
	Confidence intervals ±%				
30	19.6	•	•	•	•
50	14.9	14.6	•	•	•
80	11.6	11.4	10.7	•	•
100	10.3	10.1	9.5	8.0	6.0
200	7.2	6.9	6.6	5.8	4.0
400	5.0	4.9	4.6	4.0	3.0
500	4.5	4.4	4 1	3.6	2.6
800	3.6	3.6	3.3	2.9	2.2
1000	3.2	3.1	2.9	2.5	1.9
2000	2.2	2.2	2.0	1.8	1.3
2500	2.1	2.1	1.9	1.7	1.2
10000	1.0	1.0	0.9	0.8	0.6

The confidence intervals in Table 11.1 illustrate further the second criterion concerning the choice of sample size: that is that the necessary sample size depends on the type of analysis to be undertaken. If many detailed comparisons are to be made, especially concerning small proportions of the population, then the sample size may preclude very meaningful analysis. For instance, suppose a survey is conducted with a sample of 200 and it is found that 20 per cent of respondents went bowling and 30 per cent played tennis. The 20 per cent is subject to a margin of error of ± 5.8 per cent and the 30 per cent is subject to a margin of ± 6.6 per cent. Thus it is estimated that the proportions playing the two activities are as follows:

Bowling   14.2–25.8 per cent
Tennis   23.4–36.6 per cent

The confidence intervals overlap, so we cannot conclude that there is any 'significant' difference in the popularity of the two activities, despite a 10 per cent difference given by the survey. This is likely to be very limiting in any analysis. If the sample were 500 the confidence intervals would be ± 3.6 and ± 4.1 respectively, giving estimates as follows:

Bowling   16.4–23.6 per cent
Tennis   25.9–34.1 per cent

In this case the confidence intervals do not overlap and we can be fairly certain that tennis is more popular than bowling.

The detail of the analysis, the extent of sub-division of the sample into sub-samples, and the acceptable level of precision will therefore determine the necessary size of the sample. By and large this has nothing to do with the overall size of the original population, although there is a likelihood that the larger the population the greater its diversity and therefore the greater the need for subdivision into sub-samples.

A further point to be noted is that it could be positively wasteful to expend resources on a large sample when it can be shown to be unnecessary. For example, a sample of 10,000 gives estimates of statistics with a maximum confidence interval of ± 1 per cent. Such a survey could cost as much as £200,000 to conduct. To halve that confidence interval to ± 0.5 per cent would mean quadrupling the sample size to 40,000 at an *additional* cost of £600,000. There can be very few situations where such expenditure would be justified for such a small return.

Ultimately then, the limiting factor in determining sample size will be the resources available. Even if the budget available limits the sample size severely it may be decided to go ahead and risk the possibility of an unpresentative sample. If the sample is small however, the detail of the analysis will need to be limited. If resources are so limited that the validity of quantitative research is questionable, it may be sensible to consider qualitative research which may be more feasible. Alternatively the proposed research should be seen as a 'pilot' exercise, with the emphasis on methodology, preparatory to a more adequately resourced full-scale study.

How should the issue of sample size and confidence intervals be reported in the report on the research? In some scientific research complex statistical tests are considered necessary in reporting statistical results from surveys. In much social science research, and leisure and tourism research in particular, requirements are less rigorous. This is true to some extent in academic research, but is markedly so in the reporting of applied research. It is therefore advisable to be aware of the limitations imposed by the sample size and not to make comparisons which the data cannot support. An appendix can be included indicating the size of the sampling errors (see Appendix 11.1 to this chapter for a possible format). But a great deal of statistical jargon is not generally required: the lay reader expects the researcher to do a good job and expert readers should be given enough information to check the analysis in the report for themselves. In academic journals the rules are somewhat different and there is an expectation that statistical tests be 'up front'. It is not proposed to pursue the question of statistical tests further in this book, but Chapter 13 indicates that, once data have been prepared for computer analysis, an array of standard tests is available using computer packages such as SPSS.

Weighting

In this and previous sections situations where weighting of survey or count data may be required have been indicated. In Chapter 13 the procedures for implementing weighting using the SPSS computer package are outlined. Here the principles involved are discussed. Take the example of the data shown in Table 11.2.

In the sample of 45 interviews the number of interviews is spread fairly equally through the day, whereas more than half the actual users visit around the middle of the day (this information probably having been obtained by observation/counts). This can be a source of bias in the sample, since the mid-day users may differ from the others in their characteristics or opinions and they will be under-represented in the

Table 11.2   Interview/usage data

Time	Interviews		Actual users	
	No.	%	No.	%
9–11 am	10	22.2	25	5.7
11–1 pm	12	26.7	240	55.2
1–3 pm	11	24.4	110	25.3
3–5 pm	12	26.7	60	2.7
Total	45	100.0	435	100.0

Table 11.3 Weighting

Time	No. of interviews	Weighting factors	Weighted sample no.
9–11 am	10	2.5	40
11–1 pm	12	20.0	240
1–3 pm	11	10.0	110
3–5 pm	12	5.0	60
Total	45		435

sample. The aim of weighting is to produce a weighted sample with a distribution similar to that of the actual users.

One approach is to 'gross up' the sample numbers to reflect the actual numbers, – e.g. the 9–11 am group is weighted by 25/10 = 2.5, the 11–1 pm group is weighted by 240/12=20, and so on, as shown in Table 11.3.

The weighting factors can be fed into the computer for the weighting to be done automatically, as discussed in Chapter 13. The initial weighting factors are equal to the *user number* divided by the *sample number* for that time period. The weighted sample therefore is made to resemble the overall user numbers. It should be noted however, that the sample size is still 45, not 435! If statistical tests are to be carried out then it would be advisable to divide the weighting factors by 435 to bring the weighted sample total back to 45.

In this example the basis of the weighting relates to the pattern of visits over the course of the day, which happened to be information which was available in relation to this particular type of survey. Any other data available on the population could be used, for example if age structure is available from the census, then age–groups rather than time–periods might be used.

Further reading

Sampling and the statistical implications of sampling are addressed in numerous statistics textbooks.
See also: Hoinville and Jowell 1978, Ch. 4; Kidder, 1981.

Appendix 11.1   Suggested appendix on sample size and confidence intervals

(Suppose the survey has a sample size of 500)
All sample surveys are subject to a margin of statistical error. The margins of error, or 'confidence intervals' for this survey are as follows:

Finding from the survey	95% confidence interval
50%	± 4.5
40/60%	± 4.4
30/70%	± 4.1
20/80%	± 3.6
10/90%	± 2.6

This means, for example, that if 20 per cent of the sample are found to have a particular characteristic, there is an estimated 95 per cent chance that the true population percentage lies in the range 20 ± 3.6, i.e. between 16.4 and 23.6 per cent.

These margins of error have been taken into account in the analyses in this report.

12 Survey analysis: preparation

In this chapter the preparation of commands and data for the analysis of survey data using the Statistical Package for the Social Sciences (SPSS) are outlined.

Statistical Package for the Social Sciences (SPSS)

SPSS/PC is the personal computer version of the Statistical Package for the Social Sciences, which is available for IBM-compatible personal computers. The system is fully described in the SPSS/PC manual (Norusis 1986).

An extended list of SPSS/PC procedures is given in Appendix 12.1. In this and the next chapter only the following are described:

FREQUENCIES	– Counts and percentages.
CROSSTABS	– Crosstabulation of 2 or more variables.
MEANS	– Obtaining means/ averages.
PLOT	– Plot of 2 variables.
CORRELATION	– Correlation of 2 variables.
GRAPH	– Production of business graphics.

These chapters deal with the analysis of data from a questionnaire survey. The Student Leisure Survey questionnaire introduced in Chapter 10 is used for illustrative purposes (Figure 10.5).

This introduction to SPSS/PC does not deal with procedures for logging into a computer, file handling, or the editing procedures necessary to set up a file. These procedures vary from computer to computer and depend on the software being used. Neither does this introduction deal with the installation of the SPSS/PC software onto the computer. It is assumed that SPPSS/PC is already installed on a computer available to the reader.

SPSS also exists in a 'mainframe' computer version referred to as SPSSX. The basic file structure is the same for both mainframe and PC versions – the main differences lie in the way data files are handled and the initial instructions for activating the programs. SPSSX has more features than SPSS/PC.

Most users of SPSS/PC need to have the full manual to hand when working with SPSS/PC in order to look up details and correct errors. The information in these two chapters provide an introduction to the basics only.

Non-survey data

This and the next chapter relate to the analysis of data arising from questionnaire surveys, but SPSS/PC can be used to analyse data from other sources also. Any data which are primarily numerical can be analysed using SPSS/PC.

SPSS/PC structure

To set up an SPSS/PC job a computer file or document called an *SPSS Command File* must be created. The command file contains a set of instructions (commands) telling the computer how to interpret the survey data. It is the command file that runs the SPSS/PC program. Appended to the command file are the *data* from 50 coded questionnaires. For large data sets the data may be stored in a file separate from the command file. (See Appendix 12.2.)

For the Student Leisure Survey used to illustrate the procedures in this and the next chapter the name of the file used is STUDENT.CMD. A command file can be created using the SPSS/PC program or a word-processor. In this presentation the word-processor option is assumed, which means that most of the preparatory work described in this chapter can be done without the need to have access to the SPSS/PC program. A command file prepared with a word-processor must be saved in ASCII format. This is a special way of recording the data (American Standard Code for Information Interchange) and is the only format which SPSS/PC can read. Most word-processors have a procedure for saving files in this format, including:

WordPerfect   – use Crtl/ F5 and 1 to save the file
Wordstar   – create a 'Non-document' file.

The SPSS/PC command file

The SPSS/PC command file consists of a series of five elements:

STARRED COMMENTS
DATA LIST
VARIABLE LABELS
VALUE LABELS
DATA

The STARRED COMMENTS, the VARIABLE LABELS and the VALUE LABELS are optional. SPSS/PC will run without them.

Before examining each of these elements; data definition and the naming of variables are considered.

Data definition – variable names

In order to communicate with the SPSS/PC program it is necessary to identify each item of data in the questionnaire. An item of data is referred to as a 'variable' and is identified by a *variable name*. Figure 12.1 contains a copy of the Student Leisure Survey questionnaire annotated with variable names to be used in the SPSS/PC analysis. It is strongly advised that such an annotated blank questionnaire be prepared for reference. Every item of information on the questionnaire is given a *unique* name (no two variables with the same name!) of up 8 letters/numbers (no spaces), beginning with a letter. It is not permitted to use any of the following for variable names, because SPSS/PC already uses these names for other purposes and would get confused!

ALL AND BY EQ GE GT LE LT NE NOT OR TO WITH

The practice adopted here is to give the variables names which are shortened versions of how the item might be described – e.g. CRSE for course, and NPK for visiting a National Park. The names can be up to eight characters long, but are best kept as short as possible to save time and effort in typing out variable names when giving the computer instructions.

Note that the questionnaire number is not given a variable name because it is not intended to use the questionnaire number for analysis. SPSS/PC will ignore data which the researcher does not wish to use. Note that question 4 has two variable names, REAS1 and REAS2 because up to two answers can be recorded.

An alternative way of labelling variables is by a sort of generalised name such as VAR for variable, so a questionnaire with five variables would have variable names: VAR1 VAR2 VAR3 VAR4 VAR5.

The full version of the Command File for the Student Leisure Survey is shown in Figure 12.2. The various elements which make up the file are considered in turn below.

Starred comments

It is suggested that the command file begin with a *comment* to remind yourself, or inform others who might come across it, what the file is about! A *comment* is a message to the researcher which the SPSS/PC program ignores. A comment is indicated by beginning the line with a * (followed by a space) and ending with a full-stop. It is suggested that the first line of the command file should say that the file

Student Leisure Survey

└─┴─┴─┘
(1 – 3)

1. What course are you registered for?

Undergraduate leisure studies	1	CRSE (4)
Undergraduate tourism studies	2	
Undergraduate sports studies	3	
Post-graduate leisure studies	4	
Post-graduate tourism studies	5	
Post-graduate sports studies	6	

2. Have you visited any of the following in the last month?

a. National park	1	NPK (5)
b. Museum	1	MUS (6)
c. Zoo	1	ZOO (7)
d. Nightclub	1	NTC (8)
e. Beach	1	BCH (9)

3. Given a choice, over the next 24 hours, which *one* of these facilities would you *most* like to visit?

National park	1	PREF (10)
Museum	2	
Zoo	3	
Nightclub	4	
Beach	5	

4. What would you most enjoy about such a visit?

_____ REAS1 └─┴─┘
(11–12)
REAS2 └─┴─┘
(13–14)

5. How much would you expect to spend, for youself, on such a visit (including travel cost)?

£ _____ EXP └─┴─┴─┘
(15–17)

6. Please indicate how important the following are to you in choosing leisure activities.

	Very important	Moderately important	Not important	
Cost	1	2	3	COST (18)
Distance	1	2	3	DIST (19)
Friends' wishes	1	2	3	FRNDS(20)

Figure 12.1 Questionnaire annotated with variable names

is an SPSS/PC command file and give the name of the survey and the name of the file. A second comment line could give the name(s) of the researcher(s) and the date.

DATA LIST

The first command to be included in the command file is DATA LIST. This tells the computer the names of the variables and where each

* SPSS/PC Command file: STUDENT. CMD - Student Leisure Survey.
* Jo Bloggs, 1992.

DATA LIST/ CRSE 4 NPK 5 MUS 6 ZOO 7 NTC 8 BCH 9 PREF 10
  REAS1 11–12 REAS2 13–14 EXP 15–17 COST 18 DIST 19 FRNDS 20.

VARIABLE LABELS
  CRSE 'Course (Q1)'
  NPK 'National Park (Q2a)'
  MUS 'Museum (Q2b)'
  ZOO 'Zoo (Q2c)'
  NTC 'Nightclub (Q2d)'
  BCH 'Beach (Q2e)'
  PREF 'Preference (Q3)'
  REAS1 'First reason for enjoyment (Q4)'
  REAS2 'Second reason for enjoyment (Q4)'
  EXP 'Expenditure (Q5)'
  COST 'Cost as a consideration (Q6)'
  DIST 'Distance as a consideration (Q6)'
  FRNDS 'Friends opinions as a consideration (Q6)'

VALUE LABELS
  CRSE   1 'Undergrad/Leisure' 2 'Undergrad/Tourism'
         3 'Undergrad/Sport' 4 'Postgrad/Leisure'
         5 'Postgrad/Tourism' 6 'Postgrad/Sport'/
  NPK TO BCH 1 'Yes' 0 'No'/
  PREF   1 'National Park' 2 'Museum' 3 'Zoo'
         4 'Nightclub' 5 'Beach'/
  REAS1 REAS2 01 'Relaxation' 02 'Sense of escape'
         03 'Commune with nature' 04 'Fresh Air'
         05 'Being with friends' 06 'Learning'
         07 'Exercise' 08 'Refreshment for work'
         09 'Meet people' 10 'Fun' 11 'Other'/
  COST TO FRNDS 1 'Very Imp.' 2 'Moderately Imp.' 3 'Not Imp.'.

BEGIN DATA
00111100150407   002231
002200110410   020221
003510011111   005111
004611000501   000331
00560000010302   004123
006110011102   000333
007110001206   000131
008100000310   008122
00911100140905   025231
010110000501   000111
011100001101   000212
012100110103   004323
013100011206   002122
014210000211   000133
015210001101   002233
016211001102   005211
017211000102   004221
018200100108   000111
01920011120611   000112
020201111311   010333

Figure 12.2   Command File 'STUDENT. CMD'

```
021300011401  030233
022300001408  010133
023300000405  020222
024311111501  005222
025300011         223
0263111115022104033l
0273111005010800011l
02850110150407002222
029500011501  000122
030411111505  000133
031400011         331
032400001101  002233
03341111110701000222
03440000010703004222
035410000201  000111
036111011301  015333
037200011410  015231
03851010141009010123
039500011401  020221
04050000141005040331
04131000150708000223
042610001507  000332
043600011201  004122
044610001401  020221
045600011306  010232
046400000206  002221
047500000101  000331
04861010010107002221
049400001101  000332
050611001103  004111
END DATA.
```

Figure 12.2 Command File 'STUDENT. CMD' (*contd*)

variable is located in the data record. The DATA LIST command tells the computer which variables are in which 'columns' – CRSE is in column 4, NPK is in column 5 and so on to FRNDS, which is in column 20.

Note: the column numbers correspond to the numbers in brackets on the questionnaire.

Note: the full-stop at the end of the command.

Note: a second or third line of a command must be indented a couple of spaces (use spaces – not 'tabs') – only commands, * and data can appear in the first column, everything else must be indented.

Note: the data list in this case goes on to a second line. Any one line of information in a command file must be less than 80 characters/ spaces in length. Before reaching the end of the line, force a new line with a 'hard' return – but do not split the variable name and its column details on two lines.

If the number of columns on the questionnaire goes past 80, it is advisable to start a new line, the data from each questionnaire also being typed on two or more lines. In the DATA LIST the new line is separated with a /.

For example (not from the Student Leisure Survey questionnaire):
DATA LIST /VAR1 3–4 VAR2 5 .... VAR40 78 VAR41 79 VAR42 80
  /VAR43 1 VAR44 2–3 VAR45 3–4 ... etc.

Variable labels

The command VARIABLE LABELS gives a longer label for each variable name. This longer label will be automatically printed out on tables for ease of interpretation. Where the variable name is already self-explanatory, e.g. SEX, AGE, a variable label is not necessary. Labels can be up to 40 characters/spaces long. Labels are enclosed by inverted commas – anything can be included inside the inverted commas except inverted commas (NB leave the apostrophe out of words like dont and cant).

Note: the opening and closing inverted commas are the same keyboard character.
Note: the full-stop at the end of the list.
Note: question numbers have been included for reference; this is optional.

Value labels

The command VALUE LABELS gives labels to the values which different variables can take on. For example, CRSE can take on any value between 1 and 6:

> Value 1 indicates Undergraduate Leisure Studies,
> Value 2 indicates Undergraduate Tourism Studies,
> and so on.

Labels are included within inverted commas, and the same rules apply as for variables labels, except that only up to 20 characters can be included.

Note: the five variables NPK MUS ZOO NTC BCH are covered by the shortened statement NPK TO BCH (and COST DIST and FRNDS by COST TO FRNDS) – because they have the same codes their value labels are identified with one statement. REAS1 and REAS2 are also covered by the same value label list.
Note: labels can be only up to 20 characters/spaces long.
Note: the /separating each variable and the full-stop at the end.

The data

In Chapter 10, the process by which a completed questionnaire is coded and the information converted to a string of numbers was demostrated. The strings of numbers for five completed questionnaires were as follows:

    00111100150407002321
    002200110410   020221

```
003510011111    005111
004611000501    000331
0056000010302004123
```

To demonstrate the working of SPSS/PC, data from 50 questionnaires, including the five above, have been created and are appended to the command file, beginning with BEGIN DATA and ending with END DATA. There should be a 'hard return' after END DATA.

Non-numerical data

SPSS/PC will handle non-numerical data, such as names, or codes in the form of letters, but for reasons of space the appropriate procedures are not covered here.

RUNNING SPSS/PC

The following procedures are based on SPSS/PC Version 4.

Because of the likelihood of multiple users in an educational environment the practice of storing the command file on a floppy disk in 'Drive A:' is adopted – the command file could be stored on the hard disk, Drive C: if preferred.

Step 1 Place the floppy disk containing the Command File in Drive A.

Step 2 Type SPSSPC and press the Enter key. (Depending on the way the computer/software is set up, it may be necessary to type CD SPSS first.)
The SPSS/PC package is activated and presents the MAIN MENU in the top half of the screen and the 'scratch pad' (where your instructions will appear) in the bottom half of the screen.

Step 3 To run the Student Leisure Survey file use the down arrow to move to 'session control and info.' on the menu, and press the Enter key. On the 'session control and info.' menu select INCLUDE. A pair of apostrophes is highlighted; press the Enter key and then type:
A:STUDENT.CMD (Substitue your own file name for STUDENT.)
Then press F10 and then the Enter key.
Error check: the computer runs through the command file, including the data, checking for errors, a screen at a time. If MORE appears in the top right hand corner of the screen, press any key to continue.
If there are *errors* the programs will not run – you cannot proceed any further without correcting the errors. If there are *warnings* the program will run, but those aspects subject to warnings (usually variable or value labels) will not be printed on the output.

If there are errors or warnings, exit from SPSSPC by selecting FINISH from the MAIN MENU, and correct your file using the word processor. (*Note*: it is possible to correct the file using the editor program within SPSS/PC, but the procedures for using this are not covered here.)

Step 4 When there are no errors and no warnings analysis can begin.

● The computer is ready to accept instructions to perform analyses on the survey data. From here on the researcher can interact with the computer by selecting the commands required – as outlined in Chapter 13.

Note: In what follows, the instructions can be selected through the menu system, or typed in directly on the scratch pad. To do the latter press Alt and M together to turn 'menus off'.

Two initial instructions are advisable.

Step 5 SET PRINTER ON. This links the program with the printer, so that all subsequent results are printed out.
Select: 'session control and info.',
then: SET
then: OUTPUT
then: PRINTER
then: ON
(the printer must be *physically* turned on also!).

Step 6 SET LENGTH = 150. Enables the printer to print 150 lines at a time, rather than one table or screen at a time.
Select: 'session control and info.'
then: SET
then: OUTPUT
then: LENGTH
then: type 150

Step 7 Perform analyses – as set out in Chapter 13.

End To complete an SPSS/PC session, select FINISH from the MAIN MENU, then press F10 and Enter.

Error messages

● If there is an error in the DATA LIST command, all subsequent lines will appear as errors – even if they are OK!

● An error message 'COMMAND LINE TOO LONG ...' at the beginning usually indicates that the command file has not been saved in ASCII format.

● A similar message at the end usually indicates that a final 'carriage return' has not been entered on the command file.

● The error message indicates where a fault has been discovered by showing the message TEXT: followed by the faulty item, however, the error may in fact be on the line before – especially when the error is the omission of an inverted comma or a/ or a full stop – check for errors in that area.

● Common errors are duplicate variable names and variables spelled differently in different places in the Command File, so that the second, wrongly spelled version appears to the computer as an unidentified variable and it complains about an 'unrecognised or misspelled variable name'.

● A common error in the data arises if the letter O has been used instead of a zero.

Appendix 12.1   SPSS/PC procedures

The main analysis procedures available in the basic package are:

FREQUENCIES	Frequency counts and percents
DESCRIPTIVES	Basic statistics (mean, St. dev, range, etc.)
CROSSTABS	Crosstabulation
MEANS	Means
T-TEST	t test
PLOT	Visual plot and regression
CORRELATION	Correlation
ONEWAY	One-way analysis of variance
ANOVA	Factorial analysis of variance
NPAR TESTS	Non-parametric tests
REGRESSION	Linear regression
REPORT	Results presentation formatting

More advanced modules are available which cover such techniques as factor analysis, cluster analysis, discriminant analysis and trend analysis.

Appendix 12.2   SPSS/PC procedures

If the data set is large it can be stored in a separate file. For example, suppose the data are recorded in the file STUDENT.DAT, located on the same floppy disk as the command file in Drive B:. The command file then cross-refers to the data file in the DATA LIST command, as follows:

DATA LIST FILE = 'B:STUDENT .DAT'
    /CRSE 4 NPK 5 MUS 6 ZOO 7 NTC 8 BCH 9 PREF 10
    REAS1 11–12 REAS2 13–14 EXP 15–17 COST 18 DIST 19 FRNDS 20.

The command file then ends with the VALUE LABELS.

Note that the data file contains only numerical data.

13 Survey analysis: operation

In this chapter the process of analysing survey data is considered, and the operation of the following SPSS/PC procedures are outlined: FREQUENCIES, CROSSTABS, RECODE, MEANS, and CORRELATION. In addition the generation of graphics (including bar, pie and line graphs) is outlined, using the SPSS/PC graphics module and 'Harvard Graphics'.

Analysis

In Chapter 1 it was noted that research might be of three kinds: descriptive, explanatory and evaluative.

Descriptive research

Descriptive research involves the presentation of information in a fairly simple form. In terms of the 'Student Leisure Survey' used to illustrate the use of SPSS/PC, descriptive research involves simply establishing the leisure behaviour and preferences of leisure/tourism students. The questionnaire is of course in a simplified form for obvious reasons, but such research, in a more fully developed form, could have been commissioned, for example, by a company planning a marketing campaign directed at students (not necessarily for a leisure product), and wishing to know something about their lifestyles.

Of the SPSS/PC procedures described in this chapter, the one most appropriate for descriptive research is FREQUENCIES. This procedure presents counts and percentages for each variable. In the case of the Student Leisure Survey therefore, FREQUENCIES can be used to obtain the numbers and percentages of student respondents attending each type of course, who have engaged in the various leisure activities, and so on. FREQUENCIES is therefore used if the aim of the research is simply 'finding out'.

In addition the MEAN option can be used to obtain the average proposed expenditure (question 5) and average 'scores' on the three opinion items (question 6).

Explanatory research

Presenting descriptive data does not *explain* anything. To explain the patterns in data we must consider the question of *causality* and how data analysis can address the issue of whether A is *caused* by B.

In Chapter 3 it was noted that to establish causality it was necessary to fulfil four criteria: association, time priority, non-spurious relation and rationale.

SPSS/PCC lends itself particularly to establishing the *associations* between variables and their strength and size. The particular procedures which are appropriate for this and which are covered in this chapter are CROSSTABS, MEANS and CORRELATION. As discussed in Chapter 2, it is desirable to establish the magnitude or strength of associations and their consistency. While SPSS/PC procedures are well suited to establishing the magnitude and strength of associations the questions of the consistency of associations is more complex. Unlike the natural sciences, it is not always possible to replicate research in the social sciences to establish consistency. While reference to the literature can be relevant in this respect, in fact, the changing nature of human nature over time and space means that consistency with previous research findings is by no means a guarantee of validity.

Time priority – establishing that for A to be the cause of B then A must take place before B – is rarely testable in social science research and is more appropriate for the conditions of the natural science laboratory.

Establishing that a relationship is *non-spurious* – that is that the relationship between A and B is not mediated by a third variable C – is something which can be approached using SPSS/PC. For example, if A is related to B for the whole sample, and the two variables are also related in a similar way for, say, men and women separately, and for other subgroups, this suggests a non-spurious relationship.

Rationale, or theory, is of course not produced by SPSS/PC but should be integral to the research design. As indicated in Chapter 3, the research may be deductive in nature, with pre-established hypotheses which are tested by the data analysis, or it may be inductive in nature, in which case theory/explanation building takes place to a greater or lesser extent as part of the data analysis process. Either way explanation, or the establishment of causality, is not complete without some sort of rational explanation of the relationships found.

The 'Student Leisure Survey' questionnaire as presented does not apparently offer great scope for detailed explanatory research. While variations may be found in the activities and preferences of the different student groups (leisure versus sport versus tourism, under-graduate versus postgraduate), it is unlikely that these variations are *caused* by membership of those groups. Rather, it is likely that the causes lie in some underlying differences in values and personalities which attracted students to the different courses in the first place or to differences in ages and social circumstances between undergraduates and postgraduates. As far as explanation is concerned this type of survey is therefore likely to be suggestive rather than conclusive.

Evaluative research

Evaluative research basically involves *comparisons*. Are the survey findings higher or lower than some external benchmark? As discussed in Chapter 3, the external benchmarks may be established performance standards (e.g. a leisure centre being required to have at least x per cent of attendance by young people) or simply comparisons with previous years' figures or with comparable programmes elsewhere. The analysis called for is therefore relatively simple, is generally descriptive in nature and is easily facilitated by SPSS/PC.

The Student Leisure Survey is not of an evaluative nature, although it could become so if the results of such a survey for one group of students were to be compared with the results from another group to establish that one group was, for example, more 'culturally orientated' or more 'sports orientated' than another.

Overlaps

Analysis does not always fall exclusively into one of the above three modes. For example, in presenting a descriptive account of the student leisure survey results, it would be natural to provide a breakdown of the participation patterns and preferences of the six student groups included (provided the sample size was large enough), or of leisure versus sport versus tourism students or undergraduate versus postgraduate students. (This would involve the use of CROSSTABS and/or MEANS). While this could be descriptive in form, it would begin to hint at explanation, in that any differences in the groups' patterns of behaviour or preferences would seem to call for explanation; the analysis would be saying 'these groups are different' and would be implicitly posing the question 'why?'

Reliability

In Chapter 2 reference was made to questions of validity and reliability. It has been noted that some attempt at testing validity – whether the data are measuring what they are intended to measure – can be achieved in the design of questionnaires. In the case of reliability – whether similar results would be obtained if the research were replicated – is again a difficult issue in the social sciences, but an approach can be made at the analysis stage. If the sample is large enough, one approach to reliability is to split the sample into two or more sub-samples on a random basis and see if the results for the sub-sample are the same as for the sample as a whole. This can be achieved in SPSS/PC using the procedure SAMPLES. While this procedure is not covered in detail in this outline, full details are given in the SPSS/PC manual.

Statistics

In Chapter 10, on sampling, the implications of sample size in terms of confidence intervals were outlined. The implications are clear: that the degree of precision which can be attached to survey results, the level of detail with which analysis can be pursued and the sorts of comparisons which can be made are all limited by the size of the sample.

More sophisticated use of statistical theory is available using procedures in SPSS/PC including Chi-square tests, t-tests, and analysis of variance. While these procedures are not described in this presentation, some indications are given of the procedures available and the commands to activate them, under the headings 'Statistics note'. Further details of these statistical procedures can be found in any statistics text book and in the SPSS/PC manual; Bryman and Cramer (1990) show the use of SPSS for more advanced statistical analysis.

SPSS/PC procedures

The procedures FREQUENCIES, MEANS, CROSSTABS, CORRELATION and GRAPH are outlined below using the Student Leisure Survey as an example. It is assumed that steps 1 to 6 as outlined in Chapter 12 have been successfully completed.

In what follows the necessary instructions can be selected from the SPSS/PC menus and will appear in the 'Scratch pad' in the lower half of the screen. Once compiled the instructions are activated by pressing F10 followed by Enter. Alternatively the instructions can be typed directly into the 'Scratch pad' by first of all pressing Alt and M together to 'turn menus off'.

Note that if an error is made while compiling an instruction from the menus, it can be changed/edited by pressing Alt and E together, making the changes, then pressing Alt and E again to return to the menu.

FREQUENCIES

FREQUENCIES is the simplest form of descriptive analysis: it merely produces counts and percentages for individual variables – for instance, in the Student Leisure Survey, the numbers and percentages of respondents registered in each course (CRSE).

It is advisable to begin the analysis of a data set by running FREQUENCIES for one variable, so that the program can read through the data and establish that there are no serious problems with the data. For example, to obtain a table of the number of students enrolled in different courses in the Student Leisure Survey, from the MAIN MENU:

Select:	'analyze data'
then:	descriptive statistics
then:	FREQUENCIES
then:	VARIABLES
then:	CRSE

The following should appear in the Scratch pad:

FREQUENCIES/VARIABLES CRSE.

Press F10 followed by Enter to activate.

If the computer says MORE in the top right hand corner of the screen, press any key. The computer then presents, on the screen and on the printer, a table as in Figure 13.1.

CRSE Course (Q1)					
Value Label	Value	Frequency	Per cent	Valid Per cent	Cum Per cent
Undergrad/Leisure	1	10	20.0	20.0	20.0
Undergrad/Tourism	2	9	18.0	18.0	38.0
Undergrad/Sport	3	8	16.0	16.0	54.0
Postgrad/Leisure	4	8	16.0	16.0	70.0
Postgrad/Tourism	5	7	14.0	14.0	84.0
Postgrad/Sport	6	8	16.0	16.0	100.0
	Total	50	100.0	100.0	
Valid cases 50	Missing cases	0			

Figure 13.1 Frequencies table for CRSE (Produced by command: FREQUENCIES VARIABLES CRSE.)

In Figure 13.1:

- Values are the codes (1 to 6) for the variable CRSE.
- Frequency is a count of the numbers of respondents/students falling into each category, adding up, in this case, to 50, the sample size.
- Per cent, converts this into percentages.
- Valid per cent is explained below, under 'missing values'.
- Cum per cent, adds percentages cumulatively.

FREQUENCIES for all variables

If the single variable table has worked satisfactorily, frequency tables for all the variables can be obtained by the same procedure as above, but selecting ALL instead of CRSE, to produce:

FREQUENCIES VARIABLES ALL.

This runs frequency tables for all variables and is a common initial instruction in survey analysis: it is a good way of obtaining an overview of the results, and checking that all is well with the data. The results of this exercise for the student leisure survey are shown in Appendix 13.1 to this chapter.

Missing values

What happens when questions are not answered, either by error or design, and the particular column or columns in the data files are left blank? This can be illustrated by the frequency table for the variable PREF, shown in Figure 13.2.

PREF Preference (Q3) Value Label	Value	Frequency	Per cent	Valid Per cent	Cum Per cent
National Park	1	16	32.0	33.3	33.3
Museum	2	7	14.0	14.6	47.9
Zoo	3	4	8.0	8.3	56.3
Nightclub	4	10	20.0	20.8	77.1
Beach	5	11	22.0	22.9	100.0
	.	2	4.0	MISSING	
	Total	50	100.0	100.0	
Valid cases 48 Missing cases 2					

Figure 13.2 Frequencies table for PREF (Produced by command: FREQUENCIES VARIABLES PREF.)

Two respondents did not answer this question and PREF (column 10) was left blank. The computer calls them 'missing values' and they are listed against a full-stop,'Value' in the table. In the Percent column these two cases are included, but in the Valid percent column they are excluded. In any particular situation, the question of which set of percentages to use – the one including the missing values (Percent) or the one excluding them (Valid percent) – is a matter of judgement.

Note that as a result of the non-responses to question 3 there are corresponding non-responses and missing values in questions 4 and 5.

Checking for errors

After obtaining the FREQUENCIES/VARIABLES ALL printout it is necessary to check through the results to see if there are any oddities. For example, the table for REAS2, shown in Figure 13.3, contains an error.

REAS2   Second reason for enjoyment (Q4)

Value Label	Value	Frequency	Per cent	Valid Per cent	Cum Per cent
Relaxation	1	1	2.0	7.7	7.7
Sense of escape	2	1	2.0	7.7	15.4
Commune with nature	3	1	2.0	7.7	23.1
Being with friends	5	2	4.0	15.4	38.5
Exercise	7	3	6.0	23.1	61.5
Refreshment for work	8	2	4.0	15.4	76.9
Meet people	9	1	2.0	7.7	84.6
Other	11	1	2.0	7.7	92.3
	21	1	2.0	7.7	100.0
		37	74.0	MISSING	
	Total	50	100.0	100.0	

Valid cases   13   Missing cases   37

Figure 13.3 Frequencies table for REAS2 (with error) (Produced by command: FREQUENCIES VARIABLES REAS2.)

A 21 has appeared when the codes should only go from 1 to 11. The source of the error is a mis-keying of data from questionnaire number 26 – as can be seen in the print-out of the data in Chapter 12. This is found by 'eyeballing' the relevant columns (11–12). To find the correct code it is usually necessary to go back to the questionnaire to see what the item should have been – in this case it should have been 11 rather than 21.

The data must be corrected using the word-processor and the job run again from the beginning. But the FREQUENCIES tables need only be run again for those variables where there were errors.

Specifying several variables

The command FREQUENCIES can deal with more than one variable at a time – in fact it can deal with a list of variables. Three possibilities exist for indicating a list of variables, for example:

- FREQUENCIES/VARIABLES CRSE PREF EXP.   list of 3 specific variables.
- FREQUENCIES/VARIABLES NPK TO PREF.   list of 6 consecutive variables.
- FREQUENCIES/VARIABLES ALL.   all variables, as outlined above.

Multiple response questions

Note that the results from REAS1 and REAS2 should be added together to produce a composite table. In main-frame versions of SPSS there is an instruction (MULT RESPONSE) to get the computer to do this, but with SPSS/PC it must be done manually. If a questionnaire has large numbers of this sort of variable and it is planned to under-take cross-tabulations using them, then it may be worth transferring the analysis to the mainframe version of SPSS, if available.

RECODE

As the name implies, RECODE is a command which can be used to change the codes of variables. This can be done by adding the command to the original command file, if the change is to be fairly permanent, or by typing it onto the screen during an SPSS/PC session.

The use of RECODE will be illustrated in two situations, firstly with a non-precoded, continuous variable and secondly with a precoded variable.

The variable EXP – anticipated expenditure – is a non-precoded continuous variable. It is non-precoded in that the actual expenditure was included rather than a code. The advantage of not having the variable precoded is that it is possible to be flexible about what groupings are required and it is possible, as shown below, to use such procedures as MEANS and CORRELATION which is not generally possible with pre-coded variables.

Because EXP is not pre-coded, the FREQUENCIES command listed every single level of expenditure given by respondents, as shown in Figure 13.4. There are 12 different expenditures, including zero and no answer. In a large survey this could become hundreds.

The expenditure variable can be RECODED into groups using the following command, selected via the 'modify data or files' menu option:

RECODE EXP (1 THRU 4 = 1) (5 THRU 9 = 2) (10 THRU 19 = 3)
(20 THRU 999 = 4).

EXP	Expenditure (Q5)					
Value Label		Value	Frequency	Per cent	Valid Per cent	Cum Per cent
		0	17	34.0	35.4	35.4
		2	7	14.0	14.6	50.0
		4	6	12.0	12.5	62.5
		5	3	6.0	6.3	68.8
		8	1	2.0	2.1	70.8
		10	4	8.0	8.3	79.2
		15	2	4.0	4.2	83.3
		20	4	8.0	8.3	91.7
		25	1	2.0	2.1	93.8
		30	1	2.0	2.1	95.8
		40	2	4.0	4.2	100.0
			2	4.0	MISSING	
		Total	50	100.0	100.0	
Valid cases	48	Missing cases	2			

Figure 13.4 Frequencies table for expenditure (Produced by command: FREQUENCIES VARIABLES EXP.)

EXP	Expenditure (Q5)			Valid	Cum
Value label	Value	Frequency	Per cent	Per cent	Per cent
Zero	0	17	34.0	35.4	35.4
1–4	1	13	26.0	27.1	62.5
5–9	2	4	8.0	8.3	70.8
10–19	3	6	12.0	12.5	83.3
20+	4	8	16.0	16.7	100.0
		2	4.0	MISSING	
	Total	50	100.0	100.0	

Valid cases   48   Missing cases   2

Figure 13.5   Frequencies table for EXP – RECODED (Produced by command: FREQUENCIES VARIABLES EXP. – after RECODE)

Insert value labels for EXP via the 'read or write data' menu option, then select 'labels and formatting', to produce:

VALUE LABELS EXP 0 'Zero' 1 '1-4' 2 '5-9' 3 '10-19' 4 '20+'.

Running FREQUENCIES/VARIABLES EXP now produces the results shown in Figure 13.5.

It is also possible to change the groupings of pre-coded variables using RECODE. For instance, suppose analysis is to be conducted comparing undergraduates and postgraduates as two groups. Undergraduates, in CRSE, are coded 1 to 3 and postgraduates are coded 4 to 6. The following commands, selected as above, would RECODE them into two groups:

RECODE CRSE (1 THRU 3 = 1) (4 THRU 6 = 2)
VALUE LABELS CRSE 1 'Undergrad' 2 'Postgrad'

Running FREQUENCIES/VARIABLE CRSE now produces Figure 13.6.

CRSE	Course (Q1)			Valid	Cum
Value label	Value	Frequency	Per cent	Per cent	Per cent
Undergrad.	1	27	54.0	54.0	54.0
Post-grad.	2	23	46.0	46.0	100.0
	Total	50	100.0	100.0	

Valid cases   50   Missing cases   0

Figure 13.6   Frequencies table for CRSE – recoded (Produced by command: FREQUENCIES VARIABLES CRSE – after RECODE)

Presenting the results

SPSS/PC is extravagant with paper, as Appendix 13.1 indicates. The layout of the tables also contains more detail than is necessary for most reports. It is recommended that a statistical summary be prepared for inclusion in any report, rather than include a copy of the SPSS/PC printout. For example, the output from the FREQUENCIES/VARIABLES ALL analysis could be summarised as in Figure 13.7. As can be seen this takes far less space and is more readable.

Note: the results from the yes/no variables, NPK to BCH, collapse into a single table.

Note: it is generally not necessary to include actual frequency counts as well as percentages in reports, as long as the sample size is indicated, so that, if needed, any reader can work out the raw numbers for themselves.

Note: the scores for the attitude variables come from the MEANS procedure discussed below.

MEANS

A mean is the same as an average. It is often useful to be able to produce means, for instance mean ages, incomes, time spent, etc. Clearly means can only be produced for numerical data. Means cannot be produced for coded variables where the codes represent categories and not quantities. In the Student Leisure Survey for example, expenditure (EXP) is the only numerical item. (The attitude variables in question 6 are a special case discussed separately below.)

Two procedures are available in SPSS/PC for producing means. The simplest procedure is to add a sub-command to the FREQUEN-CIES command, as follows:

FREQUENCIES/VARIABLES EXP/STATISTICS MEAN.

(Note that this must be done *before* any RECODE of EXP, otherwise the procedure produces averages of the *recoded* values.)

This produces the result shown in Figure 13.8, which indicates that the average anticipated expenditure is £7.21.

A second way of obtaining means is by using the command MEANS. This command can be used to obtain means of suitable variables crosstabulated by other variables. For instance a comparison of the anticipated expenditure levels of the members of the different courses would be given by the command:

MEANS/TABLES EXP BY CRSE.

This produces the results shown in Figure 13.9, which indicates that postgraduate leisure studies students have the lowest anticipated expenditure at £1.14 and the undergraduate sports studies students have the highest at £15.00. The table also gives the standard deviation for each mean, which is a measure of how widely the responses are distributed around the mean.

Sample size:	50			
Course:	%			
Undergraduate: Leisure studies	20.0			
Undergraduate: Tourism studies	18.0			
Undergraduate: Sport studies	16.0			
Postgraduate: Leisure studies	16.0			
Postgraduate: Tourism studies	14.0			
Postgraduate: Sport studies	16.0			
Facilities visited in last month				
National park	48.0			
Museum	28.0			
Zoo	26.0			
Nightclub	40.0			
Beach	68.0			
Facility would most like to visit				
National park	32.0			
Museum	14.0			
Zoo	8.0			
Nightclub	20.0			
Beach	22.0			
No answer	4.0			
Enjoyment from visit to chosen facility				
Relaxation	36.0			
Sense of escape	10.0			
Communing with nature	8.0			
Fresh air	4.0			
Being with friends	8.0			
Learning something	10.0			
Physical exercise	14.0			
Refreshment for work	8.0			
Meet new people	4.0			
Fun	10.0			
Other	8.0			
No answer	4.0			

(Percentages add to more than 100 because some respondents gave more than one answer)

Anticipated expenditure on visit				
Nil	34.0			
£1–4	26.0			
£5–9	8.0			
£10–19	12.0			
£20 & over	16.0			
No answer	4.0			

Importance of factors in leisure choice	Very imp.	Mod. imp.	Not imp.	Avge score*
	%	%	%	
Cost	34	44	22	1.9
Distance	18	40	42	2.2
Friends' Opinions	44	28	28	1.8

(* Scale: Very Imp. = 1, Mod. Imp. = 2, Not Imp. = 3)

Figure 13.7 Student leisure survey: statistical summary

EXP   Expenditure (Q5)

Value label	Value	Frequency	Per cent	Valid Per cent	Cum Per cent
	0	17	34.0	35.4	35.4
	2	7	14.0	14.6	50.0
	4	6	12.0	12.5	62.5
	5	3	6.0	6.3	68.8
	8	1	2.0	2.1	70.8
	10	4	8.0	8.3	79.2
	15	2	4.0	4.2	83.3
	20	4	8.0	8.3	91.7
	25	1	2.0	2.1	93.8
	30	1	2.0	2.1	95.8
	40	2	4.0	4.2	100.0
		2	4.0	MISSING	
	Total	50	100.0	100.0	

Mean   7.208

Valid cases   48   Missing cases   2

Figure 13.8 Frequencies table for EXP–with MEAN (Produced by command: FREQUENCIES VARIABLES EXP/STATISTICS MEAN.)

Summaries of	EXP	Expenditure (Q5)			
By levels of	CRSE	Course (Q1)			
Variable	Value	label	Mean	Std dev	Cases
For entire population			7.2083	10.2562	48
CRSE	1	Undergrad/leisure	5.6000	8.3293	10
CRSE	2	Undergrad/tourism	6.2222	7.2591	9
CRSE	3	Undergrad/sport	15.000	15.5456	7
CRSE	4	Postgrad/leisure	1.1429	1.5736	7
CRSE	5	Postgrad/tourism	11.0000	14.6173	7
CRSE	6	Postgrad/sport	5.5000	6.6548	8
Total cases =	50				
Missing cases =	2 or 4.0 PCT.				

Figure 13.9 Mean expenditure by course (Produced by command: MEANS TABLES EXP BY CRSE.)

Attitude scales

Means are appropriate when using attitude or 'Likert' type scales, as discussed in Chapter 10. The scores of 1 to 3 in question 6 can be treated as numerical indicators of the importance attached to the three factors of cost, distance and friends' opinions.

For example, the three tables in Figure 13.10 are produced by the command:

MEANS/TABLES = COST TO FRNDS BY CRSE.

They indicate that the overall scores for each factor are:

Summaries of	COST	Cost as a consideration (Q6)			
By levels of	CRSE	Course (Q1)			
Variable	Value	label	Mean	Std dev	Cases
For entire population			1.8800	.7461	50
CRSE	1	Undergrad/leisure	1.9000	.8756	10
CRSE	2	Undergrad/tourism	1.7778	.6667	9
CRSE	3	Undergrad/sport	1.8750	.6409	8
CRSE	4	Postgrad/leisure	2.0000	.7559	8
CRSE	5	Postgrad/tourism	1.8571	.8997	7
CRSE	6	Postgrad/sport	1.8750	.8345	8

Summaries of	DIST	Distance as a consideration (Q6)			
By levels of	CRSE	Course (Q1)			
Variable	Value	label	Mean	Std dev	Cases
For entire population			2.2400	.7400	50
CRSE	1	Undergrad/leisure	2.3000	.8233	10
CRSE	2	Undergrad/tourism	2.1111	.9280	9
CRSE	3	Undergrad/sport	2.2500	.7071	8
CRSE	4	Postgrad/leisure	2.3750	.7440	8
CRSE	5	Postgrad/tourism	2.1429	.6901	7
CRSE	6	Postgrad/sport	2.2500	.7071	8

Summaries of	FRNDS	Friends opinions as a consideration (Q6)			
By levels of	CRSE	Course (Q1)			
Variable	Value	label	Mean	Std dev	Cases
For entire population			1.8400	.8418	50
CRSE	1	Undergrad/Leisure	1.9000	.8756	10
CRSE	2	Undergrad/Tourism	1.7778	.9718	9
CRSE	3	Undergrad/Sport	2.2500	.8864	8
CRSE	4	Postgrad/Leisure	1.8750	.8345	8
CRSE	5	Postgrad/Tourism	1.5714	.7868	7
CRSE	6	Postgrad/Sport	1.6250	.7440	8

Figure 13.10 Attitude scores by course (Produced by command: MEANS TABLES = COST TO FRNDS BY CRSE.)

Cost:	1.9
Distance:	2.2
Friends' opinion:	1.8

Bearing in mind that a high score means that a factor is not important, this shows that distance is less important in decisions on leisure than the other two factors. Figure 13.10 also shows how these scores vary among different student groups.

Statistics note

To test the statistical difference between means use the command T-TEST from the 'comparing group means' menu option. For the difference between the means of two variables, the command is:

T-TEST/PAIRS COST DIST.

For the difference between the means on one variable for two or more groups, the command (with CRSE RECODed to 2 groups) is:

T-TEST/GROUPS CRSE(1,2)/VARIABLES COST.

CROSSTABS

After FREQUENCIES, the most commonly used SPSS/PC command is probably CROSSTABS. This command relates two or more variables and marks the move from purely descriptive to explanatory analysis. Suppose, for example, it was required to compare the preferences of undergraduates and postgraduates. Having recoded CRSE, as discussed above, the following command, produced by selecting CROSSTABS instead of FREQUENCIES, produces the results shown in Figure 13.11.

CROSSTABS/TABLES PREF BY CRSE.

Crosstabulation:	PREF By CRSE	Preference (Q3) Course (Q1)		
	Count	Undergrad.	Postgrad.	
CRSE		1	2	Row Total
PREF				
1 National Park		7	9	16 33.3
2 Museum		4	3	7 14.6
3 Zoo		3	1	4 8.3
4 Nightclub		6	4	10 20.8
5 Beach		6	5	11 22.9
	Column Total	26 54.2	22 45.8	48 100.0

Number of missing observations = 2

Figure 13.11 CROSSTAB–Preference by Course (Produced by command: CROSSTABS TABLES PREF BY CRSE.)

Percentages

These tables would be easier to interpret if there were percentages available rather than just the raw figures. To produce percentages it is necessary to specify the 'cell contents'. There are four relevant options:

Counts;
row percentages;
column percentages;
total percentages.

The options are specified in the CROSSTABS command as follows and the results are shown in Figure 13.12:

A. Row percents: CROSSTABS/TABLES PREF BY
                       CRSE/CELLS = COUNT ROW.

B. Column percents: CROSSTABS/TABLES PREF BY
                       CRSE/CELLS = COUNT COLUMN.

C. Overall percents: CROSSTABS/TABLES PREF BY
                       CRSE/CELLS = COUNT TOTAL.

D. All three: CROSSTABS/TABLES PREF BY
                       CRSE/CELLS = COUNT ROW COLUMN
                       TOTAL.

Several CROSSTABS

Several crosstabulations can be produced with one instruction. For example the following command produces five tables, one for each of the variables from question 2 of the Student Leisure Survey questionnaire:

CROSSTABS/TABLES NPK TO BCH BY CRSE/CELLS = COUNT COLUMN.

The following produces four tables (Figure 13.12):

CROSSTABS/TABLES CRSE BY PREF EXP/NPK BY REAS1/BCH BY EXP/CELLS = COUNT COLUMN.

Three-way tables

CROSSTABS can also produce crosstabulations of more than two variables. For instance, crosstabulations of PREF by EXP looking at graduates and undergraduates separately would be produced by the command (assuming CRSE has been RECODEd into two groups) (Figure 13.13):
CROSSTABS/TABLES EXP BY PREF BY CRSE/CELLS = COUNT COLUMN.

Statistics note

To obtain a Chi-square test for a crosstabulation add the sub-command/STATISTICS = CHISQ. For example:

CROSSTABS/TABLES PREF BY CRSE/CELLS = COUNT COLUMN/STATISTICS = CHISQ.

A–PERCENTAGES ACROSS
Command:
CROSSTABS TABLES = PREF BY CRSE/CELLS = COUNT ROW.

Crosstabulation:		PREF By CRSE	Preference (Q3) Course (Q1)	

CRSE PREF	Count Row Pct	Undergrad. 1	Postgrad. 2	Row Total
National park	1	7 43.8	9 56.3	16 33.3
Museum	2	4 57.1	3 42.9	7 14.6
Zoo	3	3 75.0	1 25.0	4 8.3
Nightclub	4	6 60.0	4 40.0	10 20.8
Beach	5	6 54.5	5 45.5	11 22.9
	Column Total	26 54.2	22 45.8	48 100.0

Number of missing observations =   2

B–PERCENTAGES DOWN
Command:
CROSSTABS TABLES = PREF BY CRSE/CELLS = COUNT COLUMN.

Crosstabulation:		PREF By CRSE	Preference (Q3) Course (Q1)	

CRSE PREF	Count Col Pct	Undergrad. 1	Postgrad. Row 2	Total
National park	1	7 26.9	9 40.9	16 33.3
Museum	2	4 15.4	3 13.6	7 14.6
Zoo	3	3 11.5	1 4.5	4 8.3
Nightclub	4	6 23.1	4 18.2	10 20.8
Beach	5	6 23.1	5 22.7	11 22.9
	Column Total	26 54.2	22 45.8	48 100.0

Number of missing observations =   2

Figure 13.12 Preference by course, with percentages

C–PERCENTAGES OVERALL
Command:
CROSSTABS TABLES = PREF BY CRSE/CELLS = COUNT TOTAL.

Crosstabulation:	PREF By CRSE	Preference (Q3) Course (Q1)		
CRSE	Count Tot Pct	Undergrad.	Postgrad.	Row
PREF		1	2	Total
National park	1	7 14.6	9 18.8	16 33.3
Museum	2	4 8.3	3 6.3	7 14.6
Zoo	3	3 6.3	1 2.3	4 8.3
Nightclub	4	6 12.5	4 8.3	10 20.8
Beach	5	6 12.5	5 10.4	11 22.9
	Column Total	26 54.2	22 45.8	48 100.0

Number of missing observations = 2

D–ALL PERCENTAGES
Command:
CROSSTABS TABLES = PREF BY CRSE/CELLS = COUNT ROW COLUMN TOTAL.

Crosstabulation:	PREF By CRSE	Preference (Q3) Course (Q1)		
	Count			
CRSE	Row Pct Col Pct Tot Pct	Undergrad.	Postgrad.	Row
PREF		1	2	Total
National park	1	7 43.8 26.9 14.6	9 56.3 40.9 18.8	16 33.3
Museum	2	4 57.1 15.4 8.3	3 42.9 13.6 6.3	7 14.6
Zoo	3	3 75.0 11.5 6.3	1 25.0 4.5 2.1	4 8.3
Nightclub	4	6 60.0 23.1 12.5	4 40.0 18.2 8.3	10 20.8
Beach	5	6 54.5 23.1 12.5	5 45.5 22.7 10.4	11 22.9
	Column Total	26 54.2	22 45.8	48 100.0

Number of missing observations = 2

Figure 13.12 Preference by course, with percentages (*contd*)

Crosstabulation: EXP   Expenditure (Q5)
              By PREF   Preference (Q3)

Controlling for CRSE   Course (Q1) = 1 Undergrad.

PREF Exp	Count Col Pct	National park 1	Museum 2	Zoo 3	Nightclub 4	Beach 5	Row Total
Zero	0	2 28.6	3 75.0			4 66.7	9 34.6
1–4	1	4 57.1	1 25.0				5 19.2
5–9	2	1 14.3		1 33.3		1 16.7	3 11.5
10–19	3		2	2 66.7	33.3		4 15.4
20+	4				4 66.7	1 16.7	5 19.2
Column Total		7 26.9	4 15.4	3 11.5	6 23.1	6 23.1	26 100.0

Crosstabulation: EXP   Expenditure (Q5)
              By PREF

Controlling for CRSE   Course (Q1) = 2 Postgrad.

PREF Exp	Count Col Pct	National park 1	Museum 2	Zoo 3	Nightclub 4	Beach 5	Row Total
Zero	0	3 33.3	1 33.3			4 80.0	8 36.4
1–4	1	5 55.6	2 66.7			1 20.0	8 36.4
5–9	2 11.1	1					1 4.5
10–19	3			1 100.0	1 25.0		2 9.1
20+	4				3 75.0		3 13.6
Column Total		9 40.9	3 13.6	1 4.5	4 18.2	5 22.7	22 100.0

Number of missing observations = 2

Figure 13.13 Expenditure by preference by course (Produced by command: CROSSTABS TABLES = EXP BY PREF BY CRSE/CELLS = COUNT COLUMN. – with CRSE RECODED)

Weighting

Sometimes a sample turns out to be unrepresentative in some way and it is decided to correct for this in-built 'bias'. For example in the Student Leisure Survey results there are 54 per cent undergraduates and 46 per cent postgraduates. From university records, suppose it was established that the correct proportions were 70 per cent under-graduate and 30 per cent postgraduate. If the graduates and under-graduates differ in their responses to the questions then when they are added together, too little emphasis is being given to the under-graduates and too much to the graduates, so giving unrepresentative results. The imbalance can be corrected using the WEIGHT command.

In this instance the undergraduates need to be given a weight of 70/54, or 1.30 and the postgraduates a weight of 30/46, or 0.65 – the weight is the correct (population) percentage divided by the sample percentage.

To operate the WEIGHT command a new variable, the weighting variable, must be created. In this example the name of the new variable is WT. It is created by the following commands, selected from the 'modify data or file' menu option:

IF (CRSE LE 3) WT = 1.30.
IF (CRSE GE 4) WT = 0.65.
WEIGHT BY WT.

Press F10 and Enter each time to implement.
(LE means 'less than or equal to', GE means 'greater than or equal to').

The commands mean that in any analysis each undergraduate (CRSE LE 3) will be counted as 1.30 instead of 1 and each postgraduate (CRSE GE 4) will be counted as 0.65 instead of 1. Analysis can now proceed and it will be found that the ratio of undergraduates to postgraduates has been corrected.

The procedure can also be used to 'gross up' the data to produce estimates of population numbers. For example, if there are 3000 postgraduates and 7000 undergraduates in the university the survey findings can be 'grossed up' by using weighting factors of 3000/23 (= 130.4) for the postgraduates and 7000/27 (=259.3) for the under-graduates (23 and 27 being the number of postgraduates and under-graduates in the survey respectively).

If the weighting is to be more or less permanent then these three commands should be added to the original command file using the word processor. If just for a single session they can be typed interactively on the screen.

CORRELATION

Correlation is a measure of the association between two numerical variables. If both variables increase together the 'correlation coefficient' is positive; if one variable increases as the other decreases the coefficient is negative. The more closely the two variables move together the closer the coefficient is to 1; if there is no relationship between the two variables the coefficient is zero. The correlation coefficient is therefore a measure of the strength of a relationship

Correlations:	COST	DIST	FRNDS
COST	1.000	.5309**	.0013
DIST	.5309**	1.0000	.2907
FRNDS	.0013	.2907	1.0000

N of cases: 50   1-tailed Signif: * -.01   ** -.001

"." is printed if a coefficient cannot be computed.

Figure 13.14   Correlation matrix (Produced by command: CORRELATION /VARIABLES COST DIST FRNDS)

between two variables and is an important contributor to analyses seeking to establish causality, as discussed at the beginning of the chapter.

Correlation can be used to measure the extent to which the three attitude variables from question 6 are related. The 'correlation matrix' in Figure 13.14 was produced by the command:

CORRELATION/VARIABLES COST DIST FRNDS.

'Significant' correlations (i.e. correlations significantly different from zero) are marked with one or two * s. The results suggest that there is a significant positive relationship between COST and DIST – that is, students who think cost is important also tend to think that distance is important. But there are no other significant correlations in the matrix.

The use of graphics

Graphical presentation of data is generally considered to be an aid to communication. Trends and patterns can be seen more easily in graphic form by most people. Computer packages generally offer the following graphic formats:

Bar graph (or histogram)
Stacked bar graph
Pie chart
Line graph

Computers will produce all four formats from any one set of data. But all formats are not equally appropriate for all data. Data can be divided into nominal, ordinal and ratio types. Nominal data are made up of categories, such as questions 1–4 in the Student Leisure Survey questionnaire. While numerical codes are used they have no numerical meaning – code 3 is not 'half' of code 6 – the codes could equally well be A, B, C. Ordinal data reflect a ranking, as in question 6 of the Student Leisure Survey questionnaire; the 1,2,3 in this question, strictly speaking, represent the order of importance, but the code 3 cannot be interpreted as being '3 times' as high as code 1. Ratio data are fully numerical – as in question 5 of the Student Leisure Survey questionnaire. Here an answer of 4 is twice as high as an answer of 2. In the case of the question 6, even though the data are, strictly speaking, ordinal, as discussed under 'Attitude scales' earlier in this chapter, it is possible to treat them as 'scores' which have the characteristics of ratio data.

The relationships between diagram formats and permitted data types are as follows:

Bar graphs	nominal, ordinal, ratio (grouped)
Pie charts	nominal, ordinal, ratio (grouped) – when all categories/groups add to the total
Line graph	ratio

The bar graph or histogram is perhaps the most commonly used in leisure and tourism research; because it deals with categories any numerical variable must first be divided into groups – as in the RECODE of the expenditure variable from the Student Leisure Survey, discussed earlier in the chapter. The pie chart is just that – it divides something into sections like a pie – the categories making up the pie chart must therefore add up to some sort of meaningful total, often the total sample. The line graph is the most constrained and is used more generally in research in more quantified fields such as economics and the natural sciences. The line graph relates two *numerical* variables – the scales on both axes are continuous *numbers*.

SPSS/PC

It is possible to link a number of graphics software packages to SPSS/PC. These notes describe the use of Harvard graphics. Full details for installing the graphics module and for its operation are provided in the SPSS/PC GRAPHICS and the Harvard graphics manual.

The graphics module is activated by the command GRAPH. This is followed by sub-commands such as PIE, BAR, LINE, depending on which style of graphic is required. This is then followed by the variable(s) required. The computer creates a graph file with the required data in it, then swaps over to the 'Harvard graphics' program, which reads the graph file and creates the graphic. As with the SPSS/PC procedures already discussed, the instructions can be selected from the menus (choosing GRAPHICS from the MAIN MENU) or typed directly into the 'scratch pad'.

With multiple users of machines it is advisable to specify the 'outfile' into which the data should be put, rather than use the computer's 'default' graph file. Outfiles must be given a name, e.g. GRAPH1, GRAPH2, and written to the floppy disk in drive A:.

Pie chart

To produce a pie chart of the variable PREF, select or type in the following:

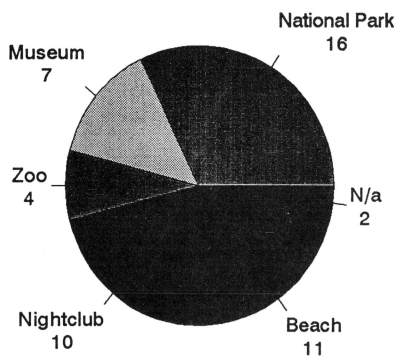

Figure 13.15   Pie chart of activity preferences Command: GRAPH PIE =
PREF/OUTFILE = 'A: GRAPH1'

GRAPH/PIE = PREF/OUTFILE = 'A:GRAPH1'.

This instruction produces the graph in Figure 13.15.

Once the computer has created the graphic on-screen, the full
facilities of Harvard graphics can be used to:

- obtain a printout of the graph;
- change its format, add labels etc.;
- save the graphic in a file for later incorporation into a report.

The pie chart can be changed to a bar graph using Harvard graphics
commands (but not to a line graph since the data format is not
suitable), or a bar graph can be created directly as described below.

Bar graph

To produce a bar graph of course numbers, as shown in Figure 13.16,
select or type the following:

GRAPH BAR=PREF/OUTFILE = 'A:GRAPH2'.

Bar graphs can include information on two variables rather than one,
the graphical equivalent of the crosstabulation. Figure 13.17 is

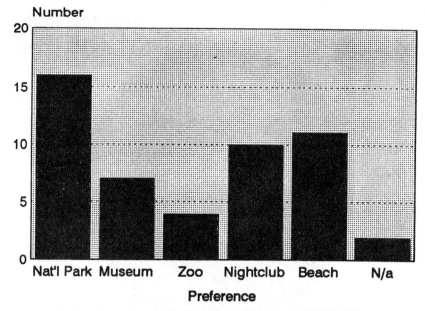

Figure 13.16 Bar graph of activity preferences Command: GRAPH BAR = PREF/OUTFILE = 'A: GRAPH2'

produced by the following command and can be manipulated within Harvard graphics to produce the 'stacked bar graph' as in Figure 13.18.

GRAPH BAR = CRSE BY PREF/OUTFILE = 'A:GRAPH3'.

Line graph

Expenditure (Q.5) is a numerical variable and the answers to question 6 are scores. Line graphs are therefore appropriate.The output in Figure 13.19 is produced by the command:

GRAPH LINE = MEAN(EXP) BY COST/OUTFILE = 'A: GRAPH4'.

To compare the three attitude scores in question 6, as shown in Figure 13.20, the following command is used:

GRAPH LINE = MEAN(EXP) BY COST DIST FRNDS/OUTFILE = 'A:GRAPH5'.

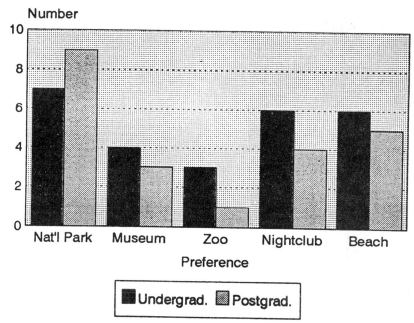

Figure 13.17   Bar graph of course by activity preference Command: GRAPH BAR = PREF BY CRSE/OUTFILE = 'A: GRAPH3'

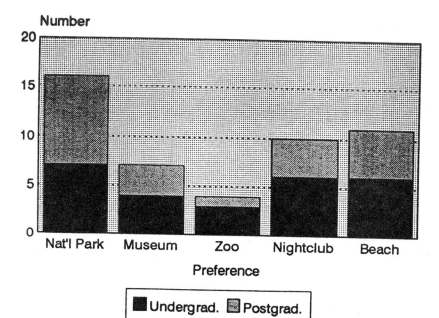

Figure 13.18   Stacked bar graph of course by activity preference Command: As for Figure 13.17: Changed within Harvard graphics

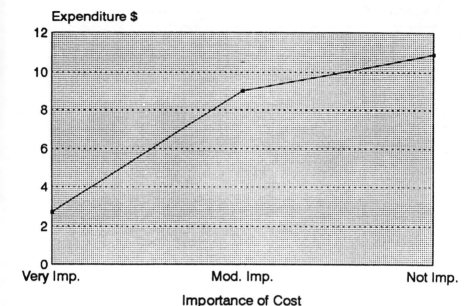

Figure 13.19   Line graph of mean expenditure by attitude to cost. Command:
GRAPH LINE = MEAN(EXP) BY COST/OUTFILE = 'A: GRAPH4'

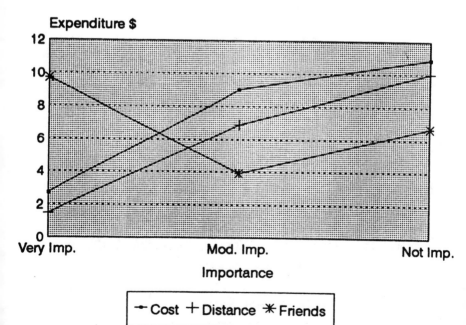

Figure 13.20   Line graph of mean expenditure by attitude scores. Command:
GRAPH LINE = MEAN(EXP) BY COST DIST FRNDS/OUTFILE = 'A: GRAPH5'

CRSE	Course (Q1)				Valid	Cum
Value label		Value	Frequency	Per cent	Per cent	Per cent
BA Leisure – PT		1	18	18.0	18.0	18.0
BA Leisure – FT		2	16	16.0	16.0	34.0
BA Tourism Man.		3	14	14.0	14.0	48.0
G Dip Leisure – PT		4	20	20.0	20.0	68.0
G Dip Leisure – FT		5	8	8.0	8.0	76.0
G Dip Tourism – PT		6	12	12.0	12.0	88.0
G Dip Tourism – FT		7	12	12.0	12.0	100.0
		Total	100	100.0	100.0	
Valid cases	100	Missing cases	0			

Figure 13.21   Frequencies weighted to 100
                    Commands: COMPUTE WT = 2
                                WEIGHT BY WT
                                FREQUENCIES/VARIABLES CRSE

Numbers versus percentages

The numbers in the pie chart and the scale in the Y-axis of the bar chart are in terms of the sample numbers rather than percentages. To get percentages WEIGHT the data first, so that the sample size becomes 100. In the case of the Student Leisure Survey, with a sample of 50, this involves weighting by 2. With a sample size of, say, 200 it would involved weighting by 0.5:

COMPUTE WT = 2.
WEIGHT BY WT.

The instruction: FREQUENCIES/VARIABLES PREF. now produces the output as shown in Figure 13.21, where the frequency column now adds to 100. Then to produce Figure 13.22 requires:

GRAPH BAR = PREF/OUTFILE = 'A:GRAPH6'.

The analysis process

The above is only a brief introduction to the mechanics of survey data analysis. While SPSS/PC is capable of much more sophisticated analyses, mastery of the procedures presented here can provide a good basis for more ambitious programmes of analysis.

Further reading

Practice rather than reading is required to master the material in this chapter. Further assistance can be found in the SPSS/PC and

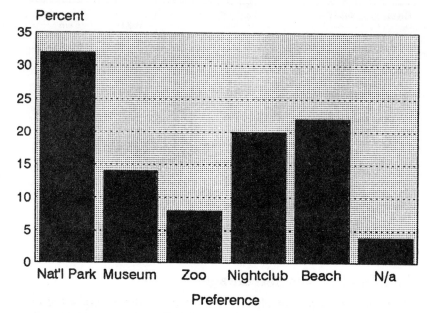

Figure 13.22 Bar graph of preferences with percentages. Command: GRAPH BAR = PREF/OUTFILE = 'A: GRAPH6'

Harvard graphics manuals, and Bryman and Cramer (1990) explore some of the more sophisticated capabilities of SPSS.

Appendix 13.1: Printout from: FREQUENCIES VARIABLES ALL

CRSE   Course (Q1)

Value Label	Value	Frequency	Per cent	Valid Per cent	Cum Per cent
Undergrad/Leisure	1	10	20.0	20.0	20.0
Undergrad/Tourism	2	9	18.0	18.0	38.0
Undergrad/Sport	3	8	16.0	16.0	54.0
Postgrad/Leisure	4	8	16.0	16.0	70.0
Postgrad/Tourism	5	7	14.0	14.0	84.0
Postgrad/Sport	6	8	16.0	16.0	100.0
	Total	50	100.0	100.0	

Valid cases   50   Missing cases   0

Page 3   SPSS/PC+   11/24/91

NPK   National park (Q2a)

Value Label	Value	Frequency	Per cent	Valid Per cent	Cum Per cent
No	0	26	52.0	52.0	52.0
Yes	1	24	48.0	48.0	100.0
	Total	50	100.0	100.0	

Valid cases   50   Missing cases   0

Page 4   SPSS/PC+   11/24/91

MUS   Museum (Q2b)

Value Label	Value	Frequency	Per cent	Valid Per cent	Cum Per cent
No	0	36	72.0	72.0	72.0
Yes	1	14	28.0	28.0	100.0
	Total	50	100.0	100.0	

Valid cases   50   Missing cases   0

Page 5   SPSS/PC+   11/24/91

ZOO   Zoo (Q2c)

Value Label	Value	Frequency	Per cent	Valid Per cent	Cum Per cent
No	0	37	74.0	74.0	74.0
Yes	1	13	26.0	26.0	100.0
	Total	50	100.0	100.0	

Valid cases   50   Missing cases   0

Page 6   SPSS/PC+   11/24/91

NTC   Nightclub (Q2d)

Value Label	Value	Frequency	Per cent	Valid Per cent	Cum Per cent
No	0	30	60.0	60.0	60.0
Yes	1	20	40.0	40.0	100.0
	Total	50	100.0	100.0	

Valid cases   50   Missing cases   0

Appendix 13.1 (continued)

Page 7			SPSS/PC+		11/24/91

BCH Beach (Q2e)

Value Label	Value	Frequency	Per cent	Valid Per cent	Cum Per cent
No	0	16	32.0	32.0	32.0
Yes	1	34	68.0	68.0	100.0
	Total	50	100.0	100.0	

Valid cases   50   Missing cases   0

Page 8			SPSS/PC+		11/24/91

PREF Preference (Q3)

Value Label	Value	Frequency	Per cent	Valid Per cent	Cum Per cent
National Park	1	16	32.0	33.3	33.3
Museum	2	7	14.0	14.6	47.9
Zoo	3	4	8.0	8.3	56.3
Nightclub	4	10	20.0	20.8	77.1
Beach	5	11	22.0	22.9	100.0
		2	4.0	MISSING	
	Total	50	100.0	100.0	

Valid cases   48   Missing cases   2

Page 9			SPSS/PC+		11/24/91

REAS1 First reason for enjoyment (Q4)

Value Label	Value	Frequency	Per cent	Valid Per cent	Cum Per cent
Relxation	1	17	34.0	35.4	35.4
Sense of escape	2	4	8.0	8.3	43.8
Commune with nature	3	3	6.0	6.3	50.0
Fresh air	4	2	4.0	4.2	54.2
Being with friends	5	2	4.0	4.2	58.3
Learning	6	5	10.0	10.4	68.8
Exercise	7	4	8.0	8.3	77.1
Refreshment for work	8	2	4.0	4.2	81.3
Meet people	9	1	2.0	2.1	83.3
Fun	10	5	10.0	10.4	93.8
Other	11	3	6.0	6.3	100.0
		2	4.0	MISSING	
	Total	50	100.0	100.0	

Valid cases   48   Missing cases   2

Appendix 13.1 (continued)

Page 10   SPSS/PC+   11/24/91

REAS2   Second reason for enjoyment (Q4)

Value Label	Value	Frequency	Per cent	Valid Per cent	Cum Per cent
Relxation	1	1	2.0	7.7	7.7
Sense of escape	2	1	2.0	7.7	15.4
Commune with nature	3	1	2.0	7.7	23.1
Being with friends	5	2	4.0	15.4	38.5
Exercise	7	3	6.0	23.1	61.5
Refreshment for work	8	2	4.0	15.4	76.9
Meet people	9	1	2.0	7.7	84.6
Other	11	1	2.0	7.7	92.3
		37	74.0	MISSING	
	Total	50	100.0	100.0	

Valid cases   13   Missing cases   37

Page 11   SPSS/PC+   11/24/91

EXP   Expenditure (Q5)

Value Label	Value	Frequency	Per cent	Valid Per cent	Cum Per cent
	0	17	34.0	35.4	35.4
	2	7	14.0	14.6	50.0
	4	6	12.0	12.5	62.5
	5	3	6.0	6.3	68.8
	8	1	2.0	2.1	70.8
	10	4	8.0	8.3	79.2
	15	2	4.0	4.2	83.3
	20	4	8.0	8.3	91.7
	25	1	2.0	2.1	93.8
	30	1	2.0	2.1	95.8
	40	2	4.0	4.2	100.0
		2	4.0	MISSING	
	Total	50	100.0	100.0	

Valid cases   48   Missing cases   2

Appendix 13.1 (continued)

| Page 12 | | | SPSS/PC+ | | 11/24/91 |

COST   Cost as a consideration (Q6)

Value Label	Value	Frequency	Per cent	Valid Per cent	Cum Per cent
Very Imp.	1	17	34.0	34.0	34.0
Moderately Imp.	2	22	44.0	44.0	78.0
Not Imp.	3	11	22.0	22.0	100.0
	Total	50	100.0	100.0	

Valid cases   50   Missing cases   0

| Page 13 | | | SPSS/PC+ | | 11/24/91 |

DIST   Distance as a consideration (Q6)

Value Label	Value	Frequency	Per cent	Valid Per cent	Cum Per cent
Very Imp.	1	9	18.0	18.0	18.0
Moderately Imp.	2	20	40.0	40.0	58.0
Not Imp.	3	21	42.0	42.0	100.0
	Total	50	100.0	100.0	

Valid cases   50   Missing cases   0

| Page 14 | | | SPSS/PC+ | | 11/24/91 |

FRNDS   Friends opinions as a consideration (Q6)

Value Label	Value	Frequency	Per cent	Valid Per cent	CumPer cent
Very Imp.	1	22	44.0	44.0	44.0
Moderately Imp.	2	14	28.0	28.0	72.0
Not Imp.	3	14	28.0	28.0	100.0
	Total	50	100.0	100.0	

Valid cases   50   Missing cases   0

14 Preparing a research report

This chapter outlines key elements of report presentation, including aspects of content, structure and layout. While much of the chapter is relevant to the writing of articles, in the main it focuses on the requirement of the consultancy report or monograph format.

Introduction

The importance of the report

In this chapter we consider the presentation of written reports. Reports are a key element of the world of management and planning. Feasibility studies, marketing plans, environmental impact assessments, recreation needs studies, tourism development plans, market research studies and performance appraisals all come in the form of written reports. The results of many academic studies are also produced in report, or monograph, format.

The medium is the message and in this case the medium is the written report. The ability to prepare a report, and the ability to recognise good quality and poor quality reports, should be seen as a key element in the skills of the professional manager. While form is no substitute for good content, a report which is poorly presented can undermine or even negate good content. While most of the researcher's attention should of course be focussed on achieving high quality substantive content, the aspects raised in this chapter also merit serious attention.

Getting started

In Chapter 3 it was indicated that researchers invariably leave too little time for report writing. Even when adequate time has been allocated in the timetable this is often whittled away and the writing of the report is delayed, leaving too little time. There is a tendency to put off report writing because it is *difficult*, and it is felt that, with a little more data analysis or a little more reading of the literature the process of writing the report will become *easier*. This is rarely the case – it is always difficult!

A regrettably common practice is for writers of reports to spend a great deal of their depleted time, with the deadline looming, writing and preparing material which could have been done much earlier in the process. There are often large parts of any report which can be written before data analysis is complete, or even started. Such parts include the introduction, statement of objectives, outline of theoretical or evaluative framework, literature review and description of the methodology. In addition, time-consuming activities such as arranging for maps, illustrations and cover designs to be produced should be done *earlier* rather than *later*.

Content

A report generally includes the following elements, and these are discussed in turn below.

- Cover
- Title page
- Contents page(s)
- Executive summary
- Preface/Foreword
- Acknowledgements
- Main body of the report
- Appendices.

Cover page and title page

The cover should include:

- Title of report
- Author(s)
- Institution/publisher (possibly on back cover or spine)
- ISBN (Back cover – see below).

The title page should include the following (starred items are sometimes on the reverse of the title page):

- Title of report
- Author(s)
- Institution/publisher, including address, phone numbers*
- Sponsoring organisation (e.g. 'Report to the Tourism Commission')
- Date of publication*
- If the report is for sale: ISBN*.

ISBN is the International Standard Book Number. All publications in the western world have a ten digit ISBN, the first five identifying the publisher. Free deposit copies of publications must be sent to National Libraries. The ISBN makes it easy to order publications through bookshops and ensures that the publication is catalogued in library systems around the world.

Contents page(s)

The contents page(s) should list:

		Page
Executive summary		xx
Preface/Foreword if appropriate		xx
Acknowledgements if appropriate		xx
I	Section/Chapter I	NN
	Subsections	NN
II	Section/Chapter II	NN
	Subsections	
III	Section/Chapter III	NN
	Subsections	
Etc.		
References		NN
Appendices		NN
1	Title	NN
2	Title	NN
Etc.		
List of tables		
1.1 Title		NN
1.2 Title		NN
Etc.		
List of diagrams/illustrations		
1.1 Title		NN
1.2 Title		NN
Etc.		

Executive summary

An executive summary is sometimes thought of as the summary for the 'busy executive' who does not have time to read the whole report, but really refers to the idea that it should contain information necessary to take *executive* action on the basis of the report.

An executive summary should contain a summary of the whole report, that is:

- the background/context/objectives;
- methods/data sources;
- main findings;
- conclusions;
- recommendations, where appropriate.

It follows that the executive summary should be written *last*.
A very approximate guide to length is as follows:

Report length	Exec. summary length
Up to 20 pages	1/2 pages
Up to 50 pages	3/4 pages
Up to 100 pages	5/6 pages

Preface/Foreword

Prefaces or forewords are used for a variety of purposes. Usually they explain the origins of the study and outline any qualifications or limitations, and acknowledgements of assistance if there is no separate 'acknowledgements' section. Sometimes a significant individual is asked to write a Foreword, such as the director of an institution, a minister or an eminent academic.

Acknowledgements

It is clearly a matter of courtesy to acknowledge any assistance received during the course of a research project. People and institutions who might be acknowledged include:

- funding organisations;
- liaison officers of funding organisations;
- members of steering committees;
- organisations and individuals who have provided access to information etc.;
- staff employed, including interviewers, coders, computer programmers, typists, etc.;
- individuals (including supervisors!) who have given advice, commented on report drafts, etc.; (collectively) individuals who responded to questionnaires etc.

Main body of the report-technical aspects

Section numbering

It is usual to number not only the major sections/chapters, but also sub-sections within chapters. One system used is as follows:

I Major section/chapter I
  I.1 Sub-section I.1
    I.1.1 *Sub-sub-section I.1.i*
    I.1.1 *Sub-sub-section I.1.2*
  I.2 Sub-section I.2
    I.2.1 *Sub-sub-section I.2.1*
II Major section/chapter II
  II.1 etc. etc.

An alternative is to adopt different number/letter series for the different levels, e.g.:

I Major section/chapter I
  A. Sub-section IA
    1.Sub-sub-section IA.1
    2.Sub-sub-section IA.2
  B. Sub-section IB
    1.Sub-sub-section IB.1
II Major section /chapter II
  A. Sub-section IIA
  etc.etc.

Paragraph numbering

In some reports paragraphs are individually numbered. This can be useful for reference purposes when a report is being discussed in committees etc. Paragraphs can be numbered in a single series for the whole report or chapter by chapter – 1.1, 1.2, 1.3, etc. in chapter 1 and 2.1, 2.2, 2.3 etc. in chapter 2, and so on.

Page numbering

One problem in putting together long reports, especially when a number of authors are responsible for different sections, is to organise page numbering so that it follows on from chapter to chapter. This can be avoided by numbering each chapter separately, for example:

Chapter 1	pages 1.1 1.2 1.3 1.4 etc.
Chapter 2	pages 2.1 2.2 2.3 2.4 etc.
Chapter 3	pages 3.1 3.2 3.3 3.4 etc.
Etc.	
Appendices	pages A1 A2 A3 etc.

Word processors can be made to produce page numbers in this form by using the header and/or page-numbering facilities.

It is general practice for the title page, contents, acknowledgements, and the executive summary, to be numbered using roman numerals and for the report proper to start at page 1 with normal numbers; again, most word processors will produce this.

Heading hierarchy

In the main body of the report a hierarchy of heading styles should be used, with the major chapter/section headings being in the most prominent style and with decreasing emphasis for sub-section headings. Such a convention helps readers to know where they are in a document. When a team is involved in writing a report it is clearly sensible to agree these heading styles in advance. With modern word processor systems and printers a large hierarchy is available:

HEADING 1

HEADING 2

HEADING 3

HEADING 4

HEADING 5

<u>HEADING 6</u>

HEADING 7

<u>Heading 8</u>

Heading 9

Typing layout/spacing

Essays and books tend to use the convention of starting new paragraphs by indenting the first line. Report style is to separate paragraphs by a blank line and not to indent the first line. Report style also tends to have more headings. A document typed/word processed in report style usually leaves wide margins which raises the question as to whether it is necessary to print documents in 1.5 or double space format or whether single spacing is adequate (and more environmentally friendly!).

Main body of the report – structure and content

Structure

The structure of a report is of fundamental importance. It needs to be discussed thoroughly, particularly when a team is involved. While all reports have certain structural features in common, the important aspects concern the underlying argument and how that relates to the objectives of the study and any data collection and analysis involved. This relates fundamentally to the research objectives, theoretical or evaluative framework and overall strategy, as discussed in Chapter 3.

A report structure, similar to the contents page, with target word or page lengths indicated, should be agreed before writing starts. While an agreed structure is a necessary starting point, it is necessary to be flexible. As drafting gets going it may be found that what was originally conceived as one chapter needs to be divided into two or three chapters, or what was thought of as a separate chapter can be incorporated into another chapter or into an appendix. Throughout, consideration needs to be given to the overall length of the report, in terms of words or pages.

When a questionnaire survey is involved, there is a tendency to structure the presentation according to the sequence of questions in the questionnaire and, correspondingly, the sequence of tables as they are produced by the computer. This is *not* an appropriate way to proceed! Questionnaires are structured for ease of interview, for the convenience of interviewer and/or respondent: they do *not* provide a suitable sequence and structure for a report.

Functions

A report can be thought of in two ways:

- the report as narrative;
- the report as record.

Narrative means that a report has to tell a story to the reader. The writer of the report therefore needs to think of the flow of the argument – the 'story' - in the same way that the writer of a novel has to consider the plot.

The report as *record* means that a report is often also a reference source where people may wish to look for information. Being a good record may involve including extensive detailed information which may interfere with the process of 'story telling'. The latter may call for only simplified information or key features of the data.

Serving both functions therefore requires careful consideration of the role of tables, graphics and appendices, as discussed below.

Audiences and style

The style, format and length of a report is largely influenced by the type of audience at which it is aimed. Audiences may be:

- popular;
- decision-makers;
- experts.

By *popular* is meant the general public who might read a report of research in a newspaper or magazine – full research reports are therefore not generally written for a popular readership.

Decision-makers are groups such as elected members of councils, government ministers, members of boards of companies, or senior executives who may not have a detailed knowledge of a particular field.

Experts are professionals etc. who are familiar with the subject matter of the report.

Clearly the amount of technical jargon used and the detail with which data are presented will be affected by this question of audience.

The narrative

The narrative of a research report usually develops along the following lines:

A. Introduction/background/purpose/objectives/statement of problem(s) terms of reference/context (one or more sections).
B. Discussion of issues/problems/hypotheses/theories/possible solutions/ informations needs (one or more sections).
C. Data collection – establishing of requirements (should reflect B)/alternatives considered/methods used/response rates.
D. Issue/topic 1
E. Issue/topic 2   } Results/analysis (should reflect B).
F. Issue/topic 3
    Etc.
X. Summary/conclusions/synthesis/recommendations (one or more sections).

The items indicated above may emerge in a variety of chapter/ section configurations. For example, sections A and B could be one chapter/section or three or four, depending on the complexity of the project.

The introductory section(s), A, should reflect the considerations which emerged in the initial steps (1,2 and 6 – see Chapter 3) of the planning stages of the project. 'Context' includes reference to the environment in which the research is situated, including any initial literature review which may be involved.

Section(s) B should reflect steps 3–5 and 7–8 in the research planning process and may include further reference to the literature.

In sections B and C it is important that the relation between data requirements and the research questions and theoretical or evaluative framework be explained, as discussed in Chapters 3 and 10. It should be clear from the discussion *why* the data are being collected – and how this relates to the planning/management/theoretical issues raised; how it was anticipated that the information collected would solve or shed light on the problems/issues raised, or aid decision-making.

In section C methodology should be described in detail; it should be clear why particular techniques were chosen, how samples were selected, and what data collection instruments were used.

Where sample surveys are involved full information should be given on response rates and sample sizes obtained and some indication given of the consequences in terms of confidence intervals, as discussed in Chapter 11. These technical aspects of the results of any survey work can be included in the methodology section of the report or in the first of the results sections.

The results/analysis section D, E, F etc., should ideally be structured by the discussion in B, around issues, elements of the research problem.

Sometimes conclusions are set out in the results/analysis section(s) and all that is required in the final section is to reiterate and draw them together. In other cases the final section includes the final stage of analysis and the drawing of conclusions. In writing the final section/ chapter it is vital to refer back to the terms of reference/objectives to ensure that *all objectives have been met*.

Not all research reports include 'recommendations'. Recommendations are most likely to arise from evaluative research.

The report as 'record'

It is wise to think beyond the immediate use of a research report, in terms of a report as the definitive *record* of the research conducted. It should therefore contain a summary of all the relevant data collected in a form which would be useful for any future user of the report. This means that, while data may be presented in the main body of the report in a highly condensed and summarised form in order to produce a readable report, it should also be presented in as much detail as possible, 'for the record'. Data included 'for the record' can be placed in an appendix or, when large amounts of data are involved, in a separate *statistical volume*.

For example the table in Appendix 6.1 would generally be considered to be too complex for inclusion in the main body of a report so would be included, as it is in this book, in an appendix. In the main body of the report a simplified table could be included, giving details of just four or five of the fastest growing activities and the declining activities – in fact those activities which would be discussed in the text. Alternatively a graphic of this limited amount of data could be presented.

In the case of questionnaire survey data it can be a good idea to provide a *statistical appendix* which includes tables from all the questions in the order they appear in the questionnaire. Any reader interested in a specific aspect of the data is then able to locate and use it. The main body of the report can then be structured around issues and not be constrained by the structure of the questionnaire.

Tables and graphics

When presenting the results of quantitative research, an appropriate balance must be struck between the use of tables, graphics and text. A number of alternatives exist:

A. No tables or graphics in the report;
B. No tables but use of graphics;
C. Graphics in the body of the report; all tables included in an appendix;
D. Graphics and simple or simplified tables in the body of the report; more complex tables included in an appendix;
E. No graphics; tables in the body of the report and/or in an appendix.

The decision on which approach to use depends partly on the complexity of the data to be presented, but mainly on the *type of audience*.

For instance, alternative A – no tables or graphics – might be used for a 'popular' summary of a study in a newspaper or magazine, when space is limited. However, in most cases such a presentation would be enhanced by the use of option B – no tables but use of graphics.

Options C or D are the most common in reports being prepared for government or private companies. If the report is intended to be read by people who are not technically qualified, for example elected council members or members of boards of companies, the tendency would be to increase the amount of graphics and reduce the use of tables. If the report is to be read mainly by qualified personnel then graphics may be less important.

Tables/graphics versus text

Tables, graphics and text each have a distinctive role to play in the presentation of the study findings. Tables provide information; graphics *illustrate* that information so that patterns can be seen in a visual way. The text should be telling a story or developing an argument and 'orchestrating' tables and graphics to support that task.

The following sentence does little more than repeat what is in the table: it says nothing to the reader about the difference between men's and women's participation patterns, which is presumably the purpose of the exercise.

Table 14.1 indicates that the top five sports and physical recreation activities for men are walking (21%), snooker/billiards (17%), indoor

Table 14.1 Sports/physical recreation participation top five activities for men and women, Great Britain, 1986

Activity	% Participating in four weeks prior to interview (most popular quarter)	
	Males	Females
Walking	21	18
Football	6	•
Snooker/billiards	17	3
Swimming – indoor	9	10
Darts	9	3
Keep fit/yoga	1	5

Source: General Household Survey/OPCS.

swimming (9%), darts (9%) and football (6%), whereas for women the five most popular activities are walking (18%), indoor swimming (10%), keep fit/yoga (5%), snooker/billiards (3%) and darts (3%).

A more informative commentary, which points out particular features of the data in the table, would be as follows:

Men and women may have more in common in their patterns of leisure activity than is popularly imagined: Table 14.1 indicates that four activities – walking, swimming, snooker/billiards and darts – are included in the top five most popular sport and physical recreation activities for both men and women. While in general men's participation levels are higher than those of women, the table shows that women's participation rate exceeds that of men for two of the activities, namely keep fit/yoga and swimming.

Typically then, the text should be developing an argument and should make reference to the table or graphic to help the argument along or, if the report is primarily descriptive, the text should draw attention to notable features of the data in a table or graphic – the highest or lowest or the greatest contrast or the lack of contrast, etc. etc.

Presentation

Diagrams and tables should, as far as possible, be complete in themselves. That is, they should be *fully* labeled so that the reader can understand them without necessarily referring to the text. They should usually indicate the source of data, but where a report is based primarily on one data source, such as a survey, it is not necessary to indicate this on every table and diagram (however, some consultants tend to do this so that if a user photo-copies just one table or diagram then its source is still indicated).

In conclusion

Ultimately the writing of a good research report is an art and a skill which develops with practice. Reports can be improved enormously as a result of comments from others – often because the writer has been 'too close' to the report for too long to be able to see glaring faults or omissions. The researcher/writer can also usually spot opportunities for improvement if he or she takes a short break and returns to the draft report with 'fresh eyes'. Finally, checking and double checking the report for typing, spelling and typographical errors is well worth the laborious effort.

Research is a creative process which, in the words of Norbert Elias with which we began this text, aims to 'make known something previously unknown to human beings... to advance human knowledge, to make it more certain or better fitting.. the aim is .. *discovery*'. It is hoped that this book will provide some assistance in that process of discovery and that the reader will enjoy some of the satisfactions and rewards which can come from worthwhile research.

Further reading

The best reading relevant to this chapter is the critical reading of research reports.

References

Age, The (1982) *The Age Lifestyle Study for the Eighties*, Melbourne: D. Syme & Co.

American Psychological Association (1983) *Publication Manual*, Washington, D.C.: APA.

Archer, B. H. (1987) 'Demand forecasting and estimation', Ch. 7 of Ritchie and Goeldner *op.cit.*, pp 77–86.

Australian Bureau of Statistics (1988) *Information Paper: Time Use Pilot Survey, Sydney, May-June 1987*. Cat. No. 4111.1, Sydney: ABS.

Bailey, P. (1978) *Leisure and Class in Victorian England*, London: Routledge.

Bailey, P. (1989) 'Leisure, culture and the historian: reviewing the first generation of leisure historiography in Britain', *Leisure Studies*, Vol.8, No.2, pp 107–128.

Baretje, R. (1964) *Bibliographie Touristique*, Aix-en-Provence: Centre d'Etudes du Tourisme.

Barnett, L. A. (ed) (1987) *Research about Leisure: Past, Present and Future*, Champaign, Ill.: Sagamore Publishing.

Barton, A. H. and Lazarsfield, P. (1969) 'Some functions of qualitative analysis of social research', in McCall and Simmons, *op. cit.*, pp 163–195.

BBC 1978 - *see* British Broadcasting Corporation.

Bickmore, D., Shaw M. and Tulloch, T. (1980) 'Lifestyles on maps', *Geographical Magazine*, Vol. 52, No. 11, pp 763–769.

Birenbaum, A. and Sagarin, E. (eds) (1973) *People in Places: The Sociology of the Familiar*, London: Nelson.

Borman, K. M., LeCompt, M. D. and Goetz, J. P. (1986) 'Ethnographic and qualitative research design and why it doesn't work', *American Behavioral Scientist*, Vol.30, No.1, pp 42–57.

Bramham, P. and Henry, I. (1985) 'Political ideology and leisure policy in the United Kingdom', *Leisure Studies*, Vol.4, No.1, pp 1–19.

British Broadcasting Corporation (1978) *The People's Use of Time*, London: BBC.

Bryman, A. and Cramer, D. (1990) *Quantitative Data Analysis for Social Scientists*, London: Routledge.

Bulmer, M. (1982) *Social Research Ethics*, London: Macmillan.

Burch, W. R. Jr. (1964) *A New Look at an Old Friend – Observation as a Technique for Recreation Research*, Portland, Oregon: Pacific Northwest Forest and Range Experiment Station.

Burch, W. R. (1981) 'The ecology of metaphor: spacing regularities for humans and other primates in urban and wild habitats', *Leisure Sciences*, Vol.4, No.3, pp 213–230.

Burgess, R. G. (ed) (1982) *Field Research: A Sourcebook and Field Manual*, London: Allen and Unwin.

Burkart, A. J. and Medlik, S. (1981) *Tourism: Past, Present and Future*, 2nd Edn., London: Heinemann.

Burton, T. L. (1971) *Experiments in Recreation Research*, London: Allen and Unwin.

Cairns, J., Jennet, N. and Sploane, P. J. (1986) 'The economics of professional team sports: a survey of theory and evidence', *Journal of Economic Studies*, Vol.13, No.1, pp 3–80.

Calder, A. and Sheridan, D. (1984) *Speak for Yourself: A Mass Observation Anthology, 1937–49*, London: Jonathan Cape.

Calder, B. (1977) 'Focus groups and the nature of qualitative marketing research', *Journal of Marketing Research*, Vol.14, August, pp 353–364.

Campbell, F. L. (1970) 'Participant observation in outdoor recreation', *Journal of Leisure Research*, Vol.2, No.4, pp 226–236.

Chase, D. R. and Godbey, G. C. (1983) 'The accuracy of self-reported participation rates', *Leisure Studies*, Vol.2, No.2, pp 231–236.

Child, E. (1983) 'Play and Culture: a study of English and Asian children', *Leisure Studies*, Vol.2, No.2, pp 169–186.

Christensen, J. E. (1980) 'A second look at the informal interview...', *Journal of Leisure Research*, Vol.12, No.2, pp 183–186.

Christensen, J. E. (1988) 'Statistical and methodological issues in leisure research', in L. A. Barnett, *op. cit.*, pp 175–192.

Cities Commission (1975) *Australians' Use of Time*, Canberra: Cities Commission.

Clarke, J. and Critcher, C. (1985) *The Devil Makes Work: Leisure in Capitalist Britain*, London: Macmillan.

Coalter, F. (1990) 'Analysing leisure policy', in I. Henry (ed) *Management and Planning in the Leisure Industries*, London: Macmillan, pp 149–178.

Cohen, E. (1984) 'The sociology of tourism: approaches, issues, and findings', *Annual Review of Sociology*, Vol.10, pp 373–392.

Coppock, J. T. (1982) 'Geographical contributions to the study of leisure', *Leisure Studies*, Vol.1, No.1, pp 1–28.

Coppock, J. T. and Duffield, B. S. (1975) *Recreation in the Countryside: A Spatial Analysis*, London: Macmillan.

Corley, J. (1982) 'Employment in the leisure industries in Britain 1960–80', *Leisure Studies*, Vol.1, No.1, pp 109–11.

Cowling D. *et al* (1983) *Identifying the Market: Catchment Areas of Sports Centres and Swimming Pools*, Study 24, London: The Sports Council.

Cumming, E. and Henry, W. (1961) Growing old: the process of disengagement, New York: Basic Books

Cunneen, C. and Lynch, R. (1988) 'The social meaning of conflict in riots at the Australian Grand Prix motorcycle races', *Leisure Studies*, Vol.7, No.1, pp 1–20.

Cunningham, H. (1980) *Leisure in the Industrial Revolution*, London: Croom Helm.

Dann, G. and Cohen, E. (1991) 'Sociology and tourism', *Annals of Tourism Research*, Vol.18, No.1, pp 155–169.

Dare, B., Welton, G. and Coe, W. (1987) *Concepts of Leisure in Western Thought*, Dubuque, Iowa: Kendall Hunt.

DASETT – see Department of the Arts, Sport, the Environment, Tourism and Territories.

Deem, R. (1986) *All Work and No Play? The Sociology of Women and Leisure*, Milton Keynes: Open University Press.

Department of the Arts, Sport, the Environment, Tourism and Territories (1988a) *The Economic Impact of Sport and Recreation–Household Expenditure*, Technical Paper No. 1, Canberra: AGPS.

Department of the Arts, Sport, the Environment, Tourism and Territories (1988b) *The Economic Impact of Sport and Recreation – Regular Physical Activity*, Technical Paper No. 2, Canberra: AGPS.

Duffield, B. S. *et al.* (1983) *A Digest of Sports Statistics*, 1st Edn., Information Series &, London: The Sports Council.

Eadington, W. R. and Redman, M. (1991) 'Economics and tourism', *Annals of Tourism Research*, Vol.18, No.1, pp 41–56.

Elias, N. (1986) 'Introduction', in N. Elias and E. Dunning *Quest for Excitement: Sport and Leisure in the Civilizing Process*, Oxford: Basil Blackwell, pp 19–62.

Ely, M. (1981) 'Systematic Observation as a Recreation Research Tool', in D. Mercer (ed) *Outdoor Recreation: Australian Perspectives*, Malvern, Vic.: Sorrett, pp 57–67.

Fielding, N. G. and Lee, R. M. (eds) (1991) *Using Computers in Qualitative Research*, London: Sage.

Fiske, J. (1983) 'Surfalism and Sandiotics: the Beach in Oz Popular Culture', *Australian Journal of Cultural Studies*, Vol.1, No.2, pp 120–149.

Frank Small and Associates (1988) *Tourism Survey Kit*, Sydney: Tourism Commission of New South Wales.

Glancy, M. (1986) 'Participant observation in the recreation setting', *Journal of Leisure Research*, Vol.18, No.2, pp 59–80.

Glyptis, S. A. (1991) *Countryside Recreation*, Harlow: Longman.

Glyptis, S. A. (1981a) 'People at Play in the Countryside', *Geography*, Vol.66, pp 277–285.

Glyptis, S. A. (1981b) 'Room to relax in the countryside', *The Planner*, Vol.67, No.5, pp 120–122.

Goeldner, C. R. and Dicke, K. (1980) *Bibliography of Tourism and Travel Research*, 9 Vols., Boulder, Colorado: University of Colorado.

Goffman, I. (1959) *The Presentation of Self in Everyday Life*, Garden City: Doubleday/Anchor.

Gold, S. M. (1972) 'The non-use of neighbourhood parks', *Journal of the American Institute of Planners*, November, pp 369–378.

Graburn, N. H. H. and Jafari, J. (1991) 'Introduction : tourism social sciences', *Annals of Tourism Research*, Vol.18, No.1, (Special Issue: Tourism Social Sciences), pp 1–11.

Grant, D. (1984) 'Another look at the beach', *Australian Journal of Cultural Studies*, Vol.2, No.2, pp 131–138.

Green, E. Hebron, S. and Woodward, D. (1990) *Women's Leisure. What Leisure?*, London: Macmillan.

Grichting, W. L. and Caltabiano, M. L. (1986) 'Amount and direction of bias in survey interviewing', *Australian Psychologist*, Vol.21, No.1, pp 69–78.

Griffin, C., Hobson, D., MacIntosh, S., and McCabe, T. (1982) 'Women and leisure', in J Hargreaves (ed) *Sport, Culture and Ideology*, London: Routledge, pp 99–116.

Griffith, G. and Veal, A. J. (1985) *Leisure Centres in Inner London*, unpublished report to the Greater London Council, London: Polytechnic of North London.

Hall, S. and Jefferson T. (eds) (1976) *Resistance Through Rituals: Youth Culture in Post-war Britain*, London: Hutchinson.

Hantrais, L. and Kamphorst, T. J. (1987) *Trends in the Arts: A Multinational Perspective*, Amersfoot, Holland: Giordano Bruno.

Hatry, H. P. and Dunn, D. R. (1971) *Measuring the Effectiveness of Local Government Services: Recreation*, Washington, D.C.: The Urban Institute.

Havitz, M. E. and Sell, J. A. (1991) 'The experimental method and leisure/recreation research: promoting a more active role', *Society and Leisure*, Vol.14, No.1, pp 47–68.

Heberlein, T. A. and Dunwiddie, P. (1979) 'Systematic observation of use levels, campsite selection and visitor characteristics at a High Mountain Lake', *Journal of Leisure Research*, Vol.11, No.4, pp 307–316.

Henderson, K. (1990) 'Reality comes through a prism: method choices in leisure research', *Society and Leisure*, Vol.13, No.1, pp 169–188.

Henley Centre for Forecasting (1986) *The Economic Impact and Importance of Sport in the United Kingdom*, London: Sports Council.

Henley Centre for Forecasting (Quarterly) *Leisure Futures*, London.

Henry, I. and Spink, J. (1990) 'Planning for Leisure: The Commercial and Public Sectors', in I. P. Henry (ed) *Management and Planning in the Leisure Industries*, London: Macmillan, pp 33–69.

Hoinville, G. and Jowell, R. (1978) *Survey Research Practice*, London: Heinemann.

Hollands, R. G. (1985) 'Working class youth, leisure and the search for work', in S. R. Parker and A. J. Veal (eds) *Work, Non-work and Leisure*, London: Leisure Studies Association, pp 3–29.

Howard D. R. and Crompton J. L. (1980) *Financing, Managing and Marketing, Recreation and Park Resources*, Dubuque, Iowa: Wm. C. Brown.

Hudson, S. (1988) *How to Conduct Community Needs Assessment Surveys in Public Parks and Recreation*, Columbus, Ohio: Publishing Horizons.

Huizinga, J. (1955) *Homo Ludens: A Study of the Play Element in Culture*, Boston: Beacon Press.

Hurst, F. (1987) 'Enroute surveys', in Ritchie and Goeldner, *op. cit.*, pp 401–415.

Ingham, R. (1986) 'Psychological contributions to the study of leisure – Part One', *Leisure Studies*, Vol.5, No.3, pp 255–280.

Ingham, R. (1987) 'Psychological contributions to the study of leisure – Part Two', *Leisure Studies*, Vol.6, No.1, pp 1–14.

Jackson, E. L. and Burton, T. L. (eds) (1989) *Understanding Leisure and Recreation: Mapping the Past and Charting the Future*, State College, PA.: Venture.

Jafari, J. and Aaser, D. (1988) 'Tourism as the subject of doctoral dissertations', *Annals of Tourism Research*, Vol.15, No.3, pp 407–429.

Kamphorst, T. J. and Roberts, K. (eds) (1989) *Trends in Sports: A Multinational Perspective*, Culemborg, Holland: Giordano Bruno.

Kelly, J. R. (1980) 'Leisure and quality: beyond the quantitative barrier in research', Ch. 23 of T L Goodale & P A Witt (eds) *Recreation and Leisure: Issues in an Era of Change*, State College, Penn.: Venture, pp 300–314.

Kelly, J. R. (1982) *Leisure*, Englewood Cliffs, NJ: Prentice-Hall.

Kelly, J. R. (1983) Leisure Identities and Interactions, London: Allen & Unwin.

Kelly, J. R. (1987) *Recreation Trends - Toward the Year 2000*, Champaign, Ill.: Management Learning Laboratories.

Kelsey, C. and Gray, H. (1986a) *The Citizen Survey Process in Parks and Recreation*, Reston, VA.: American All. for Health, P.E., Recreation and Dance.

Kelsey, C. and Gray, H. (1986b) *The Feasibility Study Process for Parks and Recreation*, Reston, VA.: American Alliance for Health, P.E., Recreation and Dance.

Kidder, L. H. (1981) *Selltiz, Wrightsman and Cook's Research Methods in Social Relations*, New York: Holt, Reinhart and Winston.

Knight, J. and Parker, S. (1978) *A Bibliography of British Publications on Leisure 1960–1977*, London: Leisure Studies Association.

Kraus, R. and Allen, L. (1987) *Research and Evaluation in*

Recreation, Parks, and Leisure Studies, Columbus, Ohio: Publishing Horizons.

Krenz, C. and Sax, G. (1986) 'What quantitative research is and why it doesn't work', *American Behavioral Scientist*, Vol.30, No.1, pp 58–69.

Krueger, R. A. (1988) *Focus Groups: A Practical Guide for Applied Research*, Newbury Park, Calif.: Sage.

Labovitz, S. and Hagedorn, R. (1971) *Introduction to Social Research*, New York: McGraw-Hill.

LaPage, W. F. (1981) 'A further look at the informal interview', *Journal of Leisure Research*, Vol.13, No.2, pp 174–176.

LaPage, W. F. (1987) 'Using panels for tourism and travel research', in Ritchie and Goeldner, *op. cit.*, pp 425–432.

Lavrakas, P. K. (1987) *Telephone Survey Methods: Sampling, Selection and Supervision*, Newbury Park, CA: Sage.

Lofland, J. and Lofland, L. H. (1984) *Analyzing Social Settings: A Guide to Qualitative Observation and Analysis*, 2nd Edn., Belmont, CA: Wadsworth.

Lucas, R. C. (1970) *User Evaluation of Campgrounds*, St Paul, Minn.: U.S. Forest Service.

MacCannell, D. (1976) *The Tourist: A New Theory of the Leisure Class*, London: Macmillan.

Marriott, K. (1987) *Recreation Planning: A Manual for Local Government*, Adelaide: Dept. of Recreation and Sport, South Australia.

Marsh, P. *et al.* (1978) *The Rules of Disorder*, London: Routledge.

Martin, S. and Mason, W. (Annual) *The UK Sports, Entertainment etc. Market*, Sudbury, Suffolk: Leisure Consultants.

Matthews, H. G. and Richter, L. (1991) 'Political science and tourism', *Annals of Tourism Research*, Vol.18, No.1, pp 120–135.

McCall, G. J. and Simmons, J. L. (eds) (1969) *Issues in Participant Observation*, Reading, Mass.: Addison-Wesley.

Mitchell, A. (1985) *The Nine American Lifestyles*, New York: Collier Macmillan.

Mitchell, L. S. (1987) 'Research on the geography of tourism', in Ritchie and Goeldner, *op. cit.*, pp 191–202.

Mitchell, L. S. and Murphy, P. E. (1991) 'Geography and tourism', *Annals of Tourism Research*, Vol.18, No.1, pp 57–70.

Moeller, G. H. *et al.* (1980a) 'The informal interview as a technique for recreation research', *Journal of Leisure Research*, Vol.12, No.2, pp 174–182.

Moeller, G. H. *et al.* (1980b) 'A response to 'A second look at the informal interview'', *Journal of Leisure Research*, Vol.12, No.2, pp 187–188.

Moeller, G. H. and Shafer, E. L. (1987) 'The Delphi technique: a tool for long-range tourism and travel planning', Ch. 34 of Ritchie and Goeldner, *op.cit.*, pp 417–424.

Murphy, J. F. (ed) (1974) *Concepts of Leisure: Philosophical Implications*, Englewood Cliffs, N. J.: Prentice-Hall.

Myerscough, J. (1988) *The Economic Importance of the Arts in Britain*, London: Policy Studies Institute.

Norusis, M. J. (1986) *SPSS/PC+ for the IBM PC/XT/AT*, Chicago: SPSS Inc.

O'Brien, S. and Ford, R. (1988) 'Can we at last say goodbye to social class? An examination of the usefulness and stability of some alternative methods of measurement', *Journal of the Market Research Society*, Vol.30, No.3, pp 289–332.

OECD – Organisation for Economic Cooperation and Development (Annual) *International Tourism and Tourism Policies in OECD Member Countries*, Paris: OECD.

Oppenheim, A. N. (1966) *Questionnaire and Attitude Measurement*, London: Heinemann.

Parker, S. (1971) *The Future of Work and Leisure*, London: Palladin.

Parry, N. C. A. (1983) 'Sociological contributions to the study of leisure', *Leisure Studies*, Vol.2, No.1, pp 57–82.

Patmore, J. A. (1983) *Recreation and Resources*, Oxford: Basil Blackwell.

Pearce, D. (1987) *Tourism Today: a Geographical Analysis*, Harlow, UK: Longman.

Pearce, P. L. and Stringer, P. F. (1991) 'Psychology and tourism', *Annals of Tourism Research*, Vol.18, No.1, pp 136–154.

Peine, J. D. (1984) *Proceedings of a Workshop on Unobstrusive Techniques to Study Social Behavior in Parks*, Atlanta, Georgia: National Park Service, Southeast Regional Office.

Peterson, K. I. (1987) 'Qualitative research methods for the travel and tourism industry', Ch. 36 of Ritchie & Goeldner, *op. cit.*, pp 433–438.

Pizam, A. (1987) 'Planning a tourism research investigation', in Ritchie and Goeldner, *op. cit.*, pp 63–76.

Plog, S. C. (1987) 'Understanding psychographics in tourism research', in Ritchie and Goeldner, *op. cit.*, pp 203–213.

Rapoport, R. and Rapoport, R. N. (1975) *Leisure and the Family Life Cycle*, London: Routledge.

Reynolds, F. and Johnson, D. (1978) 'Validity of focus group findings', *Journal of Advertising Research*, pp 3–24.

Richter, L. K. (1987) 'The political dimensions of tourism', in Ritchie and Goeldner, *op. cit.*, pp 215–227.

Ritchie J. R. B. and Goeldner, C. R. (eds) (1987) *Travel, Tourism and Hospitality Research*, New York: John Wiley.

Roberts, K. (1978) *Contemporary Society and the Growth of Leisure*, London: Longman.

Roberts, K. (1983) *Youth and Leisure*, London: Allen & Unwin.

Robertson, R. W. and Veal, A. J. (1987) *Port Hacking Visitor Use Study*, Sydney: Centre for Leisure and Tourism Studies, UTS.

Rojek, C. (1985) *Capitalism and Leisure* Theory, London: Tavistock.

Rojek, C. (1989) 'Leisure and recreation theory', in Jackson and Burton, *op. cit.*, pp 69–88.

Rojek. C. (1990) 'Baudrillard and leisure', *Leisure Studies*, Vol.9, No.1, pp 7–20.

Ronkainen, I. A. and Woodside, A. G. (1987) 'Advertising conversion studies', in Ritchie and Goeldner, *op. cit.*, pp 481–487.

Ruddell, E. J. and Hammit, W. E. (1987) 'Prospect refuge theory: a psychological orientation for edge effect in recreation environments', *Journal of Leisure Research*, Vol.19, No.4, pp 249–260.

Russell, B. (1935) *In Praise of Idleness and Other Essays*, London: Allen & Unwin.

Shadish, W. R. Jr., Cook, T. D. and Leviton, L. C. (1991) *Foundations of Program Evaluation: Theories of Practice*, Newbury Park, CA.: Sage.

Shaw, M. (1984) *Sport and Leisure Participation and Life-styles in different Residential Neighbourhoods*, London: Sports Council/SSRC.

Shih, D. (1986) 'VALS as a tool of tourism marketing research', *Journal of Travel Research*, Spring, pp 2–11.

Smith, M. (1985) 'A participant observer study of a 'rough' working class pub', *Leisure Studies*, Vol.4, No.3, pp 293–306.

Smith, S. L. J. (1983) *Recreation Geography*, Harlow, UK: Longman.

Torkildsen, G. (1983) *Leisure and Recreation Management*, London: Spon.

Tourism and Recreation Research Unit (TRRU) (1983) *Recreation Site Survey Manual: Methods and Techniques for Conducting Visitor Surveys*, London: Spon.

Towner, J. and Wall, G. (1991) 'History and tourism', *Annals of Tourism Research*, Vol.18. No.1, pp 71–84.

Tyre, G. L. and Siderelis, C. D. (1978) 'Instant-count sampling - a technique for estimating recreation use in municipal settings', *Journal of Leisure Research*, Vol.10, N0.2, pp 173–180.

Van der Zande, A. N. (1985) 'Distribution patterns of visitors in large areas: a problem of measurement and analysis', *Leisure Studies*, Vol.4, No.1, pp 85–100.

Van Doren, C. S. and Solan, D. S. (1979) 'Listing of dissertations and theses in leisure and recreation: August 1975 to August 1977', *Journal of Leisure Research*, Vol.11, No.3, pp 219–244.

Van Doren, C. S. and Stubbles, R. (1976) 'Listing of dissertations and theses in leisure and recreation', *Journal of Leisure Research*, Vol.7, No.1, pp 69–80.

Veal, A. J. (1984) 'Leisure in England and Wales', *Leisure Studies*, Vol.3, No.2, pp 221–230.

Veal, A. J. (1987) 'The leisure forecasting tradition', Ch.7 of *Leisure and the Future*, London: Allen & Unwin, pp 125–156.

Veal, A. J. (1988) 'Are user surveys useful?' in J. and N. Parry (eds) *Leisure, The Arts and the Community*, Conference papers No 30, Eastbourne, UK: Leisure Studies Association, pp 20–27.

Veal, A. J. (1989) 'The doubtful contribution of economics to leisure management', *Society and Leisure*, Vol.12, No.2, pp 147–156

Veal, A. J. (1990) *Joint Provision and Dual Use of Leisure Facilities*, London: Polytechnic of North London.

Veal, A. J. (1991) *Lifestyle and Leisure: A Review and Annotated Bibliography*, Sydney: Centre for Leisure and Tourism Studies, University of Technology, Sydney.

Vickerman, R. W. (1983) 'The contribution of economics to the study of leisure', *Leisure Studies*, Vol.2, No.3, pp 345–364.

Wade, L. L. (ed) (1983) *Political Economy: Recent Views*, Boston: Kuwer-Nijhoff.

Walker J. C. (1988) *Louts and Legends*, Sydney: Allen & Unwin.

Wells, W. D. (ed) (1974) *Life Style and Psychographics*, Chicago: American Marketing Assn.

Whyte, W. F. (1955) *Street Corner Society*, Chicago: Univ. Chicago Press.

Whyte, W. F. (1982) 'Interviewing in field research', in R. G. Burgess (ed) *Field Research: A Sourcebook and Field Manual*, London: Allen & Unwin, pp 111–122.

Williamson, J. B., Barry, S. T. and Dorr, R. S. (1982) *The Research Craft*, Boston: Little, Brown.

Wilson, J. (1988) *Politics and Leisure*, London: Allen and Unwin.

Wilson, M. J. et al. (1979) 'Styles of research in social science', in *Variety in Social Science Research*, (Block 1, Part 1 of Course DE303: Research Methods in Education and Social Science), Milton Keynes: Open University Press, pp 11–24.

Wimbush, E. and Talbot, M. (eds) (1988) *Relative Freedoms: Women and Leisure*, Milton Keynes: Open University Press.

Wynne, D. (1986) 'Living on 'The Heath'', *Leisure Studies*, Vol.5, No.1, pp 109–116.

Young, M. and Willmott, P. (1973) *The Symmetrical Family*, London: Routledge.

Index

academic research 7
ACORN — A Classification of Residential Neighbourhoods 75
activities 134–6
aerial photography 91
age 128
Age, The 6
American Psychological Association
Archer, B. 7, 10, 16
ASCII 161
attitudes 125, 137–9, 181
Australian Bureau of Statistics 147
Australian Domestic Tourism Monitor 107
Australian Recreation Participation Survey 107
author/date system 62–4

Bailey, P. 18, 25
Baretje, R. 68
Barnett, L. 26
Barton, A. 99
BBC — British Broadcasting Corporation
bibliographies 56–60
Bickmore, D. 15
Birenbaum, A. 84, 92
Borman, K. 26, 55
Bramham, P. 18
briefs 44
British Home Tourism Survey 72
Bryman, A. 196
budget 42
Bulmer, M. 102
Burch 15, 92

Burgess, R. 47, 102
Burkart, A. 18, 58, 79
Burton, T. 147

Cairns, J. 16
Calder, A. 84
Calder, B. 102
Campbell, F. 102
captive group surveys 117–18
case-studies 20, 34, 37, 76, 78
catchment areas 15, 115
causality 21, 171
Census of population 73–5, 148
Chase, D. 105
Child, E. 92
children's play 82
Christensen, J. 12, 102
cinema demand — case-study 75–8
Clarke, J. 13, 58
Coalter, F. 18
coding 139–47
Cohen, E. 14
complementary research 84
concepts 31, 36–8
confidence intervals 154–6
consultants 9
consumer testing 84
Coppock, J. 14, 25
Corley, J. 79
Countryside Commission 107
coupon surveys 53
Cowling, J. 15
CROSSTABS 183
Csiksentmihayli 17
Cumming, E. 33

Cunneen, C. 84, 92, 102
Cunningham, H. 18

Dann, G. 14, 26
Dare, B. 18
DASETT — Department of Arts,
  Sport, Environment, Tourism and
  Territories 16
data definition 162
DATA LIST 163
Dean 96
deduction 19–20
Deem, R. 13
Delphi technique 54
descriptive research 2, 21, 32, 170
Duffield, B. 79
dwelling type 133

Eadington, W. 16, 26
economic status 128
economic surveys 73
economics 15–16
education 130
Elias, N. 1, 212
Ely, M. 92
empirical research 21–2
en route surveys 53
endnote system 64–7
English Tourist Board 59
ethics 102
ethnic group 132
ethnography 95, 102
evaluative research 3, 34, 172
everyday life 84
executive summary 203
expenditure 73
experimental research 22
explanatory research 2, 21, 32

feasibility studies 6
feminism 13
Fielding, N. 25, 100
fieldwork 41
Fiske, J. 84, 192
focus groups 95, 100–101
footnote system 64–7
forecasting 6
Frank Small & Associates 47, 119

General Household Survey 70–72,
  79, 80, 107, 134, 211
geography 14
Glancy, M. 102
Glyptis, S. 15, 89, 92
Goeldner, C. 68
Goffman, E. 84
Gold, S. 92
government research 8
Graburn, N. 26
Grant, D. 84, 92
graphics 189, 210
gravity models 15
Green, E. 13
Grichting, W. 146
Griffin, C. 102
Griffiths, G. 122
group interviews 95, 100–101

Hall, S. 102
Hantrais, L. 79
Harvard graphics 190
Harvard system 62–4
Hatry, H. 34, 37
Havitz, M. 26
Heberlein, T. 92
Henderson, K. 26, 48–9, 55
Henley Centre for Forecasting 10,
  16, 79
Henry, I. 3
history 17–18
Hoinville, G. 119, 130, 147, 158
Hollands, R. 102
household surveys 106–108, 149
household type 131
housing tenure 133
Howard, D. 3
Hudson, S. 47, 119
Huizinga, J. 18
Hurst, F. 53
hypotheses 32–3

income 130
in-depth interviews 95
induction 19–20
informal recreation areas 82
Ingham, R. 17, 25
interview checklist 96, 103
interviewing 96–97, 139

ISBN — International Standard Book Number 202
Iso-Ahola, I. 17
iterative approach 22

Jackson, E. 10, 26, 58
Jafari, J. 8
journals 7

Kamphorst, T. 79
Kelly 10, 12, 13, 17, 26, 48, 55, 58, 94
Kelsey, C. 4, 10, 47
keywords 68
Kidder, L. 47, 147, 158
Knight, J., 68
Kraus, R. 47
Krenz, C. 26, 55
Krueger, R. 102

Labovitz, S. 21
LaPage, W. 54, 102
Lavrakas, P. 119
leisure centres — case-study 121–2
Leisure, Recreation and Tourism Abstracts 58
life cycle 132
lifestyle 5–6
literature review 34-5, 50, 56–68
Lofland, J. 98–9, 102
Lucas, R. 116

MacCannell, D. 14
mail surveys 110–14
management 4, 9–10
marital status 130
market profiles 5
market research 5, 94
market segmentation 5
Marriott, K. 4, 119
Marsh, P. 85, 92, 102
Martin, W. 10, 16
Mass Observation 84
Matthews, H. 18, 26
McCall, G. 96
measurement 36–8
media surveys 54
media use 136

Mitchell, A. 6
Mitchell, L. S. 15, 26
modelling 12, 14, 32
Moeller, G. 55, 102
motivation 125
Murphy, J. 18
Myerscough 16

national leisure surveys 69–72
needs studies 6
neo-marxism 13
Neulinger, J. 17
non-users 117
Norusis, M. 160

O'Brien, S. 147
observation 51, 81–92
OECD — Organisation for Economic Cooperation and Development 72
omnibus surveys 107
on-site surveys 114–17, 151
OPCS — Office of Population Censuses and Surveys 73–4, 79, 107, 148
open-ended questions 105, 125 , 140
opinions 137
Oppenheim, A.
ordering of questions 143

panels 54
Parker, S. 12
Parry, N. 25
participant observation 95, 101
Patmore, J. 15, 92
Pearce, P. 15, 17, 26
Peine, J. 92
Peterson, K. 94
philosophy 18
photography 91
pilot surveys 118–19
Pizam, A. 47
planning and management 3, 10
Plog, S. 10
political science 18
population 40, 149
position statements 5
post-modernism 13

postal surveys 110–14, 152
pre-coded questions 125, 139
prediction 12
primary data 23–4
projective techniques 54
psychology 16–17
psychographics 5–6

qualitative data analysis 98–100
qualitative vs quantitative research 24–5, 48
qualitative methods 51–2, 93–103
question wording 126
questionnaire design 120–47
questionnaire layout 144
questionnaire surveys 52–3, 104–19
quota sampling 109, 152

Rapoport, R. 13, 17, 102, 147
references 60–2
reliability 36
report preparation 201–12
representativeness 149
research
  preparation/planning 28
  process 27–8
  proposals 44–7
  strategy 38–40
residential location 132
response rates 110–11, 113
Reynolds, F. 102
Richter, L. 18
Ritchie 10, 58
Roberts, K. 58
Robertson, R. 127
Rojek 13, 22, 48, 55
Ronkainen, I. 53
Ruddell, E. 83
Russell, B. 18

sample size 153–7
sampling 41, 148–59
scales 137–8
scholarship 49
secondary data 23–4, 5, 69–79
self-completion 105
self-reported data 24
sex 127
Shadish, W. 3

Shaw, M. 6, 15
Shih, D. 6
site surveys 114–17
site use 82
Smith, M. 101
Smith, S. 15
social psychology 16–17
sociology 11–13
Sports Council 59, 107
SPSS/PC — Statistical Package for the Social Sciences (PC version)
  attitude scales 181
  command file 161–7
  CORRELATION 171, 188
  CROSSTABS 171, 183
  data definition 162
  DATA LIST 163
  error messages 168
  FREQUENCIES 170, 173, 197
  graphics 189
  MEANS 171, 179
  missing values 175
  multiple response questions 176
  non-numeric data 167
  percentages 183
  presentation of results 178
  RECODE 177
  running 167
  value labels 166
  variable labels 166
statistics 173
street surveys 108–9, 152

tables 210
telephone surveys 109–10
theory 10, 21, 33, 171
theses 8
time-budget surveys 53, 147
timetable 43–4
Torkildsen, G. 3, 58
tourism marketing plans 6
tourism questions 136
tourism strategies 6
tourism surveys 72–3
tourism trend analysis 78–9
Towner 18, 26
transport access 133
trip origin 132
TRRU — Tourism and Recreation Research Unit 15, 92, 119
Tyre, G. 92

user opinions 116
user profile 115
user surveys 114–17, 151

validity 36, 146
value labels 166
Van der Zande, A. 15, 92
Van Doren, C. 8
variable labels 166
Veal, A. 7, 10, 16, 55, 68, 119
Vickerman, R. 25
visitor surveys 114–17, 151

Wade, L. 33
Walker, J. 102
weighting 157, 187
Wells, W. 10
Whyte, W. 97, 101
Williamson, J. 19, 47, 119
Wilson, J. 18
Wilson, M. 55
Wimbush, E. 13
Wordperfect 161
Wordstar 161
Wynne, D. 101, 102

Young 18